FROM THE LIBRARY OF
BERKELEY COLLEGE

New York:
NYC (Midtown and Lower Manhattan)
Brooklyn • White Plains

New Jersey:
Newark • Paramus • Woodbridge
Woodland Park

Berkeley College Online:
BerkeleyCollege.edu/Online

Berkeley College®

Harder Than I Thought

Harder Than I Thought

Adventures of a Twenty-First-Century Leader

Robert D. Austin

Richard L. Nolan

Shannon O'Donnell

Harvard Business Review Press

Boston, Massachusetts

Library of Congress Cataloging-in-Publication Data

Austin, Robert D. (Robert Daniel), 1962–
    Harder than I thought : adventures of a twenty-first century leader / Robert D. Austin, Richard L. Nolan, Shannon O'Donnell.
      p. cm.
    ISBN 978-1-4221-6259-0
  1. Leadership. 2. Executive ability. 3. Chief executive officers. 4. Management. I. Nolan, Richard L. II. O'Donnell, Shannon. III. Title.
    HD57.7.A8494 2012
    658.4'092—dc23

                                                                2012031184

The dogmas of the quiet past are inadequate to the stormy present. The occasion is piled high with difficulty, and we must rise with the occasion. As our case is new, so we must think anew, and act anew. We must disenthrall ourselves...

—Abraham Lincoln, Annual Speech to Congress, Washington, DC, December 1, 1862

CONTENTS

Introduction   ix

1. First Day   1

2. Getting to Know SMA   13

FIRST INTERLUDE:
THE LORDS OF LEADERCRAFT 35

3. Financials and Trust   41

4. Transparency   57

SECOND INTERLUDE:
A LEADER OF MEN 71

5. Reunion   73

6. The Board of Directors   85

7. Getting Great Performance from People   101

THIRD INTERLUDE:
YOUR LINEUP IS A MESS! 119

8. Rallying the Team   123

9. Restructuring the Board   137

Contents

10. Consulting with a Peer   151

11. Implementation   163

12. Test Drive   177

13. The Agony of Defeat   189

14. Wild Card   201

15. Bluebirds Fly In   217

FOURTH INTERLUDE:
EXECUTE, EXECUTE, EXECUTE   229

16. Globalization   233

17. Execution   245

18. Public Life, Private Life   255

19. Communicate, Communicate   265

20. Partnering Risks Realized   273

FIFTH INTERLUDE:
THE LEADERSHIP MAIN COURSE   283

21. There Is a Time . . .   287

FINALE:
STILL FIGURING IT OUT   297

Ways of Using This Book   299
Cast of Main Characters   301
Glossary of Acronyms and Terms   305
Acknowledgments   307
About the Authors   309

INTRODUCTION

Harder Than I Thought invites readers to walk in the shoes of a new CEO, Jim Barton, as he navigates the challenges of transforming a twentieth-century, vertically integrated, defense contractor into a twenty-first-century, virtually integrated, commercial cargo airplane company. *Harder Than I Thought* is written for new and potential CEO leaders, those working closely with CEOs, such as board and senior leadership team members, those who want to better understand the CEO's role, students of leadership, and those who are simply curious.

While our story takes place in the context of the aerospace industry, and we do our best to represent details specific to that industry, we strive to address key CEO leadership issues that we believe are relevant to diverse industries and to companies of varying scale. We chose the aerospace context for several reasons: One of us has spent his career working for and with a major aerospace company, educating its executives and writing cases, articles, and books on company history, strategy, and leadership. Also, aerospace companies are entities that both design and manufacture complex physical machines that must unfailingly meet the highest safety standards and engage in what's characterized now as "twenty-first-century knowledge work." They manage complex networks of partnerships in a digitized landscape, engage in cocreation with key customers, and provide ongoing services over the product life cycle. The intricate integration of these activities with the former and the ability to identify and focus on core capabilities within complex networks increase the challenges leaders and leadership teams face in the design and execution of new strategies. This challenge hits home for organizations of many types.

Although this book is based on the authors' years of firsthand experience with diverse companies and leaders, the company in which our story takes place and its staff are fictional. Those readers familiar with our previous book, *The Adventures of an IT Leader,* will recognize our hero, Jim Barton. In *Adventures,* Barton was a talented general manager who, amid a dramatic company turnaround, was appointed CIO of a financial services firm and spent a year in that volatile job learning the ropes. As our current story begins, Barton, who has since been serving as COO in another financial services firm on the East Coast, is hired as CEO of Santa Monica Aerospace after other candidates turned down the job. Regard for SMA is at a low point with the investment community due to accounting tricks played by the previous CEO. Barton must stem the flow of bleeding cash and simultaneously figure out how to finance an $8 billion commercial cargo airplane redesign to save the company.

Our story follows Barton as he deals with the new set of issues, opportunities, and difficulties that face a CEO in the second decade of the twenty-first century. While these issues are raised and alternative courses of action debated and at times acted upon, not all issues are resolved in the course of the narrative. Rather, the reader is invited to consider the information at hand with his or her own experience and expertise in order to formulate recommendations. We make this invitation at each chapter's end, proposing a set of questions to guide reflection and, perhaps, discussion. For ideas on how to read this book with others, please see the section "Ways of Using This Book" at the back of the book. To assist your reading program, we also provide a description of main characters and a glossary of acronyms and terms, at the back of the book.

We hope that this book inspires reflection and makes a contribution to developing our knowledge about CEO leadership in ways that can help us meet the needs of the twenty-first century collaboratively, responsibly, and with increasing wisdom.

CHAPTER 1

First Day

Monday, October 26, 8:01 a.m....

Jim Barton barely reacted when the doorbell rang. Immersed in content streaming to a tablet propped up behind his cereal bowl, he waved an empty spoon past one ear, as if pushing away a buzzing insect, then gulped down an abrasive clump of wet high-fiber grain. Sipping coffee to clear his throat, he adjusted the reading glasses he'd begun using last week and couldn't quite get used to, without shifting attention from the editorial he'd just come across in the business section of the *So-Cal Times*. He couldn't quite believe what it said:

> Let's face it. Santa Monica Aerospace had to really be scraping the bottom of the barrel to choose Jim Barton as their new CEO.
>
> I wish it weren't true. I have friends who work for that formerly great company—friends whom I'd like to see employed and thriving. But you've got to figure a lot of people turned down this job before they found someone dumb enough take it. The fact that the guy agreed to do it speaks unflattering volumes about his judgment.
>
> Yes, I realize Barton is an SMA board member. That he "knows the company"—at least as much as a bean counter can ever know a company that really makes things. And I've heard all that

1

schlock about how Lou Gerstner was a food company CEO when he took over and saved IBM.

But I don't buy it. That was a different company, in a different situation, in a different time. IBM was in the process, then, of becoming a consulting services company, an entity perfectly suited to Gerstner's Harvard–McKinsey pedigree. That's not the case here. SMA is, still, a company of engineers, building and delivering things that have to work.

And, if the rumors about what they're paying him are true, that makes this recent development even more galling. I know, I know: East Coast finance industry pay scales, you have to pay what the market will bear if you want the talent—yada, yada, blah, blah, yada, yada, blah, blah. Yeah, I get all that. But here's what I'm wondering (and I bet I'm not alone): All that money for the wrong guy? A financial services executive running an aerospace company? I've got just one thing to say to the members of the board: "Come on, guys and gals! What were you thinking?"

Barton removed the glasses and polished them with his napkin. He rubbed his eyes and shook his head, as if to clear it. But when he once again peered through the glasses at the tablet's display, the disagreeable words remained there.

"You'd think," he said, to no one in particular, "someone might give a guy break. This being his first day and all . . ."

Shoving aside the cereal bowl, sloshing milk onto the table, Barton snapped up the tablet and flicked his finger along the edge of the screen, scanning for a byline. He quickly spotted one: *Veronica Perez.*

"Ms. Perez," said Barton to himself, "Who *are* you?"

Swirling and tapping thumb and forefinger across the tablet's display, he generated a list, refining his search with filters for journalism, business, and the name of the newspaper. Within seconds, he located three bios for Perez, information about her work with the UC Irvine alumni club, the citation for an "up-and-coming journalist" award she'd won, links to her personal pages on several social networking sites, and her "@VIPERez" Twitter ID. Seconds later, he knew that Perez had taken a master's degree in journalism about ten years earlier and had since risen rapidly to positions of journalistic prominence, first with a Northern California paper and then with her current employer.

She's practically a kid! Barton thought. *Who does she think she is?*

Three days before, someone from the *So-Cal Times*—Perez, Barton now realized, or one of her flunkies—had called his East Coast office at Erlington Financial Group for a quote he'd been only too happy to provide. Anticipating a hopeful story about a new beginning for SMA, he'd made extensive use of airplane metaphors ("soaring," "flying high") and spoken of a "new era for a great company." None of that made it into print. He'd been naive to assume the local paper would be friendly.

That's not a mistake I would have made on the East Coast, Barton thought.

In his EFG role, he'd have worked carefully with his public relations guy. He'd have known exactly who was calling and how well he could trust that person. If they'd been unsure about the caller, they might have released similar information to a more trusted outlet at the same time, perhaps offering an extra exclusive tidbit to the trusted outlet. They'd have worked on the quotes to make them seem spontaneous rather than contrived. The SMA communications office had recommended working with them in very much this same manner if Barton had occasion to interact with members of the West Coast press prior to his arrival. He'd disregarded the advice, partly because he didn't yet know his new team.

But that was not, he realized, the only reason.

Barton now recognized—with an unsettling jolt—a second reason he'd failed to take his new PR staff's excellent advice: *sentimentality.* Taking the SMA job meant coming home, to the place where Barton had grown up. Somehow he'd expected, without thinking it through, a warm homecoming. *A rookie mistake,* he thought. *I can't afford many of those.* He knew the SMA PR staff would also consider this a pretty basic mistake, and that they'd probably read into it many deeply ominous implications.

Barton was about to open Perez's vlog site to get a visual fix on his new press adversary when the doorbell chimed again. This time he heard it and stood, looking for the source of the sound in the unfamiliar company-owned apartment. Closing the tablet and stashing it in his briefcase, Barton made a mental note to check with his new PR staff sooner rather than later about this "Veronica Perez" person.

Thus began Jim Barton's first day as the new CEO of Santa Monica Aerospace.

Monday, October 26, 8:36 a.m. . . .

Barton reclined unhappily in the plush backseat of SMA Corporate Limo Number 1, surrounded by bulletproof glass and metal. A small sticker on the window assured him that the car had received a safety inspection and security sweep (to check for listening devices) that very morning. "Standard procedure," said Ben Krishnan, a dark-haired young man in wire-rimmed glasses also seated in the back of the limo.

Krishnan, it seemed, was Barton's new executive assistant.

A day earlier, at the airport, Barton had rented a Mustang convertible to celebrate returning to a land where it made sense to drive with the top down in October. He'd intended to enjoy the great weather on his drive in to work. So the arrival of a limo surprised and appalled him.

I'll stop this executive perquisite right now, Barton thought, as he comprehended the meaning of the car's sudden appearance. *I'll send a message to the entire company in my very first act: this CEO drives* himself *to work.*

But Krishnan had other ideas. Barton recalled the exact words:

"No, sir, you can't."

"I can't?" said Barton, more perplexed than affronted.

"No, sir. It wouldn't be safe. You are required to use the company car."

Barton thought: *Safe? Required?* He said: "Safe?"

"Yes, sir."

Through obvious unease, the younger man explained: "Uh, SMA, you know, the company, it does defense work," he said. "And the unions, well . . . things aren't always friendly. I think insurance requires it."

As Barton settled into the backseat, Krishnan explained that the doors and windows contained soundproofing, which prevented eavesdropping by external "agents," even those using sophisticated laser technology to detect micro-vibrations on the surface of windows. "It's a completely secure meeting space," said Krishnan, expecting Barton to be impressed. "You should see the corporate jet," he added.

"I can only imagine," answered Barton, sighing and relenting.

For most of the ride, Krishnan briefed Barton on his agenda for the days to come. The sheaf of papers the young man thrust into Barton's hands went on and on for many pages. Krishnan called it a "suggested" schedule, but it rapidly became clear to Barton that a lot of care had gone into its preparation. It represented his new team's best ideas about how to bring Barton up to speed on his new company.

Barton had his own ideas about how he wanted to start, his own plans for "the first one hundred days." But he also realized he'd need to rethink those, on the advice of people at SMA. He would need to strike a balance between setting his own agenda and responding to the many suggestions and offers of help from eager staff. Early on, it would be important to listen a lot.

As he glanced through the pages, he could see there'd be ample opportunities to discuss the top challenges that faced Santa Monica Aerospace. The big picture was pretty simple: SMA needed to move out of a shrinking, mostly military transport plane business into the expanding commercial cargo plane market. The company would use its formidable engineering know-how to create a best-in-class cargo plane in a targeted market segment. In theory, it could leapfrog the competition and gain command of that segment, which would be very lucrative.

In theory.

In fact, the company had little or no access to the capital it needed for the transition. The market had soured on SMA, in part due to financial antics instigated by the previous CEO. An engineer by background, he'd become infatuated with the new (to him) world of accounting maneuvers. He'd done nothing dramatic, nothing even close to illegal, but in the end his maneuvers had backfired, undermining the confidence of analysts. Ultimately, the board decided to relieve him of his duties. But in an odd bit of political theater, to avoid seeming to admit impropriety, they'd kept him on the board of directors. Consequently, Barton would have to contend not only with his predecessor's legacy, but also with him in person, on the board.

Some prospective CEOs might have considered this detail alone a deal breaker. *Maybe some had,* thought Barton. Though he disliked Perez's *So-Cal Times* analysis, as an SMA board member, he knew she was right about one thing: he had *not* been the first person offered the job. Perhaps he'd been too accepting of the idea of keeping the former CEO on the board. Barton had agreed to it as a board member, before he'd known that *he* would be the new CEO. By the time he agreed to take the CEO position, having been an insider involved in the decisions up to that point and knowing the former CEO well, Barton thought it would seem wrong to jettison his predecessor. Time would tell, though, whether keeping him might be a bigger mistake.

As would be true of a company in the midst of such a major transition, SMA's cost structure was way out of line with what it needed to be for long-term success. Completing the transformation would require freeing up cash. This conclusion, apparent to all, had led to mounting tensions with workers and their unions, who feared they would bear the brunt of cost reductions. The mechanics union had been particularly aggressive, lodging preemptive threats of work stoppages and implying worse.

Though Krishnan did not comment on it, the folder he'd handed his new boss contained a brief CV for each of the CEO's direct reports. Barton leafed through these, contemplating the smiling head shots at the top of each page, looking for clues about whether he'd work well with them. He recognized some of them from times when they'd participated in board meetings. But he really knew none of them.

A new CEO meant change for each one of them. Some, especially those who hadn't been part of the old CEO's innermost circle, might welcome change; for them, Barton's coming meant opportunity. Others, who'd been central in the old regime, might see threat in Barton's arrival. Some of the faces in these pictures would need to change. Barton knew this and so would they. Making good decisions about the composition of his new team would be very, very important.

And also difficult. If only people would approach you on your very first day to say something like this: "Hi, I'm Judy Smith, executive vice president of this-n-such, and I've been more or less running things around here under the old boss. If I get the idea you're not going to leave me in charge, I'll passively resist, talk behind your back, and possibly try to organize a coup d'état if it comes to that. So if you're planning to make certain kinds of changes, you might as well get rid of me early on, because you're just not going to win me over. I can already tell that. You're just not my kind of guy."

Or maybe this: "Hi, I'm John Johnson, EVP of that-n-such, and the last CEO wouldn't give me the time of day, had trouble even remembering my name. If I were honest, I'd tell you the reason: while I talk a good game, I tend to have really dumb ideas, and I can't execute my way out of a paper bag. But since you're new, you don't know that. So I'll flatter you and diss your predecessor to try to get you to take me into your confidence, exactly *because* the old boss wouldn't have anything to do with me. My ideas won't get any better, but by the time you catch on, I'll have improved my situation quite considerably, thank you very much."

Unfortunately, this never happened. No, in reality, vital information about what people would or could do under a new leader would be exceedingly difficult to come by. A pity really, but people weren't so straightforward. Figuring it all out amounted to a challenge that Barton knew had to begin on his first day.

The organization as a whole would resist change too. The company, built for one purpose, needed to be reconfigured for a different purpose. At every level, the questions about the composition of teams, who would stay, and how jobs would change would necessarily recur. There would be friction, tensions, and crisis. None of this could be avoided, but it could be managed.

Krishnan finished the briefing and grew quiet. Barton glanced through messages on his phone. He listened to a voice mail from his mother. She hoped to see him on the weekend and mentioned that his high school buddy, Ace, had called to invite Jim to watch football the following Sunday afternoon. Barton considered this a good omen. Though he doubted many people realized it, his longtime friend, Acacio "Ace" Jackson, led that aggressive SMA mechanics union, the one many regarded as an insurmountable problem for the company. Barton counted on his relationship with Jackson to help with the company's transition. *My Ace in the hole,* Barton thought, smiling at the bad pun.

He took out his tablet, fired it up, and then spent a few moments reviewing previously composed thoughts about the challenges at SMA and his opening game plan:

Objective

Transform SMA from a twentieth-century aerospace company into a viable twenty-first-century commercial cargo airplane company, addressing strategy, organization, technology, operations, culture, and any other relevant factors.

My first 100 days:

- "Airborne"—Ensure near-term operational and financial viability.

- "Navigation"—Validate/adjust/remake business strategy.

- "Fuel Check"—Ensure that we have the resources—balance sheet and cash flows—we need to implement our strategy (likely to require freeing up cash somewhere).

- "Flight Crew"—Ensure that SMA has the "right" senior management team in place to effectively develop and execute plans.

- "Landing Procedures"—Develop plans for execution and risk management.

- "Air Traffic Control"—Assess organizational structure and governance arrangement.

- "Making Connections"—Assess in-house capabilities and deficits, and needs for partners—What we can do and what we can't or shouldn't do and need partners to help us with.

- "Wingmen"—Assess relationships to existing partners.

- "Member Circle"—Get to know our customers, understand how they see us.

- "Aerodynamics"—Assess IT and its ability to support change, innovation, and virtual integration.

Barton had also composed a list of reminders, key learning from previous experiences. Advice and warnings he'd heard from others, like Bob Goldman, his longtime mentor, whose advice Barton had gone against in taking the SMA CEO job. He opened that file on his tablet:

What I need to watch out for:

1. Underestimating the senior management team.
2. Not listening—coming in with preset ideas.
3. Trying to change too much, too fast.
4. Not understanding company culture and history.
5. Making changes for the sake of change.
6. Getting input from a too-narrow group of advisers.
7. Not understanding and undervaluing existing business processes and procedures.
8. Becoming a micromanaging bottleneck.
9. Vague vision, strategy, and priorities. Sending the wrong message, or conflicting messages.
10. Making poor ethical choices.
11. Getting caught up in the short-term agendas of investors and analysts, losing faith in long term, getting cold feet.

Unsure why he hadn't thought of it before, he now added a twelfth:

12. Assuming that SMA runs like a financial services business.

"We'll need to get those security checked," Krishnan said, pointing to Barton's tablet and phone. "We might need to replace them."

Barton nodded, suppressed a sigh, and said nothing.

The limo arrived at the front entrance of SMA, where an entourage awaited. Barton exited the car. He grimaced but did not object when an odd-looking young woman with spiked jet-black hair and multiple piercings hurried away with his electronic devices.

Barton began shaking hands. He worked his way down a receiving line, eventually arriving at the end where a man in a white uniform introduced himself simply as "Joe, your executive chef."

My own chef? Barton though. Surprised, again, he fell back on habit.

"I'm Jim Barton," he said, unnecessarily.

The man grinned broadly. "I know, sir," he said, in a booming voice with an accent Barton couldn't quite identify. "We've been waiting for you. You're our new CEO! And we're *delighted* that you're here!"

Reacting to the chef's exclamation, the crowd burst into applause. They gathered around Barton. Some shook his hand again. A few patted his shoulder. All spoke words of welcome. He examined the faces, one by one, detecting complex blends of emotion behind happy, outward expressions. They appeared both nervous and hopeful. They expected him, Jim Barton, to *save* them. They received him as a long-awaited rescuer.

Barton bowed his head, feeling his face warm as the applause continued, privately wondering—no, worrying—that he might be in *way* over his head.

This worry would recur and deepen in the days to come.

Reflection

Should Barton have taken this job? Should he have negotiated different conditions? Is this a game he can win?

What should Barton do about the *So-Cal Times* editorial?

Is the editorial right? Can a bean counter lead transformation at an engineering/manufacturing firm?

What should Barton's priorities be during his first one hundred days? How should he balance pursuing his own agenda with responsiveness to the ideas of his new colleagues and employees? How critical will those first hundred days be to Barton's overall success as a CEO?*

---

*For more reflection on the "first one hundred days," see, for example, Michael Watkins, "Why the First 100 Days Matters," *Harvard Business Review,* HBR Blog Network, March 23, 2009, http://blogs.hbr.org/watkins/2009/03/why_the_FIRST_100_days_matters.html.

CHAPTER 2

Getting to Know SMA

"By redesigning the process and applying the world-class ingenuity of our mechanics, who went way beyond configuration options and essentially rebuilt this equipment after it arrived from the vendor's factory, we've been able to dramatically reduce setup time and eliminate a lot of the inventory that used to accumulate at this point. This floor is largely empty now. It used to be covered with extra materials that we needed for the different setups. It's all vastly simpler now."

Barton listened and nodded. The gangly manufacturing vice president enthused about changes SMA had made to get from "batch-and-queue" to a moving line for assembling the company's aircraft. The man possessed a youthful, nerdy exuberance that didn't quite mesh with his distinguished, aging features. Something else in his manner also seemed incongruous: Barton didn't think he'd ever seen this degree of animation about the actual content of work in any financial services exec. Airplanes were exciting. Money could be exciting too, Barton knew, but not in quite the same way.

As they watched, a heavy, low-slung "truck" towed a partially built plane forward at a speed so slow Barton had trouble discerning movement. A swarm of people worked on different aspects of this grand structure on its way to becoming a complete flying machine. "Three million parts flying in close formation," Paul Marochek, the buoyant VP joked, obviously recycling a joke he'd used a thousand times.

They worked their way through the plant, keeping to the safe lane between yellow lines on the floor. Anthony—"Tony"—Gerunzi, one of three engineers in their entourage, handled most of the explanations. Marochek added commentary. Gerunzi called out to people doing the work, wisecracking and trading insults with just about everyone. Barton sensed a healthy dynamic between managers and workers that he liked a lot. Much of the banter was incomprehensible to him. *I'm surely not in Kansas anymore,* Barton thought.

But he learned as Gerunzi explained: "The line redesign project started through the lean office here. We started thinking seriously about it when we were getting ready to build the SMA 400-3."

"That was the second major redesign, right?" Barton asked.

Gerunzi nodded. "We started with the SMA 400-1; that's the original. We've had two upgrades, SMA 400-2 and SMA 400-3. Truth is, the Air Force pushed us to make innovations in the factory on the SMA 400-3. They demanded price reductions, caused a real crisis at the time, but it forced us to simplify. We ran what we call 'New Ways' innovation workshops, where our engineers and mechanics collaborated to come up with different concepts: ways of building the fuselage and wings via a moving line system. Versus what we have right now, what we had then—well, there was no moving line system; it was all monuments—huge and inflexible machine tools.

"For wings, for example, we used to load the wings into giant monument-like jigs or machine tools, and we'd get three levels of people working on them. But we'd have to push those guys out of there within two days of build, and try to get that wing out of there as fast as possible so guys didn't have to be in there so long. It was a bad place to work. So we decided maybe we could come up with a better way to do that. We thought, 'Why can't we build that wing flat, like in nature?' That's how we get the stuff in—flat. It comes in boxes flat. Why can't we build it flat? We can. Now. Took a lot of work though."

He drew Barton over to look at what appeared to be a scale model of the line, with moving pieces and small rough-hewn foam fuselages on wooden wheels. Gerunzi continued: "We use scale models like these on the shop floor. Employees can interact with this. We display this model out here so everybody can look and see what we're doing, and what kind of improvements are happening, so everybody has the knowledge of what's going to happen out here. Everyone in the value stream is working to own this problem together. It's not an 'us-and-them' thing, but a 'we.'

"Coming out of our New Ways work, we've got a new prototype model, something pretty different, for the moving wing line on the floor in the wing plant. We also got a couple of human-scale workspace simulations set up, just with simple plastic and plywood parts. People see it, move around in it, interact with it, and get ideas for better ways. We used to have to move that wing around. Now that we got the moving line running, it goes directly from build, to seal and paint, to this building, to the airplane. But we can always make it better.

"We call using quick and dirty prototypes 'trystorming.'* With 'brainstorming,' you think up a lot of ideas fast. With trystorming, we not only think up the ideas, we also *do* them fast, in prototype or simulation. It gives us a lot more insight, more opportunities for people to point out problems and improvements."

Marochek interjected: "It's the same idea as what we used to try to do with just computer simulation, try things quickly and cheaply, try many more things in the computer than we could afford to try in real life. But these quick and dirty physical prototypes, they're cheap too, and people can interact with them better. We used to think we'd move everybody into the 'knowledge economy.' You know, no paper, no physical models, nothing physical; we'd all work with computers. But we found out that the more we got into working with knowledge and innovation—which are intangible things—the more we needed the tangible, physical models. It's ironic, but it's true. The more the business gets to be about knowledge, the more we benefit from touching and trying—from physical experience with things."[†]

*For more on trystorming and the transition to lean manufacturing in the aerospace industry, see Robert D. Austin, Richard L. Nolan, and Shannon O'Donnell, "The Boeing Company: Moonshine Shop," Case 9-607-130 (Boston: Harvard Business School, 2007).

†For research on the design of systems that allow people to improve and innovate, prototype, and also permit easy interaction with them, see Robert D. Austin, Lee Devin, and Erin Sullivan, "Accidental Innovation: Supporting Valuable Unpredictability in Creative Process," *Organization Science*, August 24, 2011, http://orgsci.journal.informs.org/content/early/2011/08/24/orsc.1110.0681.abstract.

Nodding, Gerunzi picked up the thread and provided an example: "Everybody who works on wings, and some people that don't, will tell you their opinion about things in a scale model. Lots of opinions that point us to better ways of doing it."

Another engineer, Nate McCoy, who'd been introduced but stayed quiet until now, spoke up. "We're also after the crazy ideas," he said, glancing over at Gerunzi to make sure it was okay to jump in and receiving a nod of encouragement. "What I mean is," continued McCoy, "we want a culture where crazy ideas are okay. Because at the end of the day, no ideas are crazy. Maybe we can't do them right now, maybe we can't afford them, but if it's worth doing, we won't forget them. We have interns stationed in the areas of the New Way workshops who listen, capture ideas, and post them on our New Ways whiteboards and blogs.

"You go to most of our plants, you'll see a whiteboard full of things that they want to get to, and supervisors walk by everyday—me too, I walk by that list every day, and it nags at me! I think, 'Why haven't we tried that?'"

"But still," Marochek conceded, "change is hard; it's hard for anybody. And we've changed so many things. People still worry that change might cost them their job or make their job harder. People naturally want to do what they already know how to do, what they're already good at. But I think people believe in us now, in our approach, because they participate in making these changes."

Gerunzi continued: "When we started this redesign, we thought we were going to do a pulse line. Everybody was happy, everybody bought into it, until the *sensei** came and said, 'No, that's monument thinking. You don't want monuments in your factory.' And he was right. Those monuments, they're expensive, hard to move around and reconfigure; they clog up our process flows, bad, real bad. Make them hard to improve.

---

*Sensei is the English spelling of a Japanese word used to describe a person of authority, someone acknowledged to have achieved a certain level of mastery of a field. It can be generally used to describe clergy, doctors, or teachers, or any acknowledged master. Here the word is used as it has been adopted into lean manufacturing practice; thus, it means an authority on lean operations. See James P. Womack and Daniel T. Jones, *Lean Thinking: Banish Waste and Create Wealth in Your Corporation* (New York: Free Press, 1996).

"Now everything in final assembly is on wheels. There's not a thing that's not on wheels. Everything moves. Everything flows—quicker, better, faster. Parts and components come in just-in-time from suppliers. Inventory management, the old kind with warehouses and stacks of stuff on the floor, is practically obsolete. And people are cool with that. They have to learn new things sometimes, but it makes their jobs better."

"What you've done here," Barton commented, as they neared the end of the tour, "is *very* impressive."

He meant it. These guys, their ways of working, exhibited real know-how. They, and the others around them, had capabilities SMA would need for the transition. It was beyond encouraging. It was inspiring.

On the verge of effusing further, of adding to his earlier words of approval, Barton became suddenly aware of a change in Gerunzi and the others in his entourage. He no longer commanded their attention. They'd begun whispering and gesturing. Barton looked across the floor and saw several men wearing yellow hard hats in some sort of informal gathering.

"Everything okay?" asked Barton.

"Yes, fine, Mr. Barton," said McCoy. "We're just noticing unusual activity."

"What's going on?" Barton asked.

"I expect *you* might be the reason, Mr. Barton," said Gerunzi. "They're union reps. Some of those guys are from other plants and buildings. The guy on the end, he's from the fabrication plant. Doesn't spend much time here."

Barton spotted the man Gerunzi referred to and was startled to recognize him: Ace Jackson, his old high school buddy.

"I know that guy," said Barton.

The four men surrounding Barton turned to him in unison, astonished.

"*You* know Ace Jackson?" said Gerunzi.

"We went to high school together," Barton answered.

He let slip a bemused smile at how far the other men's jaws dropped. Succumbing to a mischievous urge, Barton added: "In fact, he saved my life once. We were surfing. I would've drowned."

This revelation elicited more amazement. Gerunzi, who Barton already had pegged as a person not inclined to hold his tongue, blurted, "Well, maybe he was a nice guy then, but he's kind of a pain in the ass now."

This prompted nervous laughter from the others.

Barton smiled reassuringly, "I expect things have changed since I knew him."

Jackson looked toward them. Barton thought he saw a flash of recognition cross his old friend's face. Jackson looked away, leaned in to the group, and said something, apparently about Barton since the others in the group then turned to look.

"Jackson remembers you, too," said Gerunzi, "Ain't that sweet?" His joke met with stony silence. Undaunted, he started off again, continuing the tour, talking a mile a minute. Barton hung back to take another look at the group of union reps and then turned to follow Gerunzi.

As they came to a place where the path turned, Barton, still a short distance behind the others, cut a corner to catch up. He started across an area no more than ten feet wide, never wandering more than five feet from the path outlined in yellow. Gerunzi, glancing over his shoulder, caught sight of this and flew into action.

"Mr. Barton!" he shouted, dashing to Barton's side. Gerunzi grabbed Barton's arm and pulled him roughly back to the path. At that moment, a piece of equipment about the size of a small vacuum cleaner came crashing to the floor from high above, landing a mere foot from where Barton had been standing a moment earlier. On impact, the piece of equipment smashed into shards of metal, glass, and plastic. Barton felt small bits ricochet off his pants legs.

Dazed, Barton looked up at the scaffolding from which the thing had fallen. He expected someone to come rushing down to apologize. But he saw no one. Barton turned back to the scattered pile of rubble on the floor.

"What the hell was that?" he asked.

Gerunzi turned a reproachful expression toward Barton.

"You have to stay between the lines, Mr. Barton. It's dangerous outside the lines."

Barton felt sheepish as he realized that he'd just provided another reason for his new employees to doubt whether he was really up to *this* job in *this* industry. The story of the CEO who'd almost been killed because he didn't know to stay in the safety lanes would be told far and wide, throughout the company, in the coming days.

McCoy offered an apology: "We're really sorry that happened, Mr. Barton. We'll look right into it."

"Looks like some kind of cleaning equipment," Barton suggested, stooping to pick up a fragment from the remains.

"Looks to me," said Gerunzi, "like a message, Mr. Barton. Probably from your old high school friend."

The others awaited Barton's reaction to this conjecture. He nodded to acknowledge Gerunzi's speculation, but decided not to continue that conversation.

"Between the lines, you say," said Barton.

"Yes, sir," Gerunzi answered.

"Between the lines I shall stay then."

"Thank you, Mr. Barton," said Gerunzi.

The tour continued.

Wednesday, October 28, 12:32 p.m. . . .

"With the SMA 400-2, we mastered the process of designing and proto-typing digitally. We've been able to do individual parts of the process that way for a while, but the real trick has been getting the data flowing between parts and pieces across the whole system. We've still got difficult interfaces, but we can now flow digital information from front to back through the engineering process, which means we can transmit, at the end of our process, precise digital specifications to suppliers. They've got their own version of this information flow problem, but some of them can now take our specs automatically into their digitally controlled manufacturing equipment. We design and generate specs; they build from the same specs, the same bits and bytes. When it works, and often it does now, parts arrive in final assembly from suppliers at just the right time and fit perfectly."

Susan Akita, SMA's chief engineer, sat across from Barton at a table in a corner of the dining room in one of the company's engineering buildings. She seemed considerably more youthful than Barton knew her to be. Though many years his senior, she moved with a vitality and energy that Barton suspected he rarely exhibited. Only her face showed signs of the

19

richness of her experience: not wrinkles or wear, but a stern seriousness that challenged others to bring their very best game to interactions with her. Judging from her reputation, she could be a very tough boss. Having reached an age when she could take early retirement if she wanted to, she instead held tightly to the reins of her organization. She remained exceptionally competent in technical matters. Her staff appeared, at times, in awe of her.

"So, Susan, you've showed me great technology and exciting prototypes, and your staff is terrific. But what," asked Barton, "*don't* we have that we need going forward?"

She pushed remnants of a salad around her plate before answering. Largely finished with a fish sandwich, Barton took a sip of iced tea, wiped his hands on a napkin, placed it folded on the table, and awarded her his full attention.

"You mean," said Akita, "if we are to successfully build the new plane?"

"Yes," said Barton.

"The plane that will save the company?" said Akita.

Barton nodded. "Yes, that's right."

Akita put down her fork and moved her own napkin from lap to table, leaving the last few bits of lettuce on her plate. Like Barton, she wanted to talk without distractions.

"Often," she said, "when companies talk about being able to leverage technology they've developed in one area—say, military applications—to another area—say, commercial applications—it's nonsense. Usually it's evidence that some biz dev type is trying to muster hype to do some sort of ill-begotten deal. And the execs around him don't know enough about their own business to know that it's BS. Sorry if that sounds cynical, but that's been my experience.

"Our situation is different. Ed Frazier had his problems as a CEO. But he knew engineering. He knew what we have—technology, process, expertise—and he realized we could do it. Now you've inherited this plan. I realize it's really Frazier's plan, but I think it would be a mistake to turn away from making this new plane. We *can* do it. There really *are* synergies between what we've been doing with the military plane and what we can do with the commercial cargo plane. We just need to charge harder at it. If we do, we're talking 'best in the world,' I think."

"Why, then," asked Barton, "did SMA go for extending the SMA 400-3 military contract rather than seeking congressional funding for a new program and contract? Why didn't SMA go for it then?"

The question stung Akita. "I didn't agree with that strategy," she said, frustration evident in her voice. "We could have won a new contract. We'd have proposed the best design. I realize I'm hardly impartial, but our design could have been the best. Our technology was best."

In her reaction, Barton detected defensiveness, perhaps even worry about the new CEO's assessment of her performance and whether she would be part of the senior team going forward. The worry was reasonable. Akita, because of her long tenure with the company and her involvement in past strategies and ways of doing things, fit the profile of someone it might make sense to replace.

Barton didn't actually think this way. As a board member, he knew that Akita's name had come up in discussion of possible candidates for SMA CEO. The consensus then had been that she remained too valuable in the chief engineer role to consider any such change. The idea of moving her from her commanding position, steward of the company's crucial engineering capability, evoked palpable concern. Her name remained in play as a future CEO, but she didn't know that.

"Design and technology would not have been the only considerations," said Barton. "What was the prevailing thinking on pricing at that time?"

"Not my department," said Akita. "I don't want to say anything critical of Jan Svendsen and his marketing team. In my experience, he and his people have got a good handle on such matters."

She paused to take a sip of her drink. "But was there a debate? Sure there was. I didn't think we should even think about coming in with the lowest bid. Not with what we would've had to offer. I know for a fact that decision makers within the military appreciated and wanted what we could deliver. I argued for a higher price and for making it clear why our proposal delivered a better outcome. But that made a lot of people anxious. In the end, the powers that be decided it would be safer to push for an extension of the SMA 400-3 contract."

"Were there political factors?" asked Barton. He'd heard that there had been.

Akita shrugged. "There's always that," she said, "and it's definitely not my forte. I'll be the first to admit that. Congressmen want jobs in their districts. Sometimes military leaders don't get what they want when Congress gets what it wants. That's one of the things I really like about the idea of getting into commercial markets. Less potential for political motivations to determine our fate."

"There'll probably still be politics, Susan, especially around some of the international orders. When we sell planes to Chinese companies, for example."

Akita nodded. "I realize that. But still, I hold out hope that a competitive marketplace might do a better job valuing some of the advantages my staff can bring to the party. Fuel economy, carrying capacity, aerodynamic properties—these things translate into money saved and profits earned for commercial cargo companies. We can't count on our advantages in these areas getting properly weighted in military contests."

"Commercial RFP processes will be different. We ready for that?"

Akita nodded. "That'll be huge. The Federal Acquisition Regulation really handcuffed us. Sometimes we couldn't build new technology into a proposal because of risks of triggering disputes from the other vendors. The legalities of the process were stupefying. You could pretty much count on a losing bidder filing some sort of a protest. Lawyers vetoed some of our design choices. The commercial context will, hopefully, have less of that. We'll put our best foot forward and be judged on merit. Not how skillfully we lobby, or how well we deal with a government bureaucracy, or the risks our lawyers are willing to take."

"But, how about my question?" Barton said.

"Do we have what it takes?" said Akita.

"That's not *exactly* what I asked," responded Barton. "I asked what we need going forward that we don't have now."

"Let me be careful in answering your question," said Akita. "What we don't have yet is the design and manufacturing scenario for a successful commercial cargo airplane that customers will buy."

Barton was taken aback by the expansiveness of this response. He let slip some sarcasm: "Is that all?"

Susan ignored the sarcasm. "You want the story straight, right? What we have now is a good first attempt. But it is uninspiring relative to the potential and the opportunity. Too expensive, due to assumptions about building it like a military airplane. Too limiting, due to assumptions about using structural components made of conventional aluminum alloys rather than carbon composites. In sum, the current conceptual design is deficient in technology and uses conservative, near end-of-life structural materials and old manufacturing processes. What we have is a defense contractor-like product rather than a commercially viable product. Our current design effort was underfunded and underdone, with deficient customer input.

"This is not encouraging, Susan."

"No, but there's a simple reason for it, if we're willing to face it: no one has been willing to bet the company. It's been a replay of the SMA 400-3 decision. No one wants to make the hard call. No one wants to face the big risk. Again. But I think the current incrementalism underestimates the mess we're in. We're up against a wall now and need to acknowledge that. We *need* to bet the company. And if we're willing, we *can* do it and we can win. You asked what we needed. What we need most is someone in charge willing to face the music rather than put things off because they're hard. Someone who realizes we need to bet the company. Incrementalism, the modes and habits we've gotten into in recent years, won't save us."

She didn't voice the obvious challenge left hanging in the air: *So how about you, Jim Barton? Are you that guy? Do you have the guts to make this hard call? Are you willing to bet the company?*

Barton opted not to answer the unspoken question. "I get that," he said. "I hear you. But if we were going to bet the company, what, specifically, do you need? Whatever it is, I'd like to try to get it for you."

"We need more expertise in key areas."

"For example?"

"I need more composite material expertise. We've used composites for parts and pieces, but now we're talking about building entire structures that way. Boeing has proven that composites can be used for large structural components for commercial airliners. Composites are not only lighter weight and have a longer life, but also enable us to sculpt wings and other essential components to achieve aerodynamics never possible with metal alloys."

"You're certain composites are the way to go?" he asked.

Akita looked at him sideways: "You're referring to this morning's paper?"

Barton nodded. That morning, the *So-Cal Times* had contained a business section story about the possible hazards of shifting to composites in the manufacture of commercial airplanes. The author was someone other than the infamous Ms. Perez, and the story had focused mostly on Boeing. But local employer SMA and its "rumored plans to rely more on composites" garnered numerous mentions, none of them favorable.

"The content of that article was erroneous in more ways than I can count," said Akita. "It was largely nonsense."

"But it did have its worrying aspects," said Barton.

Once again, Akita looked defensive. But she nodded: "Those quotes."

"That's what I meant," said Barton. Several times, the article had quoted unnamed sources within SMA, product engineers "profoundly worried" about the wisdom of relying on composites. Almost certainly they were people within Akita's organization.

"People resist change," said Akita. "Some of them take their case to the press."

"You know who it is?" asked Barton.

"I have ideas," she said, "but it would be unwise to approach them about it at this time. Respectfully, I'll ask you to leave that to me. I'll work on it, but people talk. I doubt I'd be able to stop all that prattle, even with a composite-based plane in the air."

Barton decided not to press this. He shifted back to his main topic: "What else do you need?"

"We always need more digital technology talent," she said, thankful that the subject had changed. "The frontier on digital modeling and innovation moves fast."

"Can we rely on partners' expertise in some of these areas?"

"To some extent, but not completely. We need in-house expertise to work effectively with partners. Otherwise, we'll be at their mercy when they start telling us what we have to do or can't do. It's similar to propulsion: we don't design or build jet engines for our cargo airplane; we outsource to one or two jet engine manufacturers. But we have a significant cadre of SMA propulsion engineers that work hand in glove with our outsourcers, our customers, and bridge to our propulsion outsourcers. Our cadre of propulsion engineers has the technical expertise to work in unique ways with our outsourcer propulsion engineers to ensure that our SMA 400 jet engines operate within the performance windows that we need and get effectively integrated into our airframe. Without our cadre of propulsion engineers, outsourcing engines would be a fiasco."

"How about you provide me with a list of what we need, in rank order, and how you think we should get it? And, ballpark, what you think it will cost. Not just people, but also capital investment, equipment, and facilities."

Akita nodded. "Finishing the development of this new plane will be costly." She paused for a moment, looking, Barton thought, for his reaction to this and signs of whether he'd faced reality. "A new plane," she continued, "always is. Clarke, the CFO, and his staff have been working with my folks to come up with numbers. There's always uncertainty and ways to save. But it will be a substantial amount."

"I'm meeting with Clarke tomorrow, and I'm already working on how we'll finance it."

"That's good. Ed Frazier wasn't great at that sort of thing. We're all hoping you'll be better at it."

Boldly stated, Barton noticed. Akita's outspokenness, never in short supply, seemed to be growing as she forged ahead.

"As to your broader question, as I rephrased it: do we have what it takes? Yes. We have the technology, the expertise, and the motivation. We *can* do it, if that is the direction our leaders set for us. But we also have a lot of change to deal with and a lot of learning in front of us. We need to continue our new plane design process and bring our potential customers more into the process. If we can get your support to strengthen in certain key areas, to change from a defense contractor culture to a commercial culture, I know we can win in any competition."

No hedging here, Barton thought. *On the contrary, a guarantee— almost—of victory.* He pressed a little further: "One more question: What haven't I asked you that you think I should have?"

Akita nodded. "One question you might be thinking but haven't said out loud is 'Do *I* have what it takes?' Me. Susan Akita."

Curious about where this might go, Barton didn't deny it. "Do you?" he asked.

She studied Barton before she answered. The assessing, Barton realized, went both ways. Then she began to speak:

"I've risen to the level of chief engineer in a male-dominated organization, within a male-dominated industry. My parents, loyal US citizens of Japanese ancestry, started their young family in an internment camp in Washington State. My older brother was born there. When I was born, several years later, my father and mother were still trying to recover a semblance of their lives before the war. It was hard, and they never really did it. They taught me to work hard and keep quiet. Throughout high school and engineering school, I was that quiet kid in the back of the class who got the best grades. Not just because I was smart, but because I worked. Really worked. Now and then one of my professors took exception to giving a 'girl' the best grade in the class, but I always earned it, whether or not they gave it to me. I've dedicated my life to making the best possible products for the defense of the country that interned my parents and took away their livelihood—because of how they looked, not who they were."

Barton said nothing. He had the distinct sense that he had not earned the right to speak at this moment.

"Maybe," she continued, "you're having thoughts about new blood, new ideas. Maybe that's the way it's going to go. But I assure you, there's no one in this company who has arrived at their current station in a manner more determined by hard work and merit. And if you decide to stay with me, you'll have my unqualified loyalty, my best efforts, and my most candid opinions. Just like Ed Frazier did. Just like his predecessor, Bill Ford. That's who I am. And in this—only this—I am too old to change."

She seemed finished. Barton waited, considering her words and how to answer them. Knowing he had no chance of matching her gravitas, he opted for an honest plea:

"Then please let me help you solve some of your most pressing problems," said Barton. "It's my job. I am at your service."

Akita seemed surprised. She smiled. "You mean beyond my needing composite materials people and digital tech expertise?"

"If you need that, you'll get it. Already handled," said Barton.

"And funding for the new plane?"

Barton smiled, "I'll do my best."

A new thought flashed across Akita's face, but she stayed silent, until Barton prodded her. "There is one other thing . . ." she started.

"Yes?"

"Not sure it's the highest priority, but it's important, and it's on my mind because my staff has been complaining. You want it straight?"

"I always want it straight. You just told me that's the only way you give it."

"I told you also that I know how to keep quiet. I can do that too."

"No. I want it straight."

Akita launched into a venomous diatribe: "It's the bloody merit pay system. It's total nonsense, some sort of HR brainchild. They want to pay my guys for patent applications, that sort of thing. Trivial sums. It's ridiculous, just makes my guys roll their eyes. It's based on lots of absurd assumptions about what motivates great engineers. But some-how, you exec types seem to really believe in that monetary incentive crap. Every year, it becomes a major distraction in my department. I'm sick to death of it. I don't think the system ever provides any positive motivations, but it sure does trigger a lot of fairness issues. It really upsets people. Unnecessarily. If we have to have it, I'd love to at least get it to a point where the performance management system doesn't get in the way."

"Well, if that's the best you think you can hope for from the system, it does sound like it's off the rails. I'll look into it. I'm meeting with the HR team next week, I think. Is that where it's coming from?"

"There," said Akita, "and with the board of directors' blessing."

Barton thought he did recall discussion of the merit-based pay system at a past board meeting. Others had largely driven the discussion. Barton didn't remember the details. "I'll check into it," he said again.

Akita stood to go. Barton felt unsure how to conclude the conversation. Akita, whose personal style featured a substantial abruptness component, didn't seem to be waiting for Barton to tie a bow on anything. But without getting up, he did make one final observation: "You know, Susan, *you too* are an executive in this company."

"Excuse me?" she answered.

"You talk as if executives are other people. But you are one too, and you provide important leadership. Very important."

Akita's mouth formed into a tight line. "I suppose that's true. Of course it is. But I don't think of it that way, not usually."

"Thanks for all that you do, Susan," Barton said. He stood and gathered up his tray full of empty dishes. Akita nodded and turned, with her own tray, toward the dish belt.

Barton smiled as he watched her recede across the room. He suspected it might take a while to really get to know Susan Akita. One thing he *was* sure of though: she was a keeper. Like the guys in the plant and their culture of improvement, here was another solid piece of the puzzle. *Probably she would have been a better choice for CEO than the current bozo,* he thought.

Wednesday, October 28, 2:36 p.m. . . .

With a start, Barton realized that all eyes in the room had turned to him. Every person at the meeting looked expectantly across the table at Barton, waiting for him to offer his opinion about the issue on which the conversation had deadlocked.

And Barton had absolutely no idea what to say.

He wasn't even following the discussion very well. They'd been debating something about the extent to which they should rely on simulation in the design of a braking system for the new plane. It wasn't a safety issue, Barton gathered, because the braking system would receive extensive physical testing at the end of the process, no matter what. The issue had more to do with how far into the design process they should go with simulations before moving to physical prototypes. The decision hinged on costs—simulation was much cheaper than physical prototyping—but also on how faithful simulations would be to physical reality. If they discovered, when moving to prototypes, that the simulations hadn't been very accurate, then they'd have to backtrack and do a lot of earlier prototyping where they'd thought simulation might suffice. Thus, from what Barton could follow, it boiled down to differing degrees of faith in the simulation technology they had available.

The people around the table had mostly reverted to type. The crusty old engineers didn't trust simulations much. Give them physical prototypes any day. The youngsters in the room, especially those from the digital technology group, argued in favor of more aggressive use of simulation. In their minds, this stuff was too cool not to use. The subgroups had clustered themselves on opposite sides of the table, probably in anticipation of this disagreement.

In the young faces, Barton saw energy and enthusiasm, a fondness for change and new ideas that he knew the company needed. But he also saw a wild-eyed recklessness. He understood the hesitation of the older engineers. But he also saw in the experienced staff reflexes toward resistance, fear that new technologies might render their experiences less valuable, and simple disaffection with the audacity of youth.

Barton could see all this playing out, but he didn't think his perceptions amounted to enough substance to allow him to speak in a way that would resolve anything. He'd be hard pressed, he realized, to say anything at all that sounded intelligent on this deeply technical subject.

The silence and stares became uncomfortable, and Barton concluded he'd have to say something. But Shelly Kranz, SMA's highest-profile test pilot, quietly sitting in the meeting until then, threw Barton a lifeline.

"Come on, you guys," Kranz said, "let's don't make this a religious issue." Eyes turned from Barton to the other end of the table where Kranz sat. She pushed back from the table, placed a booted foot against its edge, and joined her fingers behind her head, leaning back. The move communicated a certain *Top Gun* swagger, and Barton could see that it worked. In that moment, she claimed the credibility to resolve the debate. "It's like anything else. We ought to try new stuff. But let's don't get way out on a limb here. Get out there, but not all the way."

Coming from a test pilot, this suggestion could not have appeared more sensible. The conversation immediately restarted in a better place with a more cooperative spirit. The impasse was resolved. Debate now focused on details, not principles. Design of the new plane continued.

Krishnan tapped him on the shoulder, Barton's cue to depart. He said a few more encouraging words and told a short joke about an earlier time when he'd demanded that a group "speak English" by spelling out an acronym, only to be embarrassed to learn that the acronym he'd fixated on was basic to everyone else in the room and should have been to him, too. The joke worked, he thought. It asked these engineers, in a subtle way, to be patient with him as he learned the ropes. By poking fun at himself, he diffused criticism. Then he excused himself from the meeting and followed Krishnan out of the building.

Wednesday, October 28, 4:33 p.m. . . .

Krishnan continued to explain his way through a thick file, but Barton had lost the ability to concentrate. He'd spent most of Monday meeting people at the company's headquarters, all of Tuesday in SMA plants, and Wednesday with engineering. Exhaustion had overtaken him.

He interrupted Krishnan: "So that IT person, what's her name?"

"You mean Angel?" asked Krishnan.

"Yes, Angel. She's due when?"

Krishnan looked at his watch. "Any minute now. She said she'd come by sometime after 4:30."

Barton nodded: "Remind me of major events tomorrow and the next few days?"

"Tomorrow afternoon is Clarke Gardner, the CFO. We rearranged to fit that into your schedule, at your request. More tours the rest of the week."

"I want to meet with the communications director soon; you've got that down?"

"Yes, that's Linda Kohler," said Krishnan. "She's eager to meet with you, too. And the HR vice president, Jack Bruun, wants to talk with you. He needs approval on the merit pay plan. People get upset if that gets delayed. Both are scheduled for—" he checked his notebook to be sure— "next week."

"The CIO?"

"Jen Sharp. Also next week," said Krishnan, still referencing his notebook.

"I'd also like to talk to customers."

"We've got some scheduled."

"Tomorrow let's revisit the schedule," Barton said. "But after this meeting with . . . it's Angel, right?" Krishnan nodded. "After that, I think it's time to call it a day."

"As you wish," said Krishnan with a hint of disapproval. Barton suspected the man might go on all night if nobody stopped him. "I'll make sure your car is waiting to take you to your apartment."

"Great. And there's one more thing," Barton said.

Krishnan waited, slightly sullen. Barton continued: "I don't want to keep living in corporate housing. Find me a bungalow in Venice. I'll rent for now, or if you see something that looks like a good buy, we can talk about that."

"Venice, sir? That's not exactly an executive neighborhood."

"Nonsense," said Barton. "Have you driven around down there? Porsches and Mercedes on every curb. And lots of work to keep high-priced architects very busy."

"None of our other executives live in Venice," observed Krishnan.

"Venice is cool," interjected a female voice. Barton and Krishnan turned. Framed in the open doorway, between Barton's office and a receiving area where Krishnan usually stationed himself, stood a small exotic-looking young woman.

"Mr. Barton," Krishnan said, "this is Angel Crow."

Her face featured multiple piercings—nose, ears, eyebrows—and she was dressed entirely in black, with an emphasis on leather: leather jacket, leather boots, and leather leggings under a short knit tunic. Red- and orange-streaked spikes jutted from her dark hair, and heavy black lines encircled her eyes.

Barton recognized her as the person who had dashed away with his mobile phone and tablet on the morning of his arrival. Which prompted him to start on a different tack than he'd originally intended. Motioning her to a place at the table, waiting just a moment for her to settle in, Barton began barking, "I want my tablet back."

"We'd rather replace it, sir," said Crow, standing her ground. "It's not secure. And because of its design, we can't make it secure."

Barton considered this. "Will the replacement work as well?"

"Better," said Crow. "I promise."

Her firm manner, more than what she said, quieted Barton, somewhat. But he wasn't done complaining.

"I got my cell phone back, but now a lot of things don't work."

"We had to lock it down," said Crow.

"Lock it down?" Barton asked.

"For security reasons," she said.

"I see," said Barton, annoyed but impressed by the young woman's confidence.

"I recommend that we replace your phone, too," said Crow. "That replacement will work better too, after you spend a couple of days getting used to it."

Barton wanted to grumble some more, but instead he turned back to Krishnan.

"I need you to get Jonathan Luce on the line."

"Jonathan Luce, sir?"

"Yes. His private phone number is in the address book I gave you on Monday. Shouldn't be too hard to reach him this time of day. Unless he's traveling. It's L-U-C-E."

"Jonathan Luce, the technology guy?" asked Crow.

"That's the one," said Jim. "Serial entrepreneur and technology guy. He's a good friend of mine."

Barton didn't mention how he'd met Luce. For months, the two of them had hung out in the same sports bar, watching ball games together and talking off and on without even knowing each other's names. Barton had assumed that Luce, who seemed to him like a mere kid, did a tech job of limited significance for a local university. Only later did he discover that Luce was a veteran of many successful exit strategies lately turned venture investor, philanthropist, and nerd celebrity.

"Wow," said Crow. "I hear he's seriously great."

"Put him through to this phone when you get him," said Barton. Krishnan nodded and headed for the outer room.

Barton turned to Crow.

"I didn't call you down here to complain about my phone and tablet," he said. "I have an idea, and I'm hoping you can help. They tell me you're very good at anything tech related."

"I try," she said. "Sometimes things work out well."

"You're being modest. Someone told me you're the one they put on the really hard problems. Like protecting our technology secrets from Chinese hackers."

"Not just Chinese," she said. "But yes, that's basically correct. How can I help?"

Barton felt discomfort set in. "I'm not that technical," he said, "but let me see if I can lay this out. I've been meeting people over the past few days who are doing very interesting things with prototyping. They call it 'trystorming' in the factories. Trystorming helps us improve manufacturing faster than we'd be able to otherwise. I've also seen how simulation saves us money as we're developing airplanes. I'm also painfully aware of how many aspects of this business are entirely new to me. And I'm wondering if I can put these circumstances and ideas together with technology to give me a boost getting up to speed in this job. I need to learn *faster*."

He paused. Crow shook her head.

"I'm not seeing what you want," she said. "You want to simulate something?"

"What I want is to try out ideas and decisions *without* having to make the mistakes in real life. I want a management decision helper."

"We don't have anything like that," said Crow. "If we had anything like that, I'd know."

"Yes, well, that's where Luce comes in," Barton said. He raised his voice and called into the next room. "Krish, find Luce yet?"

"Putting him through now," Krishnan called back.

Barton's phone rang. He punched a button and put it on speaker.

"Hello, Jonathan," he said.

"Hi ya, Jim," said a high-pitched voice at the other end of the phone. "What's happ'nin, man?"

Barton introduced Crow and Luce, and then repeated, more or less, what he'd said to Crow about what he wanted. "Didn't you tell me last time you and I talked that you have an investment in a company working on something like that?"

"Yes, actually," said Luce. "Not sure it's really ready for prime time, but we've been playing around with something kind of like that. Combining a massively multiplayer, online role-playing computer-game environment with web crawling, data mining, and some artificial intelligence technology."

"Wow," said Crow, "seriously cool."

"I'm not sure how good it would be for your purposes," Luce continued, "but I think the folks there would be excited to have you try it out and give them feedback. Let me make a few calls and get back to you."

"Get back to Angel here. I'm told she's our best, so I'm trusting you not to recruit her away from us." The steady mask of the young woman's face verged on a smile. "Work with her to see what you can set up."

"If this gets interesting, we might need to get formal about intellectual property arrangements," said Luce. "We'll need to get nondisclosure agreements in place."

"Our lawyers will talk to your lawyers," said Barton. "Let's not let them get in the way of doing something great here, though."

"We're on the same page there, brother," Luce said.

Crow and Luce exchanged contact information and the call concluded. Crow stood, eyes bright despite their heavy black liner.

"Thanks for including me in this project, sir," she said.

"Call me Jim," he said.

Crow gave a skeptical nod, and rose from her chair. When she had departed, Barton suddenly remembered how tired he was. Krishnan came to the door.

"Done for the day?" he asked.

Barton nodded.

"I'll call your driver then."

My driver, Barton thought, as he sighed. He'd caught himself sighing far too often these last few days. *I need to start doing something about that . . . tomorrow*, he thought.

Reflection

What is your assessment of SMA's assets and strengths (and weaknesses) as revealed so far? How can Barton leverage these assets and capabilities to meet the needs for transition?

Which meetings should Barton prioritize in the first two weeks of his job as the new CEO?

Assuming Gerunzi was right and the "accident" on the plant floor was in fact a warning message from the unions, what should Barton do with that information?

FIRST INTERLUDE

The Lords of Leadercraft

SSEER, a simulated senior executive experience role-play by Simavatar Studios

Three men stand on the balcony of a futuristic mountain citadel. In the distance, against snow-crowned peaks, a large bird with wings outstretched sails higher on a warm air current. Although partially obscured by wispy, purple clouds, the bright sun shines strong blue light across the landscape, casting shadows, creating regions of light and dark with sharply defined boundaries.

On the balcony, two men stand together. One leans against the rail of cold, polished alloy, inattentive to the magnificent view, while the other stands back from the ledge, gesturing emphatically. They appear deep in serious conversation. The third man stands further away, also at the rail but looking out toward the mountains and disengaged from the other two.

"It's not too late to admit you've made a mistake," says Bob Goldman, CEO of Erlington Financial Group, the figure standing back from the rail, "As I've told you before, Jim, I don't think this is a good idea."

Jim Barton, the man at the rail—CEO of Santa Monica Aerospace, former COO at EFG— turns to answer: "I'm hearing you say that, Bob, but I'm still struggling to understand why."

Goldman has been a mentor and longtime personal hero to Barton. Goldman had wanted Barton to remain at EFG, but that's not the reason for what he's saying now. If Goldman thought taking the job at SMA was good for Barton, he'd say so.

"I don't think you're ready, Jim," says Goldman. "CEO—it's a different role than the one you're used to." His voice echoes against the surrounding rocks.

"You think it's too big a step," Barton says.

"It's a big responsibility, yes. But that's not it. People imagine that CEOs are powerful people. In some ways, that's true. But the most striking thing when you're in the job is what you *can't* do. You can't do what you were good at doing on the way up. The operational skills that earned you the CEO job aren't that relevant to it. As CEO, you set directions, send messages—everything you do or say now will send a message, whether you intend it or not."

Barton nods but remains silent.

"If you try to exert too much direct influence, you'll discover everyone is waiting for your approval before they do the next thing. Interject yourself too far into the action, even just once, and people will expect you to do it again. They'll fall into a pattern of always checking with you before they do anything themselves. You'll become a bottleneck. The company will screech to a halt. It's a different set of skills, Jim."

"I'm hardly a micromanager."

Goldman doesn't respond to this, but instead continues his lecture: "You don't have just one boss now. Every member of the board is your boss, and in the background are investors and analysts, all obsessing about short-term outcomes. You aren't going to get many second chances.

"I grew EFG to a thousand times its size when I took charge. But if I tried to do it again today, Jim, I'd never survive. I made too many mistakes. They let me learn on the job, but they are not going to let you do that. It's not that way anymore. Somehow, you'll have to figure out how to focus on the long term. You'll have to hold on to convictions while others, including board members, get cold feet. You'll get too much advice, much of it contradictory. Maybe you're already seeing some of that."

Goldman goes silent. Barton, believing the other man has finished, turns to face the landscape. Below them, a river winds through a lush green valley. Serrated crests jut into the blue sky. The large bird circles.

"Santa Monica is where I grew up," Barton says, to himself more than to Goldman. "I can see my mother more often."

"I understand," Goldman says. "Seeing your mother is important. But . . ."

"But it's got nothing to do with whether taking this job was a good idea," interrupts Barton.

"Exactly," Goldman agrees. He steps forward to join Barton at the rail. Both stare into the distance. "You are not even going to be able to tell," says Goldman, now whispering, "what's going on in your own company, unless the people who work for you tell you. No one is ever again going to say anything to you without first considering what you want to hear."

He turns to face Barton. "You are," he says, "utterly alone."

Goldman turns back to the rails and time passes in silence. With a sudden lurch, the third man swings to face them and approaches. His high-pitched voice dispels the somber mood: "That's nonsense!" He laughs. "I don't know where he comes up with this stuff."

Barton fixes his gaze on the source of the voice and speaks a single word: "Luce!"

Luce wears his signature fashion item, a black T-shirt depicting a battle between the Orcs and the Humans, highlighted in colored flames. The contrast between Goldman, dressed in conservative suit and tie, and Luce, in basic nerdwear, is comical. The two come from different worlds. Maybe different planets.

"So, Jim, aren't you going to introduce me to your friend?" Luce asks.

Flustered, Barton turns to Goldman, then back to Luce.

"Just kidding, Jim," Luce says. "I know Bob. We're on a couple of boards together. Hey, Bob."

"Hello, Jonathan," says Goldman, sounding annoyed.

"I was kidding too," says Luce, "about not agreeing with Bob. I mean, he's right about the challenges of the CEO job. But I think you did the right thing, taking the job. I mean, sometimes you have to just do it, man.

"Bob," continues Luce, "I totally hear you about the challenges. That's cool. But would another two or three years really make a big difference? If he'll be ready then, he's pretty much ready now. Or else he'll never be ready and can't hack this kind of leadership role."

Goldman doesn't respond immediately, but when he speaks, it's with attitude: "Okay, Jonathan, let's get specific. Barton knows nothing about airplanes or the airplane business. He's spent his career in financial services."

"Bob, Bob, Bob." Luce shakes his head, and joins the other two at the rail. "That's twentieth-century thinking," Luce says.

"Here we go again," says Goldman to Barton. "He's playing the youth card."

"You think it's important," says Luce, "what people know."

"I do," Goldman agrees.

"You think it's important what resources and capabilities an organization has within it. What it owns and what it can keep."

"I do," Goldman agrees again.

"Yeah, okay. I can go with you part of the way on that. Who you've got on your team matters a lot. But this is the age of Google, Bob. Hello!"

With this, Luce slides a threatening-looking sleek device down his forefinger. It looks like some kind of ray gun. Then he points it at Barton, causing a small search screen to appear on Barton's shirt, startling the two older men. "You don't need to know everything already. You don't need to own it. And you don't need to keep it." Having enacted an instant search, Luce now scrolls through a stream of personal data detailing Barton's career, schooling, finances, and even personal photos. "You just have to be able to search for it, secure it for long enough, get the right people involved with it, and then move on again, ahead of your competitors. On to the next search."

Barton jumps out of the device's path, and the search disappears. Luce laughs at Barton's action. "What?" he asks. Then he flicks his eyebrows up and down and delivers his summary statement: "It's not about being, man. It's about becoming."

Goldman shakes his head. "That's a gimmick, Jonathan. Magic thinking. Let's be serious. You know and I know you've got to have a core," he said. "You've got to be good at something. You've got to be able to do something no one else can do as well."

"Uhhhhh, well, yeah. Again, okay, to a point. But that's, like, so internally focused, man. While you worry about your core, competitors catching the wave of the twenty-first century will be focused externally, accessing the wisdom of crowds; developing better, faster search and recombination; building webs of partners, inside and outside the company. Figuring out ways to access and control resources without establishing inflexible, static linkages and structures. Putting people into conditions in which they can produce outlier value, not trying to squeeze people into predefined roles. They'll be open-innovating while you try to push-start the closed kind."

"Pie in the sky," says Goldman. "The latest trendy silliness."

"Yeah, whatever. 'Nobody bothers to know things anymore.' Right? 'Kids today read blogs instead of books.' End of the world and all that. But maybe, just maybe, there's some wisdom in the new way, Bob. And face it. The old way brought us repeated financial cataclysms, bubbles that inflate and pop every few years, and way too many examples of serious business misbehavior. Ongoing eco-disasters. Self-interested catfights every time somebody tried to really do something about it and a trade-off had to be considered. And that's just the late twentieth century."

"Yes. Well there are babies and there's bathwater," says Goldman. "Plenty of good things happened in the twentieth century. But let's stick to the subject, shall we? Barton's got to make airplanes that won't fall out of the sky. SMA isn't a twenty-first-century company. It's a twentieth-century company, with twentieth-century capabilities and reflexes. Even if what you're talking about makes any sense, which I seriously doubt, this company doesn't know the first thing about becoming anything you're describing. It's a defense contractor trying to become a viable commercial company. Most companies that attempt such transitions fail. It's not a thing I like seeing Jim leap into."

"I know," says Luce. "You like Jim. You want what's best for him. I hear that. And I agree that a lot good happened in the twentieth century. Your points, Bob," he continues, "are good points. Nevertheless, we've all got to move on. What brought us to this place will not take us where we need to go. To go to the future, you have to live in the future, at least to some degree."

He turns to face Barton. "The CEO's job is a learning job. No one's ever really ready to do it, even the people who were one already. So," he concludes, "Godspeed, Jim." With this, Luce swings himself over the rail and leaps into the abyss. Immediately, he transforms into a large bird identical to the one in the distance. The Luce bird soars away, rising into the blue sunlight.

Barton stands, unmoving. He turns to Goldman, who shakes his head almost imperceptibly. Neither speaks.

CHAPTER 3

Financials and Trust

Sitting at his desk, Barton studied the SMA financial briefing book, preparing for a meeting with Clarke Gardner, the company's chief financial officer. The book had been waiting on Barton's desk when he'd arrived Monday morning, as he'd requested in advance. Tours and getting-acquainted sessions kept him from cracking the book open until today. But now he'd been able to spend more than forty-five minutes with it. He'd insisted on setting aside time for this in week one, both studying of the financials and the meeting with the CFO, for two reasons.

The first reason was practical: he needed to be sure he had a good handle on the company's situation. Barton's financial background made "the numbers" an important point of entry for him, a way of starting to form an overall picture that might offer him deeper insights and ideas. Having been a member of SMA's board of directors, he knew quite a lot already but needed to drill down into the details. And he wanted to compare his interpretations with someone knowledgeable, someone who knew the numbers and had been closer to the action at SMA.

Barton had seen Gardner give presentations to the board on numerous occasions and considered him extremely knowledgeable. Based on limited interactions, Barton had formed a strongly favorable opinion of Gardner's intellect and a belief that the CFO could be a huge asset. Expertise and brainpower would not be Gardner's shortcomings. But Barton feared that the CFO might just have another shortcoming, a potentially serious one. And *that* was the second and primary reason that Barton had insisted on rearranging his planned schedule to meet with the CFO in week one.

SMA's accounting practices under the previous CEO, Ed Frazier, had cost him that job. Technically, there'd been no wrongdoing. But the approach SMA had adopted, aimed at painting an optimistic picture of the company's situation, had been too aggressive. Companies choose accounting practices that make them look good all the time, and everybody understands that. But under Frazier, SMA had gone too far. It had created an impression within the broader financial community of trying to present an *overly* optimistic picture of the company's situation. SMA critics accused the company of engaging in "financial engineering"—a term that had taken on a pejorative meaning. The effect had been to undermine confidence in the company and its management. The outcome of this confidence issue made Barton's challenges as the new CEO tougher.

Now Frazier was gone (to the board of directors, unfortunately), but Gardner, the CFO who'd helped Frazier execute these questionable maneuvers, remained. What role Gardner had played—whether he'd recommended the questionable practices to his engineering-trained, not very financially savvy boss, or whether he'd advised against them and the blunder had been Frazier's alone—Barton needed to know.

Put simply, *Barton had to know if he could trust Gardner*. Quite apart from financial acumen, Barton had to know whether the man was fundamentally honest—of sound judgment and substantial character— enough for Barton to rely on him in the months and years to come. If the poor judgment had been Frazier's, then knowing this would help Barton manage his relationship with the board. With Frazier still around, Barton also had to know where Gardner's loyalties would lie in a crisis. Barton's assessment would depend to a great extent on how forthcoming Gardner appeared in response to Barton's questions.

Barton had *not* already decided to fire Gardner, though that was a possible outcome of the meeting. Gardner might well arrive at the meeting expecting to be let go. That would be a likely reason for a new CEO to insist on an early meeting with the CFO, especially given SMA's recent financial history. And firing the CFO could have advantages; it would send a strong signal to the financial community that the new CEO would not tolerate the accounting practices of the recent past and perhaps begin restoring confidence in SMA. Barton had intentionally made no effort to diffuse Gardner's expectation that he might be sacked. It might be useful to see how Gardner would bear up under the stress of that worry.

Barton looked around the office, deciding how to use the space for the meeting. Offices on the executive floor of the SMA headquarters were well appointed and technically up to date, but didn't possess the opulent, overdesigned quality of Barton's prior digs in a big-city, high-rise financial services headquarters. He'd seen all the offices on the floor by now, as first Krishnan had walked him around and then later he'd made a point of walking around by himself, looking in on members of the executive team to meet them, chat, or just say hello.

Barton had noticed that pretty much everyone had great airplane models in their offices, a not-so-subtle way of showing off the programs they'd worked on, at SMA and elsewhere. Several had Boeing, McDonnell Douglas, or Airbus models, which he assumed conveyed particular credibility and experience with the industry "big boys." Barton had no models of his own, of course, but someone had thoughtfully placed some SMA models in Barton's office, so he wouldn't feel out of place (in this regard at least).

Barton's office contained a large desk, a pair of nice chairs, a small table for informal meetings, and a large leather sofa that Barton thought he could comfortably sleep on. Through one door, just off the main office, a formal conference room with a long table and a high-technology setup awaited. Just beyond this and through another door, the CEO's private dining room beckoned. Also off the main office, tucked into a corner was a combination dressing room and bathroom, complete with a shower. Not quite as fancy maybe, but much bigger all together, than his former office at EFG.

Barton decided he'd keep the meeting with Gardner informal, that they'd sit at the small table in the main office.

On a notepad—paper, since he still hadn't received his new electronic tablet—Barton began listing questions for Gardner. Most were standard questions, ones he tended to ask about any company. First, he'd want to get at the big picture:

Are we winning or losing?

And:

What do we need to do as a company over the next three years, for the good of our customers, shareholders, and employees?

Then, in terms familiar within the CFO's world:

If we did these things, what would this look like in our pro forma financials?

And by extension:

What would need to change from what we see today?

From what Barton had been able to see so far, in the briefing book and in his wider research, there would be a cash problem, especially if the company planned to finish the development of its new commercial cargo plane, which he understood to be key to any path forward. He added questions about this:

How much funding do we need to finish development of the new plane?

Barton reckoned they needed about $8 billion for this, but it would be interesting to see what Gardner thought, having worked through the numbers with Susan Akita's engineering team. This demand for financing led directly to other questions:

Where will we get the money?

Some of it, Barton and everyone else had concluded, had to come from adjusting the cost structure of the existing organization. SMA was paying for things it had needed historically as a military contractor, but wouldn't need as a commercial aircraft company. People, organizations, services. Adjusting cost would be difficult. Everyone—analysts, investors, journalists, anyone else who cared enough to form an opinion—had concluded that this would mean layoffs, outsourcing, and other measures unpopular with key organizational constituencies. Barton had to admit that he saw no way around such conclusions. The path to these outcomes appeared treacherous, paved with potentially explosive problems with employees, unions, partners, municipalities, and even elected officials. The potential for these problems led Barton to several more questions:

Will we have cash flow problems? Other crises we can anticipate? If so, when? And what might we do to avoid them? Or at least schedule them in a manageable way?

SMA needed to use the money generated from its declining military business to transform itself into a commercial cargo plane provider. One good thing: the schedule for purchase of the last of the SMA military planes was reasonably certain and known, because it was specified in the contract. Barring unexpected and unlikely congressional action, SMA knew, more or less exactly, when it would get its remaining payments from the government and how much they would be. Legislators had not procured funding for development of a new military cargo plane, choosing instead to repeatedly extend funding for the SMA 400-3.

But this could not continue. The SMA 400-3 could no longer claim to be state of the art; the military wanted something better, but the government budget situation didn't look encouraging for a next-generation military cargo plane program. Events had reached an impasse, and although it remained possible that there would be a new program, SMA might not even win the contract, and the timing of funding for such a program would remain uncertain. This situation had led most observers, including Barton, to the conclusion that SMA could not rely on the military business to sustain it.

Barton wondered whether cutting manufacturing costs once again and lowering the price on the old plane might coax the military into extending its buy with SMA yet again, for at least a few more planes. This ploy had worked before. Ironically, SMA's success in previous cost cutting and price reductions had probably staved off congressional funding for a new plane program in the past, when the budget climate had been more favorable for the initiation of such a program. At the time, it had seemed like a good idea for SMA to get its current contract extended, rather than risk losing a new contract to another company, as might have happened with a new program. This was the decision with which Akita pointedly had not agreed.

Now efforts to upgrade the SMA 400-3 seemed increasingly like "putting lipstick on a pig." Past wisdom had turned into present problems. SMA made money from sales to other governments and to specialized commercial companies, though neither in great amounts. These sources of revenue might conceivably also be expanded. And the company expected revenues for a rather long time for maintenance and services associated with planes it had already sold, though again, that wasn't big money (but perhaps it could be more?).

Even if the company could milk more life out of its historical cash cow, from what Barton could see, SMA still faced a precarious future. The business the company had long depended on was in decline and clearly lacked viability going forward. The price of the stock wasn't very exciting and remained as good as it was only because of analysts' fragile beliefs that SMA intended to focus on two "imperatives": (1) transformation from a military business to a commercial business, and (2) modernization from a twentieth-century industrial economy manufacturer into a twenty-first-century systems integrator. Commitment to these imperatives had been stated again and again, before Barton's arrival. It had become a mantra, and Barton knew eager analysts would be listening to see whether and how often he would start to repeat it. They'd notice and analyze even the slightest variations in how he described the challenge. He'd have to be very careful about this, especially given the fragility of trust that observers now seemed willing to extend to SMA.

Barton wasn't sure what "modernization from a twentieth-century industrial economy manufacturer into a twenty-first-century systems integrator" would really mean in terms of specific organizational changes at SMA. He assumed it would generally involve less vertical integration and more outsourcing, with all the challenges that entailed. Whatever it meant, though, Barton thought it sounded expensive, which brought him to the really vital issue he'd need to work on with Gardner: *How will we get access to financing?*

The previous CEO's efforts to manage the stock price had impaired SMA's access to many possible financing sources. Barton had to admit that he couldn't see a viable way forward yet, though he had some ideas and his gut told him there had to be a way. If he hadn't thought the challenge could be met, he wouldn't have taken the job. But he did genuinely hope Gardner would have some helpful ideas.

Thursday, October 29, 2:46 p.m. . . .

Barton listened quietly for most of Gardner's forty-five-minute presentation. The barrel-chested CFO had a lively and easygoing way of imparting well-structured and concise information, which revealed the ingrained habits of military training. Though not too far from Barton's age, Gardner appeared older, thanks to a receding line of graying hair, partly offset by active eyes and a youthful face. They sat together at the table in Barton's office, working their way through the binder the CFO had prepared. The two men had quickly achieved a comfortable style of interaction. Gardner had pushed back from the table, placed one leg across another and begun to massage his bald spot with one hand, a gesture Barton interpreted as thoughtful and that conveyed unquestionable informality.

His presentation had confirmed much of what Barton had concluded about the company's situation. Asked, "Are we winning or are we losing?" Gardner had been candid: "We're losing. But we haven't lost yet, and we don't have to lose."

As Barton expected, Gardner believed in the possibility of a transition into a more efficient, probably radically reorganized company, with a specialized focus on the commercial cargo plane business. "There's definitely a growing market there," he'd said. "Someone will make money selling next-generation, much more efficient cargo planes. It might as well be us."

But, he conceded, again earning points with Barton for honesty, that he didn't see yet how to get there. The cash they'd generate from declining businesses would not be sufficient to pay for the development of the new plane, and the equity and debt markets didn't look very friendly.

"One possibility that's always lurking out there," Gardner said, "is that we become a much smaller company. A supplier to the big commercial airliner manufacturers, say. We already do some of that. We could focus on that and separate other parts of the business."

"That's the default option," agreed Barton. "Assuming we didn't wait too long to decide, that could work. But it would mean ceding that big, growing cargo plane market to someone else. So it would be nice to figure out another way. A way we might become a bigger, more prosperous company—the leader in our market space."

"Yes," agreed Gardner, "that would be better for all involved, including our surrounding communities."

"A major partner? A joint venture?" suggested Barton.

"Similar problem," said Gardner, "as with equity and debt. The terms wouldn't be very favorable, even if we could find a partner."

"Might it depend on whom," offered Barton. "Someone in a similarly tight spot?"

Gardner smiled. "Someone who could double our current troubles? I think we've all been hoping you might know someone helpful in the financial world." He said this with a wink. Barton chuckled. He liked Gardner. And he felt an undeniable sense of relief to be talking with a finance person. They shared a common language.

"Seems like we'll need a new philosophy for working with partners," Barton suggested. "The old vertical integration bias can't be the way forward. We'll have to discover, maybe invent, new organizational arrangements that will likely be more global, virtual, and tightly integrated and collaborative with people outside the boundaries of this company."

"I think you'll find the finance organization ready to go that route," Gardner said, "for a very practical reason: subspecialization or disintegration—outsourcing, to use a less popular word—often, but not always, looks better in the numbers. But other organizations, like engineering, manufacturing, and HR, will like it a lot less. Those words you just said mean something to me, but to others they sound like fluff, management-speak. They'll say we can't protect our IP, maintain quality and safety, or keep our people happy if we go that route. That's what they always say."

"We'll have to be careful about all that," conceded Barton. "What's the analysts' consensus?"

"About what you'd expect," said Gardner. He leaned forward, put both feet on the floor, becoming more formal. He knew where this part of the conversation was heading. "They look at us, see confusion," he continued. "They're not sure we can do it. Moving from military contractor to competitive commercial company, that's a big change. Not many companies make that kind of transition successfully."

"But," said Barton, "I doubt the markets are ready to see us turn away from our commitment to that transition. That decision is already made, don't you think?"

"It would be difficult to back away from that commitment. Though as a new CEO, you might have a window of opportunity," agreed Gardner.

"Like Gerstner, when he took over IBM. He decided to reverse the decision to break up that company into thirteen separate businesses."

"That's the example I had in mind."

"The rub is this," Barton said. "'Don't make the transition to a twenty-first-century company' is not quite the same kind of option as 'don't break up the company.'"

"No, it's not. I have to admit, I don't see another way."

"Would you invest your own money in this company?" Barton asked.

"I have. I do."

"No, I don't mean through your benefit plans or because of executive obligations. If you were an independent investor, with your current assessment, knowing what you know and applying your best judgment—would you?"

Gardner didn't think about it very long.

"No. The possibilities are there, but execution has been a problem. I'd want to see this company reestablish its ability to execute. I'd like to see a plausible financing plan, something convincing on how to adjust the cost structure without starting World War III with the unions. So, no. If I were an independent investor, outside the company, knowing what I know now, I wouldn't invest in SMA, not at the moment. Though I'd keep it in my hot file, to see what you might do with the company. If you're able to do something about the financing problem, I might move closer to making a wager. If I thought you had a way of dealing with the cost structures, especially the unions."

Barton didn't mention his "Ace in the hole." He still held out hope that his old friend, Ace Jackson, could be counted on. Though it had rattled him somewhat, he hesitated to consider what had happened on the factory floor as anything more than a misunderstanding and an accident. Regardless, he agreed with Gardner's assessment. "I wouldn't invest in us either," he said. "We're, what, a $6.5 billion company, and I'm guessing we might need to take out $800 million or so in cost?"

"I'd say between $600 million and $1.2 billion," Gardner offered. "I've done quite a bit of benchmarking. There's no doubt about it, our costs are way too high. For years, we've done much of our business with the government on a 'cost-plus' basis. We charge them what it costs us, plus an allowable profit margin. In recent years, that's changed some. We've seen more 'cost plus award fee,' which rewards us with higher profits when we keep costs down. But overall, these arrangements haven't led us to create a viable commercial cost structure."

"And we need how much to get the new plane to market?"

"At least $5.5 billion. Details are in your binder, behind the last tab. At worst . . ." Gardner looked hesitant. "Well, I can envision unhappy scenarios in which it might take $10 or $12 billion."

"If it costs that much, we're toast."

Gardner nodded. "Burnt crisp and ready for history's garbage bin."

"So can we agree that the problem is how to execute the transition? Not whether it's the right thing to do?"

"I'm certainly riding that train and have been for a while. Though if you have other ideas, I might be willing to get on board a different train. If I believed in it."

Gardner's statement hung in the air. He'd inadvertently—or perhaps intentionally—moved the discussion to the issue of his support for the new CEO and his plans. Barton decided it was time to go there.

"Whose train were you riding when you executed those stock buybacks for Ed Frazier?"

Gardner closed the binder he'd been referencing, which they'd pretty much finished with anyway. He pulled up to the table, folded his hands on it, and made a point of looking directly at Barton.

"That was Ed's train all the way, Jim. I tried to stop it. I realize that might sound like an excuse—"

"What happened?"

Gardner sighed, looked down at his hands.

"As you know, Ed isn't a finance guy. He's an exceptional aeronautical engineer and felt, naturally enough, that bringing out the best airplane was always the 'winning hand.' If SMA had been able to stay on this strategy, everything would have been all right, I think. But the world changed. No money for a new plane, so he needed to 'chew gum and play the piano' at the same time. Ed had trouble with this. Even if the climate had been right for a new cargo plane program, just building the best cargo airplane in the world is probably no longer enough to win. Unable to play his best hand, he began casting about for other options. He didn't like the financial side of things much. He didn't like talking to analysts and investors, wasn't good at it, and left most of that to me. Which is fine."

Barton interrupted, a little more aggressively than he intended: "That's not fine. To lead a twenty-first-century corporation, to provide effective oversight, the CEO and board members must become facile with accounting and the financial model, enough so that we can have a productive dialogue on big decisions. So we can collaborate in coming up with sound judgments."

Gardner nodded, waited to make sure that Barton had finished, and then continued: "Yes, well, he did start to become involved, though not the way you mean. Over time, Ed became fixated on the stock price. He celebrated every time it went up a little. And he noticed that he could do things that would influence the price."

"That's what a CEO does."

"Yes, but not all the things you do to increase your stock price are equally worthy. He had trouble with that. He underestimated the financial sophistication of the analyst community. He thought they'd go along with things they didn't."

"You didn't think so?"

"No, and I told him that. That we were being too aggressive, that it could all backfire and wasn't worth the risk. You were there at the board meeting where I urged caution. The auditors did, too. It was all legal. We had to admit that. Ed worked it all out with the audit committee, which you clearly should have been on—"

"I was on governance; I couldn't be—"

"Yes, I know," said Gardner, "but you'd have been way better than Van Busin, who chairs the audit committee."

"I'd have stopped it," said Barton.

"You almost did anyway, you and Owens," said Gardner.

"And Smithson," said Barton.

"Maybe I should have resigned," said Gardner. "But he'd have pointed to my resignation as the reason why the markets reacted the way they did. If I'd resigned, he'd have tried to stick it all on me. He might still be CEO if I'd resigned."

Gardner paused. He'd said the "R" word. When Barton didn't immediately throw him a lifeline, Gardner continued.

"Jim, I'm prepared to resign right now, if you think that's appropriate."

Barton nodded. He stood and walked to his new desk, lifting from its cradle the model of an SMA military plane. Like the company that had produced it, this plane projected an immense industrial accomplishment that had now become a little quaint. There would be no mercy in their brave new commercial world.

Barton sighed and returned to the table and sat. He knew what Gardner would be thinking: that Barton had obtained the information he needed from the CFO, that now it was time for the closing ceremony, the parting of ways.

The end of a career.

Gardner reached for his copy of the binder and stood: "I'll go get the letter. I've written it. It's on my desk. I should have brought it with me, but I thought . . . I hoped . . ."

"Sit down, please," said Barton.

Gardner complied, unable to hide his fear.

"You want to be part of this?" said Barton. "What we're going to do here to turn this company around?"

Gardner nodded. "I do," he said quietly. "If you think I can help."

"I don't think it's time for you to go, Clarke. If I want your resignation, I'll let you know. But I don't want it right now."

At first relieved, soon Gardner became newly distraught. "Right now?" he said. "Can you give me a sense of where I stand? I'd like to help, but I won't be effective if I'm on pins and needles."

Barton nodded. That was reasonable. "Clarke, I think you've been straight with me today. If I find out you haven't been, you'll be fired before you resign. So if you think back through what you've told me and decide you haven't told me the truth, I recommend you go get that letter and bring it back here. If you do, I'll accept it, because I'll know what that means."

"It's true, Jim, all of it. It's actually more important to me that you believe that than that I keep this job."

Barton smiled, for the first time extending a modicum of reassurance.

"You don't have to choose between me believing you and your job. You're on the team. For now. Just like the rest of us. We're all on this team just for now. Nothing's settled. If you haven't noticed, I'm on thin ice here, too. But let's see if we can't move toward more prosperity and security for all of us."

He had decided to confide in Gardner. Barton knew he'd need someone with whom to share confidences, to bounce around ideas. He slid back from the table and stood again.

"So here," said Barton, "is the rough outline of what I have in mind. My entering idea, on my very first week of work. Of course, it will have to change, and almost nothing about it is worked out. I'll need your help with it. But I would not have taken this job if I didn't think it might work."

Gardner sat back and replaced one leg atop the other, all ears and clearly delighted to remain a part of the conversation.

"As you noted before," Barton said, "I have some connections in the financial world. This is confidential, but I want to get my former boss, Bob Goldman, onto the SMA board. We'll work with him to arrange the financing we need. I've got nothing in place, and no assurances. Goldman actually thinks we're a lost cause and disapproves of my decision to take this job. But I'm pretty sure he'll work with us, give us a fair chance. We'll have to work our butts off to get this thing together, and it'll be constructed like a house of cards. The slightest puff of wind, a weakness anywhere in the structure, and it'll all come tumbling down. But we might, if we work hard, be able to get it together for long enough to shore it up and make it sturdier. It'll be delicate work, and I'll need a lot of help from you."

Gardner nodded.

"Of course, the financing won't happen unless we can demonstrate that we'll be able to reorganize, restructure, and gain some concessions from various stakeholders."

"You mean the unions," said Gardner. "That's going to be tough."

"As a matter of fact, I have a connection there too. I'm fairly confident that together we can work something out."

Barton had been imagining Ace Jackson as the cornerstone in his house of cards. Gardner didn't look convinced, but he didn't say so. Barton continued.

"Organizationally, we're going to have to be very careful about what we need to do inside the company, and what we can do outside it. Those will be complex, multifaceted decisions."

"My staff can provide info that will help with those decisions," said Gardner. "You'll need to know what's costing us a lot, and what isn't, comparatively speaking."

"Yes, I need that from you. As soon as you have it."

"We'll get right on it."

Barton stood and so did Gardner.

"Think about what we've talked about," said Barton. "I want you to punch holes in it."

Gardner nodded, turning to go. "Thanks for the meeting," he said. Barton smiled and moved toward his desk. When Gardner reached the door, however, he turned back.

"Jim?"

Barton looked at him.

"Yes."

"Thanks for this opportunity. You won't be sorry."

"I'm counting on it," said Barton. "Now, go do great things. We're going to need a lot of them."

"Yes, sir," Gardner said, delivering a quick mock salute before turning to leave.

Thursday, October 29, 5:52 p.m. . . .

"Jonathan Luce on line one," Krishnan called out from the outer office.

Barton snatched up the phone.

"Jonathan."

"Hi, Jim. You get a chance to try that sim we sent over? It's still rough—"

"It's fantastic, Jonathan. I tried it this morning."

"Well. Great to hear, Jimbo. You'll be glad to know we think we can make it a lot better."

"It's still pretty videogame-like," said Barton. "You turned into a bird toward the end of the session."

"Well, until not very long ago, it *was* a videogame, Jim," Luce pointed out. "A bird, huh? Did that bother you? Want it less videogame-like?"

"No, it's fine," Barton said. "The simulations of you and Goldman were very realistic."

"That's a result of the data mining and AI applications. We sucked in all the info we could find on the web to build simulated characters. Shortly, it'll be dynamic. We should be able to set it up so that it's always taking in new info, always updating the characters and what they have to say."

"I recognized some of what the Goldman character said from a published interview in *Forbes*," said Barton. "But it made more of an impression being delivered by an animated character like that. That definitely added value."

"We'll get you a new version to test soon," said Luce. "By the way, you were right about Angel, she's a major talent. At some point, I will be forced to hire her away from you."

"But not today," said Barton.

"No," said Luce, "not today. Say, I need to get onto an airplane here, Jim, so I'll talk to you later."

"No problem," said Barton. "I look forward to the next iteration."

"We aim to please," said Luce, as he signed off.

Reflection

What is your assessment of the previous CEO Ed Frazier's choices? How should Barton manage his relationship with Frazier?

Should Barton trust Gardner?

Are Barton and Gardner asking the right questions to determine the financial health and future of SMA?

How well do you think Barton is navigating assessment of his new senior management team (Gardner, Marochek, Akita)? How can he best use them as he moves forward in developing the new strategy at SMA? How should leaders best go about building and using their senior management teams?

CHAPTER 4

Transparency

"Jim," said PR director Linda Kohler, "I've been in this business for a long time—a *long* time—and experience suggests that what you're proposing would be a big mistake—a *big* mistake."

She pumped up the volume with each utterance and had an annoying habit of repeating phrases in order to shift the pitch of key words up an octave. At first, she'd sprinkled a lot of false humility and "with all due respects" into their conversation. But now she'd abandoned even that thin semblance of deference. Barton abhorred kowtowing, and he'd expected this meeting to be difficult. But he hadn't counted on it being *this* difficult.

Kohler sat forward in a chair at the small conference table in Barton's office. Earlier, as she'd lectured him, he'd stood up to walk off his growing annoyance. Eventually, he settled on the couch, across the room from her. Now the two of them stared daggers at each other, far past any hope of rapport.

Barton thought they were discussing a divergence of philosophies, about how open or closed a company could remain in an age of blogs, mobile phones, and social networks. But Kohler clearly thought she was teaching a new, inexperienced CEO how the PR process had to work in a "real" company. She was trying to avoid a repeat of the kind of amateur mistake he'd made when he took a phone call from the *So-Cal Times*—apparently from Veronica Perez herself—though he had not known that at the time.

Barton knew he'd screwed up. He'd admitted as much to Kohler, right off the bat. Nevertheless, she felt compelled to explain to him, repeatedly and in full detail, how carefully the communications department had orchestrated his introduction as the new SMA CEO and how he'd fouled that up.

First, she explained, they had carefully composed announcements for customers, employees, investors, the press, and other interested parties, each specially targeted to its audience. The announcements contained selected biographical information and a carefully vetted and tested message from the new CEO, designed to inspire confidence but avoid making promises. SMA communications had composed these announcements and planned the timing of their release with impeccable precision.

Second, in the lead-up to the announcement, the communications group had discreetly contacted reporters at the *Wall Street Journal, Financial Times,* and a few other prominent outlets, both print and online, to give them advance warning. Early notice allowed these newspapers to prepare thorough and well-researched stories, which would be published in sync with the SMA announcement. The particular reporters chosen understood and honored a tacit agreement: they'd keep getting such scoops, as long as they cooperated with SMA on the timing of the news release. They'd done it this way a thousand times, so no one expected surprises, and there had been none. The stories appeared at appropriate times; other news outlets picked up, reprinted, and quoted from these friendly accounts.

Third, and shortly before the announcement, the communications staff had alerted a larger group of friendly writers that important information would soon be released. The writers would be given privileged access for interviews with the new CEO. SMA PR developed a schedule that controlled when and how long Barton would speak to each reporter, in the process enforcing an understanding of how a journalist got added to the favored list and how one moved up the list to get earlier access when there was breaking news from SMA. PR had also designed the schedule to provide maximum access to Barton while making the best use of his limited time. All of this, too, had gone completely according to plan.

Indeed, *everything* had conformed to plan, until Barton had agreed to take a call from a certain "Ms. Veronica Perez" of the *So-Cal Times.* At that point, Barton had, in colloquial terms, "gone off the reservation." In the minds of PR staff members, he'd made "a rookie mistake." As Kohler saw it, the editorial in the *So-Cal Times* that had irked Barton on his first day at SMA had been the predictable result.

Barton protested, accurately he thought, that Perez could have written that editorial whether she'd talked to Barton or not. It included no information that she'd obtained from Barton during the call.

To Kohler, however, this made no difference. He'd made a mistake, and he needed to avoid making it again. If the consequences had been mild, well, that didn't change the facts.

Barton thought his admission of error and apology should have ended that line of discussion. But now they kept circling back to it, as they discussed how to handle Perez at a charity event where he was certain to encounter her.

Kohler and Perez had a history that explained the former's vehemence in this matter. Perez had been on none of the favored lists because of past misbehavior. So it galled Kohler that she'd gotten past SMA's PR defenses to talk to Barton before he arrived at the company. In what Barton now understood to be an ongoing war between Perez and Kohler, Barton had helped Perez win a battle. In taking that call, Barton had undermined the implicit "code" that allowed precise execution of plans, like the one designed for introduction of the new CEO. He'd let Kohler's team down and undone their good work. As Kohler perceived it, he'd been disloyal to her personally.

It was a lot to overcome in a first meeting.

"I don't think you should say two words to Ms. Perez this evening," Kohler repeated. "She's been trouble in the past; she'll be trouble again in the future. There's simply no upside for SMA in engagement with her."

"If we ignore our critics," said Barton, "we antagonize them. And we have no channel through which to influence them."

"That's simply not true," said Kohler. "Maybe that's the way a financial service firm runs, but we're in the defense business. We have secrets that must be kept. We have to *control* information."

"Linda, I've had some experiences, too. Once upon a time, in an earlier life, I presided over a team responding to an attack on our computer systems. We had trouble figuring out what was going on, and that created serious disclosure issues for us. We tried to control information about the incident. But in the weeks that followed, we discovered several examples of ways the information had gotten out, despite our best efforts. Employees blogged about it. Analysts put two and two together. And none of it had the negative effects we feared. In these times, we have no choice. We're going to have to be more open. More transparent."

"Maybe we should post all our national security secrets out on the public Internet," said Kohler, sarcastically.

"Of course we won't do that!" responded Barton, angrily, "I'm not saying that at all. It's not that black and white. We're going to have to be smarter than that."

"Smarter than I am, I guess." Kohler crossed her arms, sat back in her chair, and rolled her eyes.

Barton tried to cool things down. In a calm, measured voice, he stated his position: "If Veronica Perez has been a problem in the past, that's all the more reason to engage with her. Yes, she'll cause us more trouble, but if we engage with her, maybe we'll have a better sense of what she's up to and maybe even influence what she writes."

"That's optimistic, to say the least," said Kohler. "Possibly even naive."

She'd finally said it. That word, *naive,* had been prominent in the subtext of her comments throughout their conversation.

"How about if we try it my way?" suggested Barton. "Rather than ignore Perez, which hasn't been working very well, let's surprise her by *approaching* her. What do you think?"

Kohler exhaled in frustration. "I well understand," she said coldly, "that a lot of men would like to *approach* Veronica Perez. She's an attractive woman."

"Come on!" protested Barton. "That's not remotely what I meant! I've never met the woman. I have no idea what she *looks* like, nor do I care. How she looks has nothing to do with what we're talking about."

Kohler pulled back. "Well, you'll discover how she looks soon enough." She stood. "I've made my recommendations. You're the boss. Try it your way. I think it's a mistake, but go ahead."

"I'll use my judgment. You're going to have to trust me."

"And you, me."

"Fair enough," said Barton.

And with that, Kohler, arms still folded, whirled and hurried away.

Harder Than I Thought

The gala event to raise money for a new library had been under way for roughly forty minutes when Veronica Perez made her entrance. Barton, while half-listening to an older woman recounting her difficulties "flying commercial," noticed a disturbance on the other side of the room. At first, he couldn't see what caused it.

He'd arrived in the ballroom of the Wilshire Grand twenty minutes earlier, accompanied by Bobbi Smithson, an SMA board member and head of the fund-raising committee for the new library. Smithson had been walking Barton around, introducing him to other guests. Though he felt uncomfortable, as always, in the stiff tuxedo, Barton knew what was expected of him. Smile pleasantly. Nod often. Shake hands warmly. Act distinguished, but betray signs of humility. Say vague and complimentary things about SMA and its employees. As appropriate (but not too often), deliver a reliable stock phrase—"That must be a very fascinating business right now . . ." This always produced a period of five or ten minutes in which he didn't have to say anything and could return to smiling and nodding. Now and then, he managed to meet someone to engage in more stimulating conversation, but he had not yet been so fortunate this evening.

The lady relating her airline adventures had also noticed the commotion across the room. She stopped and craned her neck: "I wonder who . . ." she said. Then, suddenly, she tipped her head toward the ceiling. "Oh," she said, oozing disdain. "It's *her*." Barton couldn't see who *she* was, so he stepped forward to get a better look.

A shatteringly beautiful woman emerged from the crowd, wearing a very short, glittering, dusty gold dress. When she turned, Barton saw that the back of the dress plunged to reveal tanned shoulders and (he thought, but could not be sure) a tattoo at the base of her spine. Her luxurious dark hair converged into a sleek knot at the nape of her neck. The dress displayed long, strong, tanned legs, which stiletto heels drew into an elegant line that hastened Barton's heartbeat.

"Wow," he said.

The older woman at his side heard him. "You men," she said, shaking her head. "Put a short dress on a tall woman and you go all to pieces."

Having made this observation, she turned away and sought an audience with a female friend.

Barton didn't notice.

Summoning his composure, he noticed that Perez—for this could only be the infamous Veronica Perez—was accompanied by a mobile-device-laden entourage. An immaculately coiffed young man wearing a lavender plaid suit and an ironical expression tapped at a smart phone, apparently transmitting Perez's every move to an adoring (or at least interested) public. Another young man, lanky and dressed in a green tuxedo, recorded her movements on what appeared to be a compact video camera. He occasionally turned to scan for other interesting subjects, always turning the camera back to Perez.

Kohler had warned Barton about the media gang that Perez took places with her. This assistant with the video camera, who captured encounters between Perez and the other guests for the famous VIPERez Vlog, seemed particularly hazardous. "Under no circumstances should you allow them to videotape you," Kohler had commanded. "You do *not* want to appear on her vlog!" Though he differed with Kohler on many points, he thought here her advice was surely impeccable.

Barton turned away from the cluster of people forming around Perez and moved toward the bar, intending to switch from drinking wine to sparkling water. It took a surprising amount of will not to glance back at her, but Barton was determined. He had a policy against lavishing attention on women accustomed to having attention so lavished. Let Perez do her thing; he'd talk with the other guests.

After exchanging a mostly untouched glass of wine for a full glass of mineral water, he wandered over to the tables where a silent auction was under way, to check on his bids. Chatting here and there with a few other guests, he upped his bid on a VIP membership to the local botanical gardens and decided to bid on a brightly colored abstract painting by a "hot" new artist who was somewhere in attendance at the gala. The painting didn't really appeal to him, but he thought he might send it to his ex-girlfriend Maggie Landis. The two of them had a long-running disagreement about the merits of abstract art. Since he didn't like it much, he thought she'd probably love it. Taking a sip of water, he realized that he rather missed Maggie. Maybe he'd give her a call later.

As he contemplated a bid on dinner for two at a celebrated area restaurant (*who would he go with?*), a soft-spoken voice interrupted his thoughts.

"Avoiding Veronica Perez?"

Barton turned to face a short, dark-haired man in his midthirties. He looked out of place in a tux, but his manner conveyed self-assurance. "I'm sorry," Barton said, not willing to answer the question until he had a better idea who was asking, "who do you mean?"

The other man nodded. "Smart man. I keep away from her too." He extended a hand. "Robert Zealand," he said. "I'm part of your external legal counsel team at Coffin & Storm, but we haven't met yet. I know you because your picture's been in the papers. You probably get this a lot."

"It's been known to happen," admitted Barton. "Goes with the job."

"One of the many perils," said Zealand.

Barton smiled. "Are there other perils I should be particularly worried about?"

"Nothing in particular," said Zealand, "It's a general comment. We live in fascinating times. The perils and opportunities are evolving, often faster than we can assess them. Especially for a business like SMA."

This interested Barton. "Do go on."

"Take the issue we were just circling around," Zealand said. "Exemplified by Perez and her social media entourage. Secrets are important to a company like SMA. But what secrets can you keep? What secrets can you afford to protect?"

"If you're on my legal team, shouldn't I be asking *you* these questions?"

"We're just talking here. This is not legal advice."

Barton smiled at the lawyer's reflexive disclaimer. "Okay," he allowed. "We're just talking."

Zealand looked at Barton, as if to gauge whether the interest was sincere, then seemed to decide that it was.

"Real secrets—national security secrets, key proprietary technical secrets—must be kept. Multilayered defenses. Defended at the data item level. Spending on defenses in proportion to the value of the specific data item. You want to spend just the right amount protecting specific secrets, because overspending on one thing means underspending on defense of something else. So abandon the idea of protecting everything equally well and also the idea that secrets won't ever get out. The optimal number of revealed secrets is not zero."

"So, as a CEO," said Barton, "I can't just say, 'don't let it happen, ever.'"

"Oh, you can say that. But you'll almost certainly produce activity that overprotects some things at the expense of things that could use greater protection."

"Great. This argument has a cost-benefit flavor. As a bean counter, I get that. May be hard to put into practice, but I get it in principle."

Zealand nodded. "Hard to put into practice. Not everyone will get it."

"What else?" Barton asked.

Zealand shrugged. "You can't protect too much. You can't afford it. Some secrets we used to think we could keep are a lost cause now. Stuff will leak."

"So that's that. Just get used to it, and everything will be great."

"I didn't say that," Zealand responded. "The tough thing is that the spin around leaks is hard to control and hard to counter. A message with just a little bit of truth in it, with a whole lot of crap surrounding that truth, is a very hard thing to manage. That's the sort of thing Perez specializes in. Enough truth to be credible, plenty of crap to make it compelling and give her career yet another boost."

"So what's the answer?" Barton asked. "What do we do in this fascinating new world?"

Zealand shook his head. "That remains to be figured out, I'm afraid. But I suggest you get on it."*

"Well, I see the two of you have met," said Smithson, rejoining Barton. "Robert, as I'm sure you've gathered, is one of Coffin & Storm's whiz kids. Probably their best."

Zealand executed an exaggerated bow. "The lady flatters me," he said.

"It's not flattery," she said, "if it's true."

"Thank you, mi'lady," said Zealand, in a manner that suggested past membership in the campus medieval club.

---

*For more on security and risk management, see Daniel E. Geer, "The Evolution of Security," *ACM Queue*, April 1, 2007, http://queue.acm.org/detail.cfm?id=1242500.

Smithson turned to Barton. "I've got to go. I've got another event to attend this evening, I'm afraid."

Barton feigned disappointment, but was secretly delighted. Once she left, he'd make his own exit. He'd made the required appearance, met the people he needed to meet, according to Smithson and Kohler, and steered clear of Perez. Kohler would be proud.

He exchanged pleasantries with Zealand and helped Smithson get into her coat. When she had departed, Barton wandered onto a balcony to look out at the city. The difference from the East Coast skyline could not have been more obvious. *Not in Kansas anymore,* he thought. *Or in New York, Boston, or Philadelphia.*

He turned to look back toward the party, leaning against the balcony rail, his eyes searching for the goddess in the golden dress. She wasn't difficult to locate. Not that far away from Barton, just inside the doorway to the balcony, she stood still surrounded by people, smiling and talking. She said something to her entourage, and they fanned out into the room.

Safe within the darkness of the balcony, watching Perez move around and interact with others in the lighted ballroom, Barton felt grudging admiration. The image she projected was deftly composed. A woman so skilled at imagery would be mind-bogglingly good at a great many things, but especially journalism. If she was as smart as people said, she would be a dangerous person to encounter, especially for a new CEO.

Without warning, Perez turned and strode toward Barton. As he tried to guess where she was going, she distanced herself from other guests, several of whom looked very disappointed, and passed from the lighted room through the doorway onto the balcony. Realizing *he* might be her destination, Barton hastened to compose a reaction. Instinctively, he extended a hand in greeting, intending to say something formal: *I don't believe we've met . . .*

Perez walked right by him, laughing musically, and took up position beside him at the rail, facing outward, toward the city lights. He turned to face outward alongside her.

"Hello, Mr. Barton," she said, and laughed again. "Yes, I know who you are. I couldn't help noticing you were looking my way."

Startled, wondering how she could have noticed—skeptical, in fact, that she could have—Barton nevertheless felt his face warming. He was grateful for the concealment of the balcony's darkness.

She turned toward him.

"Don't punish yourself," she said. "You're not married, so I thought there was a chance you might play for the other team. But I can see now that you don't." She made a show of examining his face, which Barton thought had probably become red, though still he wondered whether that would be visible in the dark. "Definitely not gay," she said, as she turned back to the rail.

Barton thought she might be executing a routine, assuming his reactions rather than seeing them in the dark. If true, that would suggest amazing arrogance on her part. Off balance and annoyed, he made an attempt to strike back: "You have a high opinion of yourself."

"Yes, I do," said Perez. "Am I wrong?"

Barton kept quiet.

"Do you like my dress?" Perez whirled in a circle, swayed from side to side, placing a hand on one hip. The move threw Barton further off balance. He worried that others might have seen and might think he'd said something to prompt it. Nothing he could think of to say seemed clever enough. So he remained quiet. She pursed her lips, disappointed.

"I noticed," she said, turning back to the rail, "that you've been betting on an annual membership to the botanical gardens. You interested in orchids, Mr. Barton? I don't usually think of the CEOs of major aerospace firms as sensitive souls."

"For my mother," Barton grunted.

"Ahhhh," said Perez. Her momentary silence gave Barton the idea that he might have done the impossible and fazed Perez, if ever so slightly. Her teasing tone, at least, abated. "How . . . sensitive."

His eyes wandered to the tattoo at the base of her back. Thanks to a perfectly placed beam of light from the ballroom, he could just make out its form: a viper. She noticed him looking.

"What," Perez asked, "about the painting? For your girlfriend?" Barton didn't answer, so she continued: "Another surprise, you know. I wouldn't have figured you for a fan of abstract art. You're turning out to be full of surprises, Mr. Barton."

"Surely you're mistaken, Ms. Perez," said Barton. "How surprising, really, can a 'bean counter' be?"

Perez laughed. "Ah. My editorial. Kohler warned you not to talk to me, didn't she? And you didn't listen . . . Doesn't matter though. You've got much bigger things to worry about than my little ol' editorial."

"Yes," said Barton, "I do."

"If I were you, I'd worry more about that dip in the stock price that happened right when they announced you."

"I didn't notice."

"I bet your staff noticed."

"It recovered the next day," he said.

"Yes, it did," she said. "I noticed that too. But I'm sure Kohler was furious that you took my call. It surprised me too."

"You seem very certain of yourself," said Barton, "and yet you're often surprised. Shouldn't that tell you something?"

This modest parry constituted, in Barton's estimation—and by quite a large margin—his most clever response in the conversation so far. Perez failed to appreciate it.

"What *you* can be certain of," she said, drawing close to him, "is that the word gets out. I will find out. So get over it. Okay?"

Barton kept quiet. They shared the view from the balcony. The sun had dipped below the horizon. The sky displayed a range of hues, from deep purple to orange, its spectral breadth a result of the quantity and variety of hydrocarbon particulates suspended in the atmosphere over the city.

"Enchanting," she said.

"Very," said Barton.

"So, Jim Barton," she said, without looking over at him, "how would you like to take me home with you tonight?"

Barton considered how to navigate the situation. He wondered if a camera or audio recorder might be running somewhere nearby. He opted for simplicity. "Of course, I would," he said, in an obviously facetious tone.

She turned toward him. "I don't usually date, you know," she said. "My career comes first. Leaves little time for romance."

"Your question, then," said Barton, "was rhetorical."

"Informational," said Perez. "I'm trying to figure out what kind of man you are, Jim Barton."

"Making any progress on that?"

"Some," she said. "Some."

"Be careful, Ms. Perez. A person can become addicted to external reinforcement and superficial affirmation."

"Wise words," said Perez. "Interesting, too, coming from a new CEO."

"I bet half the men here would answer yes to that question."

"Only half, Mr. Barton?" She pretended to be hurt. "More, I'd say. Especially if you stipulated that there'd be no adverse repercussions with wives. Not a problem for you, of course. Oh, but there's that girlfriend . . ."

"No girlfriend," said Barton.

She smiled. "Most men are basically victims of their insecurities and involuntary urges," she said. "Like the insecurities that made you angry when you read my editorial. Like the urges that make you want to take me home with you."

"And what are most women like?"

"Women? Most of them follow men around like puppies, trying to patch up their insecurities and satisfy their urges. Not this woman, though. I'm not easily satisfied."

"There you go, being sure again," said Barton.

Perez laughed, an apparently spontaneous laugh this time. "So where do you live?" she asked.

"Excuse me?" said Barton.

"We're not leaving together, if that's what you thought. I won't let you put that feather in your cap."

"You really do have a high opinion of yourself, don't you, Ms. Perez?"

"It hasn't often steered me wrong." She stepped away from the rail, starting toward the ballroom. "This is it, Mr. Barton. You think I don't mean it, but maybe I do. Now you've got to decide. That's what you're supposed to be good at, right? That's why they pay you the big bucks. You want to meet me at your place? Or not?"

Reflection

How should Barton manage Linda Kohler?

In a context like SMA's, how should a firm handle openness and protection? What examples do we have of different firm approaches to transparency?

How should Barton and SMA communications handle Veronica Perez, regarding SMA business? How should Barton respond to Perez's private invitation? Do you see this as an ethical dilemma?

A Leader of Men

SSEER, a simulated senior executive experience role-play by Simavatar Studios

The interior of an executive jet. The drone of engines barely penetrates its soundproofed walls. Luce lies on his back on the floor, arms outstretched, eyes closed, absorbing flight vibrations into his body. He balances a soda can on his chest.

"So let me get this straight," he says. "You *both* dated her?"

Luce asks this question without opening his eyes. Barton, in a plush, ultramodern swivel chair, holding an expensive beer, doesn't answer right away. Goldman, sitting on a couch, places his drink—it looks like a martini—on a side table.

"Yes," Barton says finally, "we both dated her, at different times."

"Whose was she first?" asks Luce.

"It wasn't like that," says Barton.

"It's always like that," says Luce, sitting up, leaning against the bulkhead. "So she was his first."

"They were all his first. Have you seen the guy?"

"No."

"He's half Hawaiian. Lots of muscles, great tan."

"He's head of the mechanics union. I'd guess he's one tough hombre. And you stole his girl," says Luce. "That can't end well."

Barton shakes his head. "You've got it all wrong. He dated her in high school. Then she and I went to college on the East Coast. They drifted apart. Years later, Maggie and I dated."

"Well, from what I hear," says Luce, "Ace Jackson is a real 'leader of men.' Charismatic. Bright. Athletic. Aggressive."

"A formidable adversary," says Goldman.

Barton shakes his head. "He's not an adversary. He's a friend."

71

Luce and Goldman exchange suggestive glances.

"I agree with Bob," says Luce. "Things have changed. He has other friends now. How sure are you that he's still your friend?"

"Our friendship has the deepest of foundations. We went through a lot together. He saved my life once, when we were surfing. I would have drowned. We may have difficulties, disagreements, but in the end he'll work with me on this transition. We'll work together."

Now Goldman shakes his head. "Jim, you know the cost structure is far out of line with what you need. A big reason is the unions. He's their lead dog, not just of the mechanics, of all of them. He's going to fight you, tooth and nail. He can see it coming, and he's fighting already. You're going to have to crush him. You'll have to break their backs and outsource their jobs, and he's not likely to consider that very friendly."

"That's my decision," says Barton. "And I haven't decided to do it that way yet."

"I guess," says Goldman, "we shall see."

Luce nods. Barton squirms. The sound of the jet engines changed slightly as the plane began its descent.

CHAPTER 5

Reunion

"She's a beauty, don't you think?"

Jim Barton ran his fingers along the bright red fender of the vintage Ford Mustang convertible, nodding in agreement with Ace Jackson, who called out to him from the front porch. Barton had detoured up the driveway to get a closer look at the magnificent car, freshly waxed and gleaming in the Southern California sun. His own current-year Mustang rental car stood parked at the curb at the edge of the yard of this modest bungalow in a nice middle-class neighborhood. Jackson, who'd caught sight of Barton from inside the house and emerged with fingers curled around the necks of two freshly opened beer bottles, sat down on the porch step to let Barton finish his encounter with the car.

"What year?" Barton asked.

"1964 and a half. Officially 1965, according to the VIN. They were all that way, '65 VINs. But this is one of the early ones."

"I thought so," said Barton. The shiny white of the interior reiterated the spotless whitewall tires. White convertible top. *Great color scheme for this car*, Barton thought.

As if reading his mind, Jackson said: "Rangoon red exterior, white vinyl inside. As original as I could make it," he added. "Under the hood, too."

"She's totally gorgeous," said Barton, finally looking up and smiling. Jackson placed the two beers he held on the top step and stood, advancing across the yard toward Barton, who extended a welcoming hand. Jackson bypassed the hand entirely and engulfed Barton in a massive bear hug. The CEO of one of the world's major aerospace companies succumbed like a small child, his face pressed awkwardly against his friend's shirt, which smelled of tanning lotion and car wax. *Smells of my youth*, thought Barton.

"It's good to see you, Jim," said Jackson. "It's been a long time. I'm glad you've come home."

When Jackson let him, Barton pulled back to arm's length, without letting go. "You're exactly the same, Ace. Still a chick magnet, I bet. It's good to see you too, my friend."

Jackson swung his arm around Barton's shoulder and turned them toward the front door. He leaned over to pluck up the two beers as they mounted the steps, handing one to Barton.

"Come on," said Jackson. "Let's drink beer and watch football. Raiders versus those pansy-ass New Englanders today."

Barton could have mentioned that he'd become a fan of the New England team during his time on the East Coast, or that he'd often watched their games from corporate luxury seating. But he said or thought none of this and instead lapsed happily back into a long-ago pattern of shared fanaticism for the Raiders. Barton strained to recall the team's top players, so he could get into his role better.

Once inside, Barton was touched to see that Jackson had put a lot of effort into his old friend's visit. The living room extended left from the front door through which they'd entered; a large-screen TV beamed pregame programming toward two seriously cushy recliners, each with built-in side tables already stocked with bowls of potato chips. To the right of the front door, through an archway, a table in the adjoining dining room overflowed with sandwich fixings: three loaves of different kinds of bread in wrappers; piles of roast beef, ham, and turkey laid out on plates; and what looked like coleslaw and potato salad in plastic containers, surrounded by an abundance of condiments, from ketchup, mustard, and mayo to exotic-looking hot sauces, relishes, and pickles. Right in the middle of the table, positioned as the centerpiece, a galvanized steel tub held a lavish supply of beer bottles in different domestic and Mexican brands, necks poking up through gallons of melting ice.

It looked incredible.

Jackson laughed, noticing that Barton seemed almost as transfixed by the sandwich spread as he had been by the vintage Mustang.

"Make a sandwich, Jim," he said, "and settle in. I'm going to pull the car into the garage. Then I'll come in and make one too."

When Jackson left, Barton took the opportunity to look around. His old friend kept a tidy house, free from clutter, a few pictures on the walls of beach scenes, a sports magazine here and there. The only items of interest sat on a small shelf behind the TV. On the top shelf, Barton recognized three surfing trophies—two from high school days—and two photos, one of Jackson's mother, the other of three bright-faced youngsters—Ace, Jim, and Maggie, at about age sixteen.

Down on a lower shelf, Barton spotted something draped with a big beach towel. He walked over and poked at it, moving one corner of the towel aside. Underneath, he found some sort of machine, metal with rods and connections, and a wire harness attached to it, mounted on a wooden platform. A plate in the corner of the piece of wood said, "Property of Santa Monica Aerospace," which prompted Barton to raise an eyebrow. Carefully, he put the towel back and went to get food.

Balancing a loaded plate of food, he'd just begun to wonder which of the recliners to take when Jackson returned, apprehended his quandary, and pointed: "You take that one. View's a little better from there, I think."

Barton sat, positioning his plate in an almost stable arrangement, while Jackson moved in on the sandwich fixings. Barton glanced at his watch and noted that the game would begin in about fifteen minutes. He wondered if there'd be time to broach the subject of SMA's business situation with Jackson. That wasn't the purpose of their get-together today, and Barton didn't want to make it too much about that, but he did want to start a conversation with Jackson. If nothing else, he wanted to try to diffuse some of the anxieties workers might be feeling with the arrival of a new CEO, especially a finance guy.

Barton had already heard grapevine whispers about "Neutron Jim." Longtime General Electric CEO Jack Welch had earned the nickname "Neutron Jack," supposedly for tendencies, like those of a neutron bomb, to get rid of people while leaving buildings and other physical assets intact. Variations on the title tended to recur anytime a finance person took over a company. "Neutron Bob," "Neutron Jen," "Neutron Jim"—it worked well with pretty much any name, and it expressed a common and understandable dread. He hoped Jackson had been telling fellow workers and union members that they had less to fear from Jim Barton than that.

He also hoped that would be true. Barton favored a way forward that involved an alliance between management and the unions. Many, maybe most, people seemed to think that would be impossible. He realized too that the idea that such an alliance couldn't be achieved, if widely held within the community of analysts, investors, business press, and even white-collar employees, might pose a daunting difficulty for him, whether or not it really was true. Barton would not only have to achieve the alliance, but also have to convince the other stakeholders whose support he needed that such an alliance would hold and that forging it would be the smart way to go.

As Jackson sank into his own chair, Barton tried a question about SMA. "So what's your assessment of how things are going at work?"

When Barton spoke, Jackson had just picked up the remote. Now he unmuted the TV and voices blared from it, too loud. Barton watched as Jackson adjusted the volume down and placed the remote on a foldable tray between them.

"Sorry about that," Jackson said. He offered no response to Barton's question. Barton wondered if he'd heard.

"Did you see," asked Jackson, "that college game yesterday where one team was down by two, not quite in field goal range, and let seventeen of the twenty-six seconds left tick off the clock before they called time out? They passed down to the six-yard line on the next play, but couldn't get the field goal team on the field in time. The clock ran out. Dumbest way to lose a game I ever saw."

Barton shook his head. "I missed it."

"Head coach ought to be fired," Jackson said. "Team played great, came through in the clutch. Management screwed things up. As always."

Barton wondered what to make of this. It sounded like a not-very-subtle dig at his "management" friend. Was it friendly jesting, or more serious? Barton couldn't tell. Jackson looked straight ahead, focused on something the televised talking heads were discussing.

Suddenly Jackson turned, grinned, and used his fork to fire a dill pickle slice at Barton. The pickle smacked against the side of Barton's cheek and slid down onto his plate. Jackson raised both hands in celebration: "Score!"

He winked. "I'm just messing with you, man." He let loose a long, loud infectious laugh, in which Barton joined. Barton picked up the pickle slice and flung it back toward Jackson. It missed, flew past Jackson, and vanished behind the couch.

"Oh, man," said Jackson. "Look what you did. That'll be lost back there for the next ten years." Again, they laughed, and took swigs from their beers.

Jackson stood. "Before the game starts, I'm going to move those beers over here between us, so we can reach them without getting up."

"Excellent idea," agreed Barton.

Barton watched Jackson easily lift and relocate the very heavy-looking tub of ice and beer. As he passed near the shelf behind the TV, Barton asked him about the machine on the lower shelf.

"What the hell is that thing?"

Jackson sat the tub down and looked where Barton pointed.

"That's totally legit, checked out from the shop, by the book," said Jackson, more than a little defensive.

"I'm not busting you, man," said Barton, smiling, "but what is it?"

"Geez," Jackson laughed, sitting down in his chair and grabbing another beer from the tub, checking the reach distance. "It's part of an SMA 400's thrust reverser. It's one of the ways we get the planes to stop after they land. Been trying to figure out why one of the parts wears too quickly. Works fine, but I think we might be able to change the design a little, maybe the assembly process, to make it better. I'm communing with it, you know, trying to understand the depth of its soul."

"Don't the engineers handle those kinds of issues?"

Jackson shrugged. "Sure. They do, too. They know the system. But I'm the one who *really* knows it. They have their drawings, their simulations. Which are pretty cool, I got to admit. But they can only take you so far. Deep down, it's my system. They know it like an acquaintance. I know it like a lover."*

---

*For more on the knowledge that comes from manual work, see Matthew B. Crawford, "Shop Class as Soulcraft," *The New Atlantis*, Summer 2006, 7–24.

Barton, trying to gauge how serious Jackson was, looked perplexed, which amused Jackson. "Jimmy, you've got some things to learn about airplanes. But not now. Let's watch the game."

Barton dropped the subject, and they watched the last of the pregame show.

He tried only one more time for talk unrelated to football: "Hear anything from Maggie?" Barton asked, during a commercial break, while Jackson, back at the table, smeared mustard onto a ham sandwich.

"Maggie who?" Jackson responded. Barton thought he was joking again, but then the dots connected: "Oh, you mean Maggs. Nawww. Not for a long time. Not for a long, long time."

That was it. The commercial break ended and Jackson sat down, intent once again upon the TV images.

The game commenced. The teams appeared well matched. The Raiders scored first, a touchdown on a twenty-three-yard pass. The New England team answered quickly with a seventy-three-yard drive and a three-yard scoring run, then edged ahead after a Raider punt with a shorter drive and a long field goal.

Beers disappeared from the tub. Barton got up to make another sandwich. Jackson vanished into the kitchen, off the dining room, to retrieve a bag of cheese snacks, which he sat between them. Those disappeared quickly.

At some point, the number of beers consumed reached a point that would have diminished the quality of any serious conversation. Barton couldn't remember how many he'd had, but he thought Jackson had downed more. An empty beer bottle forest had grown between the two chairs by halftime.

At the half, New England led twenty to seventeen. Jackson stood.

"Let's go toss a football around," he proposed.

"Say what?" Barton said. He was feeling impaired, his stomach full of junk food and beer.

"Let's toss the football, like old times. You can run patterns. I'll be QB."

"I don't know, Ace. I'm pretty full. I haven't played much football lately."

"Don't be a wuss," said Jackson. "Come on."

Jackson exited through the kitchen. Barton heard a screen door slam somewhere out back of the house. He stood, vowing not to overdo it, get sick, or injure himself. But he followed Jackson out through the kitchen and back door.

The small, fenced yard ran the length of the house and backed up to a neighbor's yard. *Not unlike the arrangement of my own place in Venice*, Barton thought. He was pleased with his new place; it suited him perfectly, the diversity and energy. To one side lived a modernist composer; toward the back, a neighbor he hadn't met, but who kept the most unusual gardens. Jackson's neighbor in the rear seemed less intriguing; whoever lived there appeared uninterested in cutting the lawn, much less gardening.

Jackson stood in the doorway of a small shed, bent over, rummaging. As Barton approached, Jackson triumphantly turned and held out an old football.

"Found it!" he said, "And there's even air in it. Go deep."

He dropped back a couple of steps like a quarterback and pointed somewhere behind Barton. Barton looked back and said, "Deep? If I go deep, I'll be in your neighbor's garage."

"Well, okay, down and out, then," said Jackson, sounding exasperated. "Quick, the defensive end is coming at me and he's a big mo-fo."

Barton sighed but did as he was told. He jogged away from Jackson. About five yards out, Barton turned sharply at a right angle. Jackson pretended to evade two defenders, then smoked a spiral into Barton's gut. The ball hit Barton hard, stung his hands, and knocked the wind out of him. He dropped the pass and fell to his knees trying to recover his breath.

"Geez," said Barton, when he could get his breath back. "That's a bit hard for such close range, don't you think?"

Jackson strolled over to pick up the ball. "Jim, man, you dropped the ball. I put it right in your hands, and you couldn't hold on. Let's do it again, come on. How 'bout you really run this time? None of this lollygagging."

Barton felt a tinge of anger, probably, he realized, alcohol enhanced. But he didn't care. He pulled himself to his feet.

"Fine," he said. "Let's do this."

Barton fell back to near where Jackson stood. Jackson readied himself to take a fake snap, calling out a cadence:

"22-red-34-19-hike-hike!"

Barton dashed into the yard and turned in his pattern. Jackson dropped back, pump-faked long, then zipped the ball on a line, again directly into Barton's stomach. If anything, this ball was thrown harder, but Barton held on out of sheer determination. It hurt like hell, again knocked the wind out of him, but he refused to let on that he felt anything. Instead he suppressed a wheeze and returned to the imaginary line of scrimmage. When he got close to Jackson, Barton whipped the ball hard at his friend, catching him by surprise, but not really hurting Jackson, whose muscular abs took the blow easily.

Jackson laughed. "Atta boy. That's the way we like it, a little spirit, a little heart," he said. "Let's do it again."

They ran more plays, variations of all kinds, until Barton began to feel genuinely ill. After a while, only sheer resolve kept him going and only pride kept hidden how much he was suffering.

"Don't you think we ought to see if the game is back on?" Barton tried. "Raiders are down by three, you know."

Barton added this last little bit out of anger, rubbing it in that those "pansy-ass" New Englanders were, at least for the time being, beating Jackson's rough, tough Raiders. Jackson, already a little annoyed that he hadn't succeeded in breaking Barton's determination, reacted.

"Let's try one more thing," he said, "then we'll go in."

"What?" asked Barton.

"I'm the QB," said Jackson, "and you're the defender. I'm going to throw an errant pass, which you'll intercept. Then you'll try to return the interception for a touchdown. I'll try to stop you."

"Stop me?"

"You just have to get to the edge of the yard." He pointed. "Over there, by the sprinkler."

"I'm not sure this is a good idea," said Barton. "We're both a little drunk, and I'm already about to puke my lunch. Now you want to play tackle?"

"What the hell?" said Jackson. "We used to do this all the time. Sometimes when we were a lot drunker than this. Don't you remember?"

Barton did remember. It had been a pretty good game. Jackson had always been bigger, but Barton remembered sometimes having a speed and agility advantage over his large friend. Mostly, he recalled, Jackson had been able to stop him. But not always.

He remembered one particular play he'd thought most successful in those days, because Jackson was faster to his left than to his right. It involved a fake to the left, a spin to the right, and a sprint through a split-second opening. Barton wondered if his much older body could still execute the play. If it could, he'd avoid physical contact with Jackson, which would surely be best. He'd get past Jackson, score, and they could go back inside and watch the game.

"Okay," Barton said, "let's try it."

He wondered whether Jackson also remembered the play and expected him to try it. *If so,* Barton thought, *this is gonna hurt . . .* But he moved into position, ready for the play to start.

Jackson hiked the ball to himself. Barton fell back, acting the role of a defender. Jackson zipped the ball, again very hard, at Barton, who caught the ball and started to Jackson's left.

As he began to angle toward the corner of the yard, Barton noticed that Jackson had taken on a grim expression, an almost deranged look. Barton realized with a start that his friend might actually be willing to hurt him, if they came into contact. That prospect added half a step to Barton's quickness, and when it came time to turn and spin, he realized Jackson had taken the bait and had fallen out of position. Barton accelerated to the right toward the opposite corner of the yard and, in the next instant, moved past Jackson, who whirled and grabbed air. A moment later, Barton stood in the "end zone" holding the ball aloft, shouting "touchdown, touchdown!" and doing a not-very-cool victory dance. Jackson advanced toward him, slowing in recognition that the play had ended, slouching under the realization that Barton had scored.

It was over and Barton had won.

Then, without warning, Jackson accelerated and executed a hard tackle of Barton anyway, throwing him fiercely to the ground.

"What the—!" blurted Barton, before the lawn materials forced into his mouth prevented any further utterance.

Angry but unable to move or speak, Barton waited for Jackson to get off him. Instead, Jackson flipped over, twisting in what Barton recognized as a wrestling move, and pulled him up into an immobilizing headlock. He still couldn't really see Jackson, but he could speak again, his face no longer pressed into the ground.

"The play's over, you jerk," said Barton, spitting out grass and dirt. "I scored. That's a late hit. Unsportsmanlike conduct. It'll cost you fifteen yards on the kickoff and a fine from the league. Maybe even a suspension. That was blatant, man."

Barton realized that one of his ankles didn't feel so hot. It had rolled at an angle when Jackson hit him.

Jackson said nothing but held Barton in the wrestling lock for a few more seconds, then pushed him away, throwing him free. Angry, Barton pivoted, still sitting, to confront Jackson.

Then Barton stopped. Jackson was shaking with rage. Barton's fury subsided into a weird mixture of fear and concern for his friend.

"You think," said Jackson, in a quiet, cold, stony voice, "that this is *your* company now. It's not. You can't just come in here like this. These are my people. My company." His voice faltered. But he continued. "I can save it. Or I can kill it. Not you."

Jackson stood and went toward the back door.

From some place deep inside himself, Barton mustered what he thought later just might have been the perfect response to this outburst by Jackson: "That was an unfair tackle, Ace, and you know it! What a bunch of crap!"

The screen door slammed and Jackson was gone.

Barton stood, gingerly, and found that his ankle would bear weight. But it was tender and already starting to swell. He limped across the yard and through the back door, crossed the kitchen to the dining room and living room, and returned to his chair. He reached down, grabbed another beer, twisted off the top and threw it at Jackson, who dodged.

"Screw you, man," Barton said. "Look at what you did to my ankle."

Barton threw off his shoe and propped the ankle on a stool.

Jackson said nothing. Over the next twenty minutes, a lump the size of a baseball grew on the outside of Barton's foot.

They watched the game in silence. At the start of the third quarter, Jackson stood and disappeared somewhere into the back of the house. He returned with a plastic bag of frozen peas, which he draped over Barton's foot.

"Keep that there. It'll help," he said. He opened a paper bag he carried and extracted an elastic wrap, some felt pads, medical tape, and a pair of scissors. "I'll wrap it later, after we ice it a while. I wrap a mean ankle. I'm good at it, lots of practice."

"Damn good thing," said Barton, "cause that's feeling like a mean ankle."

"It's not broken," Jackson said. "But it's gonna be tender, and it'll turn all badass blue, and purple, and yellow."

"Excellent," said Barton. "Just what I need."

When a few minutes remained in the game, Jackson positioned himself on the floor in front of Barton, off to the side so they could both see the TV, and carefully wrapped the ankle, cutting the felt pads into a U-shape and positioning them under the bandage to protect the area around the bone where a lot of the pain centered. When he was almost done wrapping, Jackson spoke again, quietly.

"I meant what I said, Jim. I got people to watch out for now. You and me, we go way back, but you joined a different team. A team that's mostly been headaches for me and mine.

"You can watch football with me whenever you want. I've had a really good time today, though I'm sorry I hurt you. But if you're counting on me to do stuff for you, *don't*. Cause I *won't*. Being honest about that—and wrapping this ankle—these are the last favors I'm going to do for you. From here on out, we negotiate for everything. My people got to get something if they're going to give. Got it?"

Barton frowned. "Yeah, Ace, I got it."

"Try standing up now," Jackson said. Barton did.

"It feels better," admitted Barton.

"You're going to need that support for a while," Jackson said, collecting his materials back into the paper sack. "It's hard to do a wrap like that for yourself, so stop at a drugstore on the way home and buy an elastic ankle brace. Does the same thing, but it's easier to get on." He stood and started toward the back of the house. "I'll put on some coffee. We need to sober you up before you leave."

"I'll probably just call a taxi," said Barton.

"Whatever," said Jackson, as he vanished into the kitchen.

Barton sat wondering what he'd say to Perez about the ankle. She'd spent a fair amount of time at his place this past week. No way could he keep her from finding out. No way could he tell her the truth, either. He'd have to make up a story about clumsiness on a stairway or something like that.

Another thought nagged at him, too. His first board meeting was scheduled for Thursday, in just four days. The symbolism of limping into that meeting after only two weeks in his new position didn't thrill Barton. Kind of made it look like the job was kicking his ass.

He had to admit that at that moment, sitting there next to the top guy in the mechanics union who had nearly broken his ankle, and considering how his plan for collaboration with the unions seemed to be in shambles— well, Barton thought maybe this job *was* kicking his ass.

Jackson came back just as the smell of coffee brewing wafted into the living room. He sat in his chair and they watched the end of the game in silence.

The Raiders lost to New England thirty to seventeen.

Reflection

What do you make of Jackson's behavior toward Barton? Is Barton out of line to expect his friend to work with him differently than he would another CEO?

Do you think Barton and Jackson will be able to work out an alliance at some point in the future?

How would you advise Barton to manage SMA's relationship with the unions? What are his best options?

CHAPTER 6

The Board of Directors

Jim Barton hobbled on crutches into his first board of directors meeting as CEO of Santa Monica Aerospace. Martin Van Busin, who'd missed the dinner the night before, turned a spotlight on Barton's injury: "Bloody hell, Jim," the dean of MIT's engineering school exclaimed in his signature Americanized Australian accent, "what happened to you?"

Barton had heard this question a lot in the past few days and from the other board members twelve hours earlier. He'd consistently responded with a vague story about jogging and a patch of uneven ground. He now offered this account to Van Busin. The jolly, balding academic answered with a joke Barton had heard by now in many variations and hadn't liked very much the first time: "Looks like the new job's been kicking you around a bit, mate."

Van Busin's quip drew no reaction from around the conference room, where board members waited for the start of the meeting. A few spoke on cell phones. Van Busin wandered off to get another cup of coffee.

Barton made eye contact with his CFO, Clarke Gardner, who nodded (*Yes, all's ready with the presentation*). A quick look around the room confirmed that everyone was present. Barton moved to an open chair, careful to avoid snagging his crutches on anyone or anything. He sat and removed a notebook and pen from his briefcase, which he then put by his feet and slid under the table. Bobbi Smithson asked if he wanted a cup of coffee and kindly retrieved one for him. Unexpectedly, for no reason he could fathom, Barton felt nervous.

The dinner the night before had given him little cause for worry. All present had reiterated earlier congratulations, and Barton had given a short, not entirely impromptu speech in which he'd reiterated how honored he felt to be elected CEO.

"I realize," he'd said at one point in his remarks, "that I was not the first choice. Hell, I was there," he said, smiling, "when three other candidates turned us down." The others laughed. "However, I've learned a great deal about this company over the past three years. And I bring a different profile to the job than the candidates we'd been seeking. I'll be bringing that and every other fiber of my being to bear on finding success for this company.

"I believe," he'd said, finishing, "that we have the talent, the organizational capabilities to create a twenty-first-century company that makes the world's most advanced, high-quality commercial cargo jet. The challenges are great—we should not underestimate them—but the strength of SMA, its people and culture, are more than equal to the challenges. I've seen evidence of that again and again in the short time since I arrived on the job. We'll need a great deal of support from all of you, of course, and I'm grateful that you've so generously offered so much of it already. Together, I hope—no, I *know*—that we can take this great company forward into an even greater future."

The group, sequestered in a private room at the back of a nice restaurant, applauded politely, not loudly enough to interrupt diners in adjoining rooms. This response, Barton thought, had been appropriate to the setting and suggested that he'd hit the right notes. He'd almost said he was "overwhelmed" by the support that board members had offered him, but he'd decided that "overwhelmed" was not a word a new CEO should utter, especially when standing on one leg and propped against a stabilizing crutch. He suspected some had thought it though, for it was just then, as they settled into their places at the table, that Ed Frazier joked about Barton's ankle.

He interpreted Frazier's kidding as a sign of the easy familiarity of his relationships with these people, not as a pointed barb. Having been a member of this board prior to becoming the CEO, Barton had come to know them all very well, assisted in this by his past role as chair of the governance committee (which he'd promptly resigned upon accepting the CEO position).

As committee chair, he'd exercised considerable authority, which he'd used, along with fellow governance committee members, to separate the CEO and board chair leadership roles. At SMA, as at many companies, the roles had been combined historically. In recommending separation of the roles, the governance committee advocated state-of-the-art thinking about "good board practice." The board had agreed to this change, and Ron Haas was elected the first nonexecutive chairman of the board. Frazier gave up the chairman title but continued (at that time) as CEO.

Frazier had never seemed bothered by this loss of power, but Barton could not avoid speculating about his real feelings, whether he might secretly resent the change and blame Barton for it. Influenced by Bob Goldman's past mentoring, Barton had definitely led the charge for separation of roles. Add to this the fact that Frazier had eventually been removed from the CEO position, too, and that Barton had ended up in the role, and you had the potential for serious tensions.

These had never surfaced, however. As far as Barton could see, Frazier appeared unbothered by insecurities. The only possible evidence Barton could see that Frazier had taken anything personally was an occasional tendency toward pointed commentary, such as his joke about Barton's ankle injury. But Frazier had always exhibited a sharp wit, so nothing had really changed, as far as Barton could see.

Nevertheless, Frazier's presence made today's presentation trickier. Barton and Gardner had to be careful not to imply too much criticism of past strategies and actions, while also proposing thinking that did not seem to others like the same old thing. In any case, they'd be talking to an entire group responsible, quite literally, for oversight of the firm's past directions. The board had approved Frazier's ultimately controversial stock buybacks, for example. In addition, Bill Ford, an SMA chairman and CEO from several years past, also remained on the board. To some extent, this sensitivity, the difficulty of presenting change to people who had approved or even implemented what SMA needed to change *from*, was inevitable.

It helped that Barton had been there alongside them for much of it, participating in the decision making. If they were culpable for past mistakes, so was he. To perform well, the board collectively had to achieve a degree of magnanimity, enough to discuss past decisions openly, transcend personal insecurities, and change its mind. Barton hoped the members were up to it.

He had doubts about this, however. As governance committee chair, Barton had also carried out the annual review of board member performance. He'd employed outside consultants to develop and administer a patterned interview. Then he'd reviewed and interpreted the results. The outcome of the board self-evaluation permitted Barton to report back good-to-excellent performance, with no significant dysfunctional incidents that required follow-up. Barton had welcomed this outcome, as the process of addressing board difficulties could be delicate and awkward.

But in truth he also doubted that the performance review process was really calibrated to show whether the board had what it took to oversee the transformation required at SMA. The consultants' approach was, Barton had to admit, pretty generic. Even so, reading between the lines (Barton had full access to the raw data, unlike other board members), the consultants had surfaced worrying signs that not all board members were fully engaged and capable at the level required to achieve major changes. Barton hoped he was wrong about this, because he had other worries. He worried, for example, that the twelve-member board might be too large and too oriented toward the past military business to guide a successful transformation.

The move from governance committee chair to CEO now placed Barton in a very different position in relation to his colleagues on the board. Before, Barton had orchestrated assessment of *their* performance. Now he, in effect, worked for them, and they'd be assessing *his* performance. They'd determine his compensation, the size of his bonuses, and, if he failed to perform in a way that met their approval, they'd have a responsibility to shareholders to remove him from his position. This first meeting launched him into his new role.

It began the Jim Barton era at Santa Monica Aerospace.

As if to mark the occasion, a thought crystallized in Barton's mind's eye, and it hung there, almost like a prayer: *There is a time for every CEO to make a contribution. And there is a time for every CEO to make an exit. Please don't let me overstay my time at SMA.*

The meeting agenda—plotted by Barton and Gardner in consultation with board chairman Ron Haas and sent to all board members in advance—began promptly at 8:15 a.m. Haas called the meeting to order and issued a formal welcome from the board to new CEO Jim Barton. Murmurs of encouragement followed. As planned, Haas then turned the meeting over to Barton.

"I made my little speech last night," he said, "so my inclination this morning is to get right down to business." He saw nods around the table. "Good," said Barton. "In many ways, not much has changed since our last meeting. As you all know, this company is committed to a transformation from twentieth-century defense contractor to twenty-first-century best-in-class provider of commercial cargo aircraft. In my assessment, we are too far down that path to consider other strategic alternatives. We're committed to this transformation. Ed and the rest of you have had the right idea. Next, we must make it happen. The first challenge has to do with access to the financing necessary to complete the development of a new, extremely advanced cargo plane. After that, we have to execute, to deliver.

"As you all know, we have to take out cost. The organization must change. And change is hard. We'll have to convince a lot of people who fear the worst that we'll help them get to a better place, or else they'll resist us at every turn. Or we'll lose key engineering and management talent that we badly need. That can delay us or even kill us. The situation is volatile. We could debate, and argue, and spin our wheels right out of existence. But I believe there's a way to fly through this dangerous turbulence if we make the right choices, act resolutely, and communicate effectively to our people.

"That's what *I* think. I could say much more, but, as you know from the agenda sent out in advance, today I'd like your input. To set the stage, I've asked Clarke Gardner, whom you all know, to summarize the financial situation. Sound okay?" Again, the others nodded. "Clarke?"

Gardner stood and held up a short stack of paper, copies of a one-page financial summary. "We distributed this financial summary with your advance board materials, but I have more here if you need them."

Half the board members reached for a copy as the stack made its way around. "It shows the profit-and-loss statement for this year and last year, along with a number of business performance ratios."

Gardner presented for almost forty-five minutes, covering the material with great thoroughness. At the beginning and end, he summarized, making three main points.

"Right now our finances depict a declining defense contractor with a single product nearing its end of life. While our cash position is relatively healthy, on current trends, cash flow will become a problem in the not-too-distant future.

"Return on equity has declined from a healthy 15 to 20 percent into dismal single digits and will probably decrease further, especially if debt burden increases significantly as the company acquires financing for development of the new plane.

"Stock share price has been declining, and our investors are divided in their opinions of what SMA should do. One group of investors is reluctant about new investments and is calling for cash to be distributed; this points to growing worries that SMA can't develop a new successful product, and that shareholders would be better off if the company were sold and cash value returned to them. Another group of our shareholders comprises strategic investors who believe in our proposed new direction—to enter the growing commercial cargo airplane market. Those investors are encouraging us to make the investments required to transform the company. And probably another third of our shareholders are sitting on the fence; they're intrigued by the idea of going into the commercial cargo airplane business, but are concerned this will distract us from profitably winding down our cash-generating military cargo airplane business."

During Gardner's update, Barton discreetly studied the reactions of individual board members. Patricia Shanahan, a former pharmaceuticals company CIO, stifled a yawn and sat up straighter. Chris Harden, a retired US Air Force general, doodled on a pad of paper. Both, Barton suspected, were a bit out of their depth in such a detailed financial presentation, as Gardner rapid-fire referenced acronyms and ratios, and pointed out conclusions based on the DuPont ROE framework analysis. Van Busin thumbed at his smartphone throughout the presentation, occasionally looking up and nodding, but apparently quite occupied

TABLE 6-1

Santa Monica Aerospace Company annual income statement

Santa Monica Aerospace Company		P&L
Annual income statement ($000,000)	Previous year	Most recent year
Price per military plane ($000,000)	250	250
Number of military cargo planes sold	24	24
Net airplane revenue	6,000	6,000
Other revenue		
Other revenue, spare parts	105	242
Other revenue, maintenance	240	264
Total revenue	**6,345**	**6,506**
Cost of revenue	4,886	5,010
Gross margin	**1,459**	**1,496**
Research and development	800	800
Depreciation	250	250
Selling and general administrative expenses	317	325
Operating income	92	121
Interest expense	63	65
Net income before taxes	**29**	**56**
Provision for taxes	30%	30%
Net income after taxes	**20**	**39**
Cash and market securities	777	780
Performance ratios:		
Earnings per share (actual $)	**$0.12**	**$0.23**
Return on sales	**0.32%**	**0.60%**
Revenue per employee (actual $)	**$423,000**	**$433,733**
Gross margin percent of sales	**23%**	**23%**
Number of employees	**15,000**	**15,000**
Share price	**$29.42**	**$27.30**
Outstanding shares (millions)	**170**	**170**
Return on equity (ROE)	**2%**	**5%**
Return on net assets (RONA)	**0.68%**	**0.79%**

with something going on elsewhere. Bill Ford, a former SMA CEO, and John Elliot, a former ambassador to Japan and Wall Street securities lawyer by background, could follow the analysis, Barton felt sure, but they both appeared bored, as if they didn't think they needed all this additional information to decide anything.

In contrast, Bobbi Smithson, true to her own CFO background, listened attentively and asked Gardner a number of detailed questions. The two of them, Smithson and Gardner, had a history of rancorous relations; something of a young hotshot (she was thirty-eight), bright but not always diplomatic, Smithson had often made Gardner uncomfortable. Today he had little difficulty with her questions, and Barton thought their interaction primed the pump for exactly the kind of detailed discussion he hoped all would join later. Smithson, for instance, pointed out the current rate of airplane production of twenty-four planes per year and asked about the capacity of the SMA factory. To which Gardner responded that capacity was much higher, but their contract was for only twenty-four planes and would be declining. This opened up a general discussion about production rates for commercial planes, to which Gardner contributed by citing a recent analyst report stating Boeing's production of its 737 passenger jet was nearing forty airplanes per month.

When the discussion following Gardner's presentation had finished, Haas turned the meeting over to Barton again, who elaborated on Gardner's presentation to enumerate and underscore the challenges that he believed the company's senior management and the board of directors needed to address. These included:

- Obtaining front-end airplane development investment monies.

- Collaborating with global manufacturers to realize more value from their relationships, including aerospace design and advanced manufacturing capabilities, something not previously done.

- Understanding and serving commercial customers.

- Designing and building a technologically advanced, breakthrough-operating, efficient, commercial cargo airplane.

- Restructuring the company from a defense contractor to a lean commercial company.

Barton emphasized how formidable these appeared and explained that he and his senior management team would be assembling a proposed plan to meet the challenges. He hoped to present the proposal, at least in summary, he said, at the next scheduled board meeting.

Then he turned to the next item on the agenda, which called for going around the table, round-robin style, to receive advice from each board member, input on what the plan should include, or how they should go about realizing the transformation.

Elliot volunteered to start, but he took the discussion in an unexpected direction: "Given that some major investors seem interested in cash distributions, as Clarke pointed out, I think it's our responsibility to at least look at the value of the company if we divided it into pieces and liquidated it," he said. "This would, at the least, provide a bogey for us. If we cannot then justify a better risk-return ratio to our shareholders, we have a fiduciary responsibility to sell. This transformation looks hard. As you said yourself, Jim, it might not happen. Might be a lot easier and better for shareholders, if we sell. Some tough-minded private equity types might be better at winding down the company in a manner that would maximize shareholder value."

Ron Haas squirmed noticeably at this suggestion, but he said nothing, perhaps feeling that, as meeting chair, he should let others jump in first. Having just expressed his commitment to the transformation, and given that he was leading the current discussion, Barton also felt he should leave the next word to others. He felt quite eager, though, that someone should oppose Elliot's suggestion. That discussion wasn't where Barton hoped to spend their scarce time. When no one said anything, Barton reached out to Haas: "Ron? That looked like a reaction to John's comment."

Haas nodded. "It was. Not sure it was the right reaction, in this context, though." Everyone waited for him to continue, so he finally did. "Well, as you all know, I'm into lean manufacturing. And I've seen what those private equity guys John mentions mean when they say 'lean.' They implement lean by firing half the workforce. It's not the way I'd like to see things go, but I guess, as John says, it's our job to look at all the options."

Russell Rigby, a former California lieutenant governor, weighed in predictably: "That'd be a disaster for the region. It'd ripple through the supply base."

"Not our problem, the way I see it," said Elliot. "The region isn't a shareholder."

Several board members shifted uncomfortably.

"Many people and institutions in the region *are* shareholders," said Rigby.

"That's a different matter," said Elliot. "We're accountable to all our shareholders, including our small minority shareholders."

Ed Frazier spoke, annoyance obvious in the tone of his voice: "I thought we'd agreed we're committed to a strategy of transformation."

"What John is proposing, however," said Bill Ford, the past SMA CEO who had been closely involved in the long-ago spin-off of SMA from a larger aerospace company, "could make all of the shareholders and us a lot of money. We should have done it back when we did the spin-off. We'd have a lot fewer cost issues now if we had."

Frazier glared at Ford. "We'd have no company now, if we had," said Frazier. The tension between Ford and Frazier was personal. The former had been the latter's mentor throughout his career, and Ford had handpicked Frazier as his successor. But the two had increasingly diverged in their views in recent years. Barton thought Ford might have moved on and gained other interests in retirement, as his time at SMA receded into the past. Perhaps so much so that Ford had stopped being deeply interested in the company's future, Barton feared. Or perhaps it was more complex than that. On occasion, Ford made cracks about how SMA had ceased to be a real airplane company. With a deep background as a legendary aeronautical engineer, maybe he'd just become disconnected from what excited him about the company.

"Depending on the strategy we adopt," said Smithson, "we're looking for very different kinds of investors. The transformation approach requires strategic, long-term investors. The chop-up and sell-off option requires efficient pillagers." This provoked nervous laughter from some in the room. "That probably tells you," she finished, "which way I'm leaning on the issue."

A lull descended, so Barton steered things back to the round-robin, beginning to the right of Elliot, who had opened, where Charlotte Owens sat quietly: "Charlotte?"

Owens had once been a popular Stanford Business School professor. Upon retirement, she'd been invited to participate on several corporate boards, as well as some nonprofit boards, which kept her very busy.

"Well, I've just finished teaching an executive program on audit committees, and I haven't had as much time to put thought into this as I'd like," she began. She then launched into a general comparison of "stakeholder" versus "shareholder" board responsibility, adopting a lecturing tone that carried over from her teaching. She was particularly critical of the share buyback, and although she had gone along on it with the rest of the board, she seemed to have conveniently forgotten this. The other board members patiently waited for her to finish so the meeting could move on. Elliot rolled his eyes. Barton controlled his reactions, but felt disappointment. Her comments had disrupted the flow of the meeting and dissuaded real discussion.

Finally she finished, and Barton turned to Van Busin, sitting next to Owens. He'd put his smartphone away but, like several others, he'd appeared preoccupied while Owens spoke. Now Barton surprised him.

"Huh?" he said, when Barton singled him out. "I'm sorry, I wasn't listening." Owens fixed a venomous gaze on Van Busin. Ever the clumsy jokester, he tried to pretend that he'd been kidding. "I never pay attention, you know," he said, "to my esteemed colleagues from the other side of the continent," he said, referring to a presumed rivalry between Stanford and MIT. He grinned expectantly, but no one laughed. "Well," he said, moving on, becoming more serious, "I was wondering . . ."

Van Busin zeroed in on a detail from Gardner's earlier presentation and began to build from that detail a mildly relevant argument about a possible asset-liquidation strategy for increasing ROE, based on the DuPont formula, as Gardner had discussed it. But Van Busin was out of his area of expertise, and after about six minutes of his rambling, Gardner interrupted.

"Excuse me, Martin," said Gardner. "I think I might have been a little unclear in what I said . . ." A brief exchange followed, which made it obvious that Van Busin had in fact misunderstood the detail on which he had built his strategy suggestion. Gardner explained the detail and how it should be interpreted, whereupon Van Busin essentially said, though not in exact words, "Oh—never mind." Then he yielded the floor by turning to the person next to him, Phil Shepard.

To Barton's immense relief, Shepard, an influential CEO from a high-tech company, who'd made many fortunes on tech start-ups and investments, restored the meeting to a productive track by suggesting a vision for virtually connecting with partners to rationalize the supply chain and take out cost. He talked for a good fifteen minutes and at one point stood and drew some diagrams on the whiteboard. He also offered to "be active" in financing efforts, which Barton took to mean that he'd summon money, his own or from investment portfolios under his control, to be a strategic investor in SMA. Many around the table welcomed this statement of support for the transformation plan, which seemed in doubt since Elliot had begun the discussion. Barton felt immensely grateful to Shepard.

But the favorable trend didn't hold. Patricia Shanahan, a board member with CIO training, tried to build on Shepard's comments, but mostly succeeded in making it clear how long ago she'd retired, and how different the technologies for partner interaction had been then. Chris Harden, the former Air Force general, had little to say, and what he did say had a lot more to do with a company in a military contracting business than one in a commercial cargo business.

Things continued in roughly this pattern. Occasionally, things moved in a productive direction, but then they'd circle back. Smithson and Shepard continued to be the stars, with Gardener joining them in discussions that many others seemed not to follow. Frazier and Ford continued to disagree, responding mostly to each other. The discussion ranged widely, often shooting off in different directions, but never going very deep.

By the end of the meeting, Barton was discouraged. Whether he had a right to be, he wasn't sure. Much of the work had to be done down in the details. This job really belonged, Barton thought, to the SMA management team. But he had certainly hoped for more substantive contributions from the board. Elliot had closed the meeting on an ominous note.

"I have to say, folks, that nothing I've seen today has changed my idea that we still need to be looking carefully at 'nonstrategic' options. My take on our discussion in this meeting is that we just don't know what to do to accomplish this transformation. Given the stature of this group, I'm inclined to consider the evidence that the transformation might be too complex for us to pull off. If so, we need to look at other options, especially ones we could be more likely to successfully execute. Splitting up and selling off the pieces has its challenges. But it may be a better course of action than what we've supposedly 'committed' to do. And there are some worrying signs that the confidence of the market in our ability to pull it off is wavering. Maybe we should just face the music. I realize this is not a popular suggestion in this room, but it might be the reality we face."

No one disagreed out loud. Barton grew increasingly uneasy as he thought about whether he'd be willing to stick around for an exercise in dissection of SMA into its most valuable pieces and parts. Instead of coming home to save the day, he'd return as villain and betrayer. That wasn't what he'd signed up for when he agreed to be CEO. Nevertheless, the day's events seemed quite consistent with how his time at SMA had gone so far. Nothing as expected.

His ankle hurt.

Thursday, November 12, 9:13 p.m. . . .

"Ugh, when will you be through with these wretched things?" said Perez, kicking over the crutches Barton had left by the front door as she dropped her cashmere wrap and made a beeline for the bar. "It's cramping my social life to have you hobbling around. You should be joining me right now at the NiveauNu opening, instead of curling up on the couch like an old man." She looked radiant, as usual, in an emerald green dress, her wrists adorned in gold rings that rang musically in time with the martini shaker. Barton remained startled, as he was every time he saw Perez, that her beauty existed in flesh and blood even more exquisitely than the image he (regularly) conjured in his memory. Before he had a chance to formulate words, Perez slipped a drink in his hand and started mixing her own.

"Don't think I'm going to do this homebody thing for long," she said, still scowling. "I'm only being nice to you because your text message was so pathetic. And I know the SMA board."

She dropped the liquid mix into her glass and slid onto the leather couch next to Barton, wrapping one long leg around the other. "So, tell me. What happened?"

Barton inched himself nearer to her on the couch, intending to be smooth, but wincing at the effect of applying pressure to his ankle.

"You asking as a friend, Veronica, or a journalist?"

"Both, of course," she replied. "Don't tell me anything so juicy that I have to put it in print. Or," she raised an eyebrow seductively, "do."

"I'm afraid there's not much we're going to be able to talk about then," Barton said.

"Oh, come on," said Perez, running a fingertip behind his ear. "I know you find it hard to believe, but I might write something helpful. You never know."

"You'd do that for me?" asked Barton. He'd meant to keep the question light, flirtatious, but his voice betrayed wariness.

"No," Perez withdrew her finger. "Not *for* you. But I might if I agreed."

"Hmm," said Barton.

Perez gave Barton something of a glare. "Obviously I wasn't at the meeting today, Jim. But I do actually know something about those people, your board members. Quite a bit. I've met some of them."

Barton remained silent. He tried to imagine what Perez meant when she said she'd met them, what kind of history she might have with which board members. The thought disconcerted him on a number of levels.

Perez softened. Taking Barton's glass and setting both of their drinks aside, she drew her legs underneath her and curled her body into his sympathetically.

"Let me give you an idea," she whispered, "of what I mean by helpful."

"Okay," said Barton, inhaling the scent of her perfume. "Enlighten me."

"Naturally," Perez teased, and then began editorializing. "While it remains to be seen how financial services veteran Jim Barton will cut it as CEO of SMA, somehow he's made it this far and has committed to moving ahead with a bold strategy to transform, and thereby save, the company. It's one thing to ask if Jim Barton, CEO, has what it takes. But here's another question for you: has the SMA board he's inherited—an unwieldy collection of military veterans and retired professors—got what it takes? Transformation from the twentieth to the twenty-first century can't be done by a CEO alone. He's going to need a whole lot of support from all kinds of places, not the least of which, from an effective, efficient, and committed board. SMA's board probably hasn't been right for the company it *has* been—the company's performance certainly suggests as much. How can it possibly be the right board for the twenty-first-century company the bold new CEO wants it to be?"

"So you think I should restructure the board," said Jim, grateful for the chance to voice his own thoughts safely in the guise of hers.

"Yes, Jim. I think you should restructure the board."

"What if I'm the first board member who should go? One could easily conclude that from your editorial on my first day at work."

"Well," said Perez, "I may have been wrong about that. I haven't decided."

"Restructuring a board is difficult, delicate work. I've never done it before."

"There're a lot of things you haven't done before, Jim. Welcome to your new life." She reached for his hand and stroked the open palm. "Call your friend Bob Goldman. He knows how. Ron Haas will go along. You need a smaller, better board."

Barton considered this. Though he would not confirm it to Perez, he'd been thinking much the same way.

"I've been thinking of writing a piece along those lines—not on SMA particularly, but generally," said Perez. "If we got a discussion going on that topic in the financial community, it might just create some cover for you to act."

"Or it might push us into doing something dumb."

"Hey," said Perez, leaping to her feet and pulling Barton to his. "You gotta take some chances in your new life, right?"

"Ow!" He exclaimed, quickly shifting his weight onto his good leg. Perez had wrapped his hands around her waist and begun swaying in dance despite his stasis. "When do you think you're going to write this piece?"

"I haven't decided that I will. Just tossing the idea around."

"Love to know what you decide," said Barton.

"You can read it," said Perez, "in the newspaper. Just like everyone else."

She grabbed her martini and spun up to kiss him, spilling a little of her drink on his shirt.

"Oh, no, you need to change clothes," she said. "Let's go take care of that, shall we?"

Tossing several gold bracelets onto the bar as she danced passed it, she sang out her standard reminder to Barton, who hobbled to catch up: "I can't stay long. I promised to make another appearance in an hour."

Reflection

How did the board meeting go? Is it reasonable for Barton to be frustrated?

Do you agree with Elliot's recommendation to examine SMA's "nonstrategic" options as well? How should SMA leadership consider its responsibility to shareholders as it designs and communicates the strategy moving forward?

What is your assessment of the SMA board members? Have they got what it takes to transform the company? What changes would you make, if any, and how would you recommend Barton go about restructuring the board?

CHAPTER 7

Getting Great Performance from People

Thursday, November 19, 10:43 a.m. . . .

"The only thing I'm asking for—the *only* thing—is approval of this year's merit pay plan for our employees," said Jack Bruun, the senior HR executive at SMA. "The checks are overdue. Everyone below the CEO level has signed off. If I can get your signature, Jim, then we can close the books on this and everyone can get their money." Bruun's tone of voice communicated exasperation.

More than seemed warranted by the situation, Barton thought. "I know. I'll sign," he said. "But I'm glad we've had this discussion. I'm grateful to you, Jack, and to you, Rajit, for helping me think through these issues."

Bruun said nothing. He obviously didn't feel at all grateful for the past forty minutes. Rajit Palepu, from R&D, mumbled about his happiness to help. They sat in silence for a moment, in the conference room just off Barton's office.

Bruun had requested a meeting with Barton alone ("fifteen minutes max, just need to handle some administrative matters"). But Barton had scheduled it for forty-five minutes and asked Akita to send someone who could explain R&D's frustrations with the merit pay system. Akita's remarks about the system had been very negative and Barton wanted to understand why. From what he could see, by the standards of the financial services industry—at least in the companies in which he'd worked—this system had few unusual features. If he could understand how such a seemingly normal system could spark such vehement opposition from Akita and her people, then that might provide him fresh insights into this new (to him) business. Perhaps he'd be able to start a conversation that might lead to development of a system that fit better in the R&D area.

Akita had sent Palepu, describing him as "probably the smartest person in the company." Palepu had taken the meeting very seriously. He'd prepared extensively, researching the theoretical foundations of merit pay and other bonus systems, which he referred to during their conversation as "the agency theory" literature.* When a question from Barton early in the meeting elicited an onslaught of incomprehensible technical explication from Palepu, the SMA CEO concluded he'd made a mistake setting up the meeting this way.

Then Palepu proved him wrong by exhibiting a talent for getting across complicated ideas. After ten minutes, Barton could see why the man was so highly regarded. Though eccentric in manner, Palepu could dive deep into technical detail, then swoop back to explain what it all meant in business terms.

We should pay this guy whatever he wants, Barton thought at about the twelve-minute mark in their meeting. When he remarked about this to Akita in a follow-up visit to her office, her response was interesting: "That's just it, Jim. He doesn't really want more money. Oh, he'd take more and be happy to have it. Who wouldn't? But what he *really* wants is to design the greatest cargo airplane ever built. Or, preferably, the best that *will ever be* built. That grand vision, an ideal he'll never realize—not in the spectacular way he's imagined it, anyway—is the thing he really

---

*For one summary of this literature, see Robert D. Austin, *Measuring and Managing Performance in Organizations* (New York: Dorset House, 1996).

cares about. Money, that's not motivation for Rajit. But it is, potentially, distraction, a source of feelings of injustice if he thinks we get it wrong when we assess 'merit.'"*

Barton had a very different impression of Bruun. A large man who carried himself in ways calculated to impress his physical stature upon others, Bruun projected swaggering pragmatism. You could tell from watching and listening to him for only a few minutes that he prided himself on "knowing how the world works [wink]" and on never deluding himself or others. He had little time for idealists of any kind, which made him just about the polar opposite of Palepu.

Palepu digressed in almost everything he said, distracting himself with each new idea, his sentences veering sideways, extending and elaborating. Bruun, in contrast, enforced linear trajectory in all his communications and thoughts, always focused on the next point, refusing to be distracted by anything or anyone. This too, Barton knew, was a valuable trait in many situations.

But the two men combined badly. Whereas Palepu valued quality of discussion, Bruun wanted to be done as quickly as possible. Released into the wild, they'd be natural antagonists. In Barton's office, Bruun proved the predator: he had a much tougher time controlling his impatience with Palepu than Palepu did his dismay with Bruun's ideas.

"So, perhaps you could explain to us," Barton had said at the outset of the meeting, "your problems with the merit pay system."

"Oh, it's not a problem for me," said Palepu. "I always get the top bonus. I just think it's silly. It's a problem for SMA. It doesn't do what it claims to do. It's a flawed idea."

Bruun bristled. "Our merit pay system results from a two-year study done in collaboration with one of the very best consulting firms in the world. We examine how it's working and refine it every year, in collaboration with those same external, international experts."

"Yes," said Palepu, laughing undiplomatically, though with no ill intention. "Isn't that crazy? So much time and money spent on such silliness . . ."

*See Robert D. Austin and Richard L. Nolan, "Bridging the Gap Between Stewards and Creators," *MIT Sloan Management Review*, Winter 2007, 29–36.

"Could you be a little more specific?" asked Barton. "'Silly' isn't an informative criticism."

That's when Palepu let loose with an indecipherable torrent of explication, rambling at length about invalid assumptions, monotone likelihood conditions, and mathematical models from economics. Bruun looked to Barton and rolled his eyes knowingly. Barton refused this invitation to join in the "isn't this guy clueless?" appraisal. Instead, he remarked to Palepu: "I didn't understand a word of that. Can you translate?"

And that's when Barton discovered that Palepu *could* translate.

"It's like this," said Palepu. He stood, moved to the whiteboard, and drew a picture: two axes, the vertical labeled "Value" and the horizontal labeled "Time." Then, between them, he drew two curves, one rising steadily, the other first rising, and then turning down to dip even below the horizontal axis. The first curve he labeled, "Merit pay system value." The second, downturning one, he labeled, "Actual value."

"Look familiar?" asked Palepu.

"Looks like a flawed merit pay system," said Barton.

Bruun scowled, refusing to play along.

"It's just about every such system," said Palepu. "This picture tells a story that's at least partly implicated in just about every organizational and economic catastrophe you can think of. The Internet bubble.

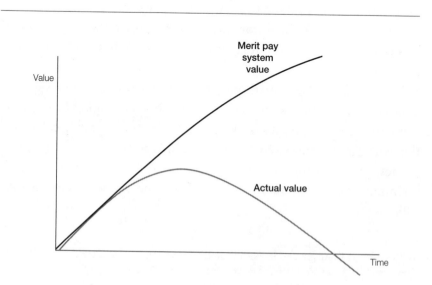

The mortgage crisis. US defense department overruns. You name it. Situations in which we maximize something that we think is value, but it eventually turns out to be driving away from real value."

"You're suggesting," said Barton, "that over time people figure out how their performance is being evaluated and drive up that performance artificially. They 'game' the system."

"That's part of it," said Palepu, "but I wouldn't put it exactly that way. Sometimes people would rather not play games, but they have to because the 'merit pay' system forces them to."

"Nonsense," muttered Bruun.

"And our system does that?" Barton asked.

"Think about it this way . . ." Palepu drew another two axes, but with different labels. On the vertical, he wrote: "Effort applied to seeking unmeasurable goodness." On the horizontal, "Effort applied to seeking measurable goodness." Then he drew a squiggly line starting at the point where the axes connected, moving out into the space between them. He labeled the squiggly line, "Ideal combination of measured and unmeasured goodness."

"Suppose," said Palepu, "that I'm an SMA R&D worker—hey, you don't have to suppose that, do you? I am one!" Palepu laughed nerdily. Barton smiled, and Bruun frowned. Palepu continued: "Now suppose

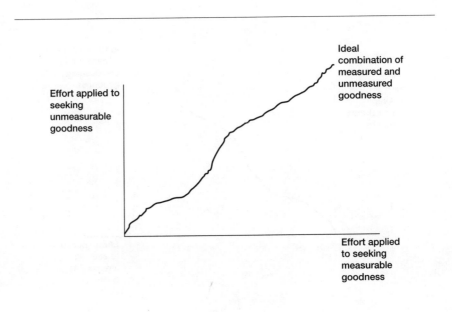

that left to my own devices, I'd be inclined to use five units of effort—don't worry for the moment about what a 'unit of effort' is; just think of it as a certain level of trying hard. Now, I could devote all five units of effort to seeking unmeasurable goodness or all five units of effort to seeking measurable goodness, or I could allocate some of the five to each, so that the total of effort applied to unmeasurable and measured goodness effort totals to five. On our picture, we draw a dotted line like this:

"Anywhere on the dotted line, the effort the R&D guy uses totals five units. But, as you can see from where it intersects the 'ideal combination' line, the R&D worker, if he can tell where that line is, will allocate a bit more effort to seeking measured than unmeasurable goodness because the 'ideal' line dips a bit at five units of effort. See? It jumps down a little bit. At this point, he's 'working smart' because he's allocating effort on the 'ideal' line. If he moves off the ideal line, he's working less smart."

Palepu pointed to where the two lines touched, where the ideal line jogged downward a little.

"You might worry that this guy doesn't know where that ideal line is. You'd be right to worry about that. It's hard to know. But you hired this particular guy into an R&D job because you thought he was more likely to know where that line is than others would. Those 'others' include, by

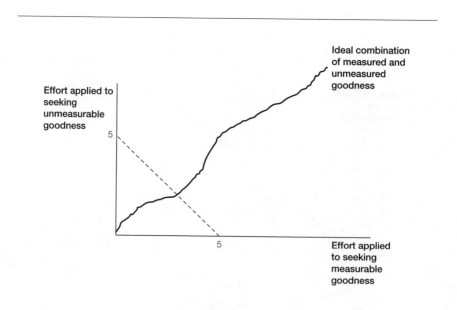

the way, his managers and the designers of merit pay systems. In other words, if he decides to put in a little extra effort, to 'work harder,' say, make it 5.1 units instead of 5, he knows best how to split that extra 0.1 units between unmeasured and measured effort. He'll move outward along this squiggly line until his effort level is at 5.1.

"The ideal line is, of course, where we create the most overall value for the business. If we move away from the ideal line, we create less value than we could for the same level of effort. That's why we call it the 'ideal' line."

Barton nodded. "When do we get to the good part?"

"Now," said Palepu. "Let's 'incentivize' this guy. We want him to work harder. That's the point of a merit pay system, right?"

"We want him to create more value," said Bruun. "We incentivize that."

Palepu grinned broadly. Barton couldn't tell whether he was simply pleased that Bruun was paying attention, or whether his reaction constituted a figurative rubbing together of hands, as in "ha, ha, ha, now you have fallen into my trap." It turned out to be the latter.

"Yes, you *want* to incentivize them to create more value," said Palepu, almost giddy, "but in fact you can only incentivize what you can evaluate. What you can measure. You ask us to set quantitative goals, milestones to stretch for."

"Yes, though we don't expect everyone to meet stretch goals," said Bruun. Barton sat back and listened. He was starting to get Palepu's point.

"Maybe," said Palepu, "you do take into account some unmeasurable factors. But the most tangible evidence of performance is what you *can measure*. So even if you tell this R&D guy that he'll be evaluated on a broad range of considerations, those measurable, quantitative performance indicators—how many patents, that sort of thing—they hang out there in space like glowing neon signs. Because those we know you can verify. The unmeasurable, intangible stuff is a lot more ambiguous.

"So—this is the good part—or rather, the *not-good* part—if I'm an unscrupulous R&D guy and I know you've got a bias toward what you can measure, or that anyway those are the clearest indicators of my performance, I might just start to slide down my effort line toward the measurable indicators.

"Since I'm moving away from the 'ideal' line, I'm reducing the value to the business, but I'm increasing my measured performance indicators. See?

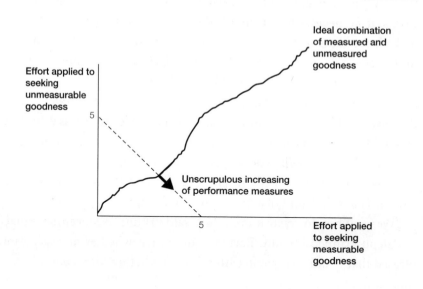

And if I do have scruples, I'm an unhappy guy indeed, because you're putting me in competition with this other R&D guy who might just be unscrupulous and willing to do whatever looks good. I might even feel that I must move away from the ideal line, as much as I might not want to, in order to prevent my managers from thinking I'm a poor performer compared to that unscrupulous guy."

"What if," asked Barton, "you allocated more effort. You worked harder?"

"Yes," said Palepu, like a teacher pleased with a question from a promising student. "That is indeed what you, as a manager, might hope. That I would have scruples. That instead of sliding down the effort line, I'd move outward along the ideal line. Like this."

Palepu added an arrow pointing outward along the ideal line.

"I, personally," said Palepu, "would do that. I'd work harder rather than move away from the allocation I knew delivered better value for the business. Because, for me, it's a matter of personal integrity. But I'd be annoyed as hell that I'm having to work a lot harder than the guys who are willing to slide down the effort line, *just* so I can look equally as good as they do."

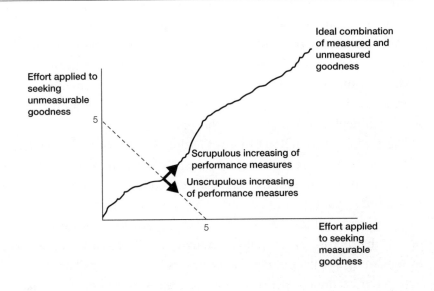

"So, Jack," said Palepu, "that's what your precious merit pay system is about. Rewarding creeps willing to compromise their integrity. Making me and my colleagues look around at each other distrustfully, wondering who might turn out to be a creep. If you want evidence, go look into the mortgage crisis. How people got paid for generating quantity, not quality, of mortgages."

Bruun shook his head. "That was a bad incentive system. Ours isn't a bad incentive system. We're smarter than that."

"Hmmm," said Palepu. "Did you know that more than 80 percent of people who drive automobiles think they're better than average drivers?" Barton thought Palepu smirked.

"So what if," said Barton, "we reward people not for specific effort, but for their results? We don't try to specify with measures how they should act, but what they should realize as outcomes?"

"Good idea," admitted Palepu, "in theory. But in practice, what results would you use for R&D? You want us to have good ideas, not just a lot of ideas. A really good patent, not just a lot of them. If we have one really, really good idea, that might be worth more than a whole lot of not-as-good ideas."

"If it's a really, really good idea, it ought to generate more profits," said Barton. "Its economic value ought to be obvious."

"Yes," agreed Palepu, "but you've still got the problem of figuring out how to allocate credit for the idea across the different members of an R&D staff. Innovation is not an individual pursuit, not anymore. Most of what we do that's really, really good we do in collaboration, and it's terribly difficult to tease apart who did what.

"Sure, those of us in R&D, those of us doing the work, know that some of us contribute more than others, some a lot more than others. But our managers' insight into that is worryingly dependent on those measurable things you've got us counting under the merit pay plan. That makes for lots of potential injustice. We do something great as a team, and you reward that person unscrupulous enough to slide down the effort line. In something as collaborative and diffuse as R&D, it's very hard to attribute credit accurately at the individual level. And we know you like to count things, so we're back to that annoyed-as-hell feeling, that you've implemented a system that some creep can take advantage of in this way."

"How do you know," asks Barton, "that we can't formulate measures that are good enough? They might not be perfect, but they might be good enough."

"That's the economist's dream," said Palepu. "But it's a pipe dream. Economists know these kinds of systems have this problem. Holmstrom and Milgrom wrote about it in 1991,* and a lot of others since. But it hasn't changed practice. Hasn't even changed their beliefs much for many of them. People persist in believing in *incentivizing* people to perform better because they're willing to assume that measures can be 'good enough.' That the measured and actual performance don't separate the way they do in my first picture." He pointed back at the first graph.

"But that's a shaky assumption," he said. "It's a much stronger assumption than its opposite, that no such measure that magically spans all the dimensions essential to value creation actually exists. Not to mention all the empirical evidence lying around waiting to be looked at. Financial crises, that sort of thing.

*Bengt Holstrom and Paul Milgrom, "Multi-Task Principal-Agent Analyses: Linear Contracts, Asset Ownership and Job Design," *Journal of Law, Economics and Organization* 7, Special Issue (1991): 24–52.

"And in R&D . . ." he shook his head. "We're rediscovering which direction the ideal line goes in and adjusting that on a daily basis, as we learn from experiments, as we react to competitive offerings, as technology makes new things possible. And managers can't see as well as we can where the next increment of effort should be applied. So when they design systems that try to influence where we allocate that effort, why should they be able to get that right? It's crazy . . . Plus, there's the time scale. Jack, how often did you say you adjust the merit pay system?"

"Every year," said Bruun.

"But our sense of what we ought to be doing in R&D changes every day, maybe several times a day. You give me merit pay targets; those become obsolete fast. In the worst case, my targets, my stretch objectives, force me to do dumb things, things that looked good when I promised to do them, but that I now know don't make sense. Again, the merit pay system forces me off that ideal line. And for somebody like me, who lives to make a better airplane, that's demoralizing."

"What if," asked Barton, "we worked harder to take qualitative factors into account, to see the whole picture?"

"You might be able to do that," said Palepu, "if your people trusted you enough to see clearly into what they do. That would be hard work though. You'd have to spend time with people, not reports of performance. And you'd have to be convincing—credible in assuring people that you wouldn't just fall back at some point on easier-to-defend, apparently less ambiguous quantitative measures."

"So what would you have us do? Avoid quantitative measurements all together?"

Palepu literally giggled. "No," he said. "We're engineers and scientists. We love to measure. We like to measure and learn. It's not the measurement; it's this 'incentivizing' idea that's a problem. Linking rewards with measures, counts, milestones.

"If you think about it, you say you want to reward good, hard work, but in fact the only reason your incentivizing works at all is because people have too much integrity to play games. They're willing to work harder, rather than compromise their integrity. So in a backhanded way, maybe it works. But it's one hell of way to treat the employees you say you value and depend on the most."

"I get your point," said Barton. "But shouldn't we be able to reward terrific employees in some way?"

"Sure," said Palepu. "But there's a big difference between, a) looking into what's really happening in a serious, wide-ranging way and rewarding people based on what you find out, and, b) setting up some sort of precise counting scheme in advance that defines performance and associates it with compensation, so that people can play games.

"And there's still another problem. Merit pay systems don't calibrate rewards very well. We invent something that makes a billion dollars for the company; you give us $5,000 in additional pay. That's just . . . insulting. Why do that? Why start down that road? We get it that we're not going to make billions when we come up with an idea that makes billions for SMA. We'd have chosen different careers if that's what we were about. We'd have been entrepreneurs, maybe. Now you want to make us silly, pretend entrepreneurs with your merit pay schemes. But, hey, news alert: we're grown-ups. We can tell it's pretend."

"You'd prefer that we'd just let you do your work," said Barton, "rather than distract you with this . . . system."

"Distract, annoy, upset . . . yes," said Palepu. "Maybe it works in some areas of the company. But it's a bad fit in R&D. You aren't buying my time; you're buying the quality of my ideas. You don't need quantity from us; you need quality, in collaboration. And, because the world changes so fast, quality of R&D is one hell of a difficult thing to measure."

"Jack?" said Barton. "Comments?"

"Seems like the whole world is wrong, then," said Bruun, "because the whole world uses these systems."

"In some places," said Barton, "there *is* an issue with getting people to work hard enough."

"Sure," said Palepu. "But there's a question how much distraction we want to create for our best people just to keep a few of our worst from 'free riding.' And getting people to work hard is pointless if they allocate effort wrong, if they slide down that effort line. At some point, skewed effort allocations can become harmful. That's when we get canceled defense programs, because a project made quiet quality compromises to stay on schedule. Or collapsing market bubbles, because people sold a lot of mortgages that shouldn't have been sold. And who knows what else."

Barton looked at Bruun. Bruun looked down at the piece of paper awaiting the CEO's signature. "Yes," said Barton, "I'll sign."

The meeting had ended quickly after that. Barton thanked them, they left, and he sat confused. Palepu's arguments displaced too much management infrastructure familiar to Barton to gain his easy acceptance. To reject "incentivizing," as Palepu called it, even for certain parts of the organization, he'd need an approach, a way of thinking, to fill the void left by that rejection. And he had no idea what that would be.

Saturday, November 21, 10:43 a.m. . . .

"My name's Clara," said the older woman in the wide-brimmed straw hat, "and if you come over here, I'll show you my babies."

Barton smiled and stepped through the gate that joined the backyard of his new residence in Venice Beach with Clara's. She stood holding open the door to a greenhouse. The windows of the house were not quite transparent, but he assumed the "children" were orchids or something similar. When he reached the doorway and peered in, what he saw surprised him: *dandelions.*

Dandelions in boxes and buckets. Dandelions in pots. Big dandelions, small dandelions. Unusually colored dandelions. All looked amazingly healthy.

"Why . . .?" Barton began, then stopped for fear of seeming rude.

"Why do I raise weeds?" she said, smiling, reading his thoughts.

He thought fast and lied: "Why inside a greenhouse?"

"You're very polite," said Clara. "Of course, my neighbors wouldn't like my babies spreading seeds into their green lawns. I keep them in here all year round. You've seen, I'm sure, how exuberantly they spread their parachutes and take to the winds." She gestured broadly, flapping both hands.

Barton smiled. "My name's Jim Barton," he said. "And I'm pleased to make your acquaintance. We're now neighbors, it seems. I've been moving in gradually. Still moving in really."

Clara dropped her arms and shook hands.

A few minutes later, Barton and Clara sat at a small wooden table on a deck off the back of her concrete-block construction bungalow, which had, at some point, gained the addition of an ultramodern second floor. Each sipped a glass of wine—"dandelion wine," Clara had explained. The sun shone, and it remained warm even so late in November.

"Until about nine years ago," said Clara, "I was the CEO of a pharmaceuticals firm." This surprised Barton, but it did explain why she might own such an expensive piece of real estate. "When I retired, I stepped well back from the business. No long-term board involvement for me. That suited them, too. It was not a completely amicable parting, really, but enough about that."

She sipped her wine before continuing: "My current claim to fame is based primarily on my expertise with these lovely creatures," she pointed toward the greenhouse. "The species *Taraxacum*, these tap-rooted herbaceous plants. A sort of second career, you might say. I've become quite well known in certain circles."

"But why . . .?" Again Barton veered off the question most prominent in his mind. She answered it anyway.

"Why grow a weed?" Barton thought she seemed disappointed in him. "Well, I realize you're the CEO of a major company, which excuses you somewhat. Your ignorance in such matters, I mean. Also, I suppose, about other things."

Barton laughed and came clean: "Okay, Clara: Why *do* you grow weeds? It seems rather, well . . . eccentric."

The characterization pleased her. She too laughed, apparently delighted. "Yes, it does, doesn't it?"

She took off her hat and gathered her thick, graying hair back with her hands, to better secure it within an elastic band. Then she straightened her pale blue linen top. Barton waited and took a sip of the wine. It was good. The bottle nearby sported a handmade label. Clara had made the wine herself. A chemist by training, perhaps, he thought.

"Tell me, Jimmy . . ." she said, then interrupted herself. "Can I call you Jimmy? I assure you, it's an affectionate moniker. My late older brother's name. You remind me of him a bit."

"I've been called much worse," said Barton.

"So tell me," she said, "what makes a dandelion a weed?"

She waited. Barton thought.

Before he could answer, she continued: "Children and some adults make them into crowns, which they wear when they play together. *Taraxacum albidum* is a lovely Japanese variety; I have some in my greenhouse. Maybe you saw them. You can make rubber from *taraxacum kok-saghyz*, native to Asia and certain parts of Europe. I have some of those also, though I don't make rubber. I stick to wine.

"The leaves are edible and contain abundant vitamins and minerals. One cup contains 112 percent of your recommended daily allowance of vitamin A. They are good sources of calcium, potassium, iron, and manganese, better than spinach in this regard. They contain beta carotene; lutein; luteolin, an antioxidant; and zeaxanthin. Some say they promote healthy weight loss and liver detoxification. The flower petals can be used, as you can taste for yourself, to make an excellent wine. Roasted and ground, the roots make a superb caffeine-free coffee. They are a natural diuretic and supply the potassium that other diuretics often cause you to lose. They reduce inflammation. There is some evidence that the leaves might normalize blood sugar. A group of researchers in Ontario have even demonstrated, in early results, that dandelion root extract can cause certain cancer cells to commit suicide.* They are important to bees early in the growing season, and they are food for butterflies.

"So I ask you again: what, precisely, makes a dandelion a weed?"

This time, Barton was ready: "People don't like them in their lawns. People invest a lot in making their lawns look nice. Dandelions spoil that."

"Making their lawns uniform," said Clara, disapprovingly.

"Yes," Barton said.

"Same species of grass. Same height. All orderly, in the right place."

"Yes," Barton said.

Clara took a sip of wine, looked up at a distant cloud, and sighed. "So what makes a dandelion a weed," she said, "is not its inherent qualities. But rather *where* it is placed. In my greenhouse, it's a source of wine, nutrition, even medicine. In your lawn, however, it's a weed."

*"Cancer-Killing Dandelion Tea Gets $157K Research Grant," CBC News, April 20, 2012, http://www.cbc.ca/news/health/story/2012/04/20/wdr-dandelion-tea-research-grant.html.

"That's it, I guess," said Barton. "Though its tendency—you called it exuberant—to propagate on the breeze to those places where it's not wanted, that seems like an inherent quality."

"Yes, but that depends entirely on your perspective. As a cultivator of dandelions, I quite appreciate how easy it is to propagate them."

"So," said Barton, following along, "if we had better ways of containing dandelions in places where they could provide benefits without drifting into people's lawns, we might have a very different view of dandelions."

"Yes," Clara said. "Then people would stop picking on my poor little babies. If we were better dandelion 'managers.'"

"As usual," said Barton, "the real problem is with management."

Clara did not answer this. Instead, she seemed to change the subject.

"Let me tell you a story about a small company," said Clara. "They've just invited me to join their board—at least in part because of my expertise with dandelions, believe it or not. They're based in Denmark. My connections with that part of the world go way back. My husband was Norwegian; we met in Tanzania many years ago, but then lived in Norway and Sweden. But that's a different story." Barton wondered if the wine had started to affect her.

"*Specialisterne*," she said, "means, literally, 'the specialists.' Their corporate logo contains an airborne dandelion seed afloat in the air, suspended from its open parachute. The company does most of its business in software testing, very specialized work that people who are good at developing software do badly. The company's consultants are very, very good software testers, some of the best in the world. They are remarkable in this sense. But the thing many people consider most remarkable about the company is something *else* about its consultants: most of them have some form of *autism*."*

Barton's attention had been starting to drift, but he now sat up straight and listened.

"That's right," said Clara. "Autism. It makes them the world's greatest software testers. They are bright, very analytical, and they enjoy the kind of repetitive activity that would make many of us batty. Their supposed

*Robert D. Austin, Jonathan Wareham, and Javier Busquets, "Specialisterne: Sense & Details," Case 9-608-109 (Boston: Harvard Business School, 2008).

disability makes them some of the world's best at this kind of task. Most of the company's employees were considered unemployable before they went to work for Specialisterne. Do you see what that means?"

Barton was getting it. "They were weeds before, because they were in the wrong place."

"Exactly," said Clara. "As it turns out, the most difficult thing about the Specialisterne business model might be all the special handling these consultants with autism require. They have to be put in just the right conditions to be world-class software testers."

"Kept out of the lawn."

"What made them unemployable—supposedly unemployable," observed Clara, "was that we kept trying to get them to fit into that uniform, single-species green lawn. Everybody the same height. Everybody the same kind of grass. But don't you see how that underachieves?"

"Sure," said Barton.

"The point is more general," said Clara. "I spent quite a few years managing research at my former company. Some of my very best researchers were, well . . . a little bit weird, frankly. Peculiar manners. Unusual work habits and schedules. If I wanted them to do great work, I accommodated this. I didn't try to force them into the same pattern as everyone else. Because I didn't need uniform, consistent performance out of them. I needed exceptional ideas from them. I needed them to be outliers. To enable them to be outliers, I had to do just what Specialisterne does. I had to put them into conditions where they could achieve outlier performance."

"You never tried to get them to fit in? To be a uniform blade of grass?" asked Barton.

"Of course I did. At first. But then I learned. They taught me. They showed me that I didn't really want them to be like everyone else."

"The problem's obvious, really, isn't it," asked Barton. "You hire them because they're exceptional, then you put them into system and try to make them behave like everyone else."

"It's not just the exceptional employees, either, Jimmy. It's all of them. In that airplane company of yours, you need all your employees to do exceptionally well. You need them all to be outlier performers. And to get them to be able to do that, you—and I mean *you*—have to create the conditions in which they can *perform*."

The two of them fell silent. Barton took a sip of the wine. It couldn't be quite noon, he thought, and he felt a bit buzzed. He hoped he'd remember this conversation and think about it some more.

"Have you seen my pond?" Clara asked. "Come see my Japanese koi and my lovely goldfish. My other babies."

She stood and started toward one corner of the lot, where Barton spotted a small pond that he had not noticed earlier. He rose and followed her.

"Next time we talk," she said, "I must explain to you the wisdom one can obtain from caring for perennials . . . they must be occasionally unclumped, you know, for their own good . . ."

Barton contemplated the deep wisdom in her statement. He felt the warm sun on his skin and thought he might be getting a bit burned.

"Next time," said Clara, wobbling a bit, "we should perhaps have coffee . . ."

Reflection

Is the merit pay plan "silliness"? What needs to change for it to better serve the needs of the R&D workers at SMA and lead to the best possible performance? What role should the CEO take in leading this change?

Can measures be formulated that are "good enough" to serve as the basis for rewarding performance in an area like R&D that involves outputs of an "uncountable" nature (i.e., responses to moving targets, collaboratively generated ideas, ideas of varying value)?

What kinds of conditions support outlier performance in your organization? As CEO, how can you ensure these conditions are provided and outlier performance nurtured?

Can grass management and dandelion management be practiced in the same organization? What possible tensions might arise between managers of each, and how can the CEO allay these tensions?

Your Lineup Is a Mess!

SSEER, a simulated senior executive experience role-play by Simavatar Studios

The crowd at the Staples Center erupts in boos. The Lakers are *not* playing well. Still in the second quarter, they've fallen behind by twenty-two points. Luce's voice rises above all others in the vicinity: "Come on, you bums! Get it together!"

Their seats are amazing. Jack Nicholson sits courtside, just in front of them. They can see Leonardo DiCaprio and other celebrities opposite. Most people anywhere nearby, including Nicholson, have noticed Luce; he's been carrying on for a while, oblivious to the disapproving stares directed his way. He's painted his face half purple and half gold, and wears an oversized team jersey that says "Abdul-Jabbar" on the back, pulled on over his trademark black tee. Luce sits on the end of a row, next to Barton.

On the other side of Barton, Goldman wears a white shirt and suit slacks, but no tie, the top button of his shirt undone. Barton has never seen Goldman with no tie, or with shirt unbuttoned, and it looks weird. Too upright in his seat, holding a box of popcorn as if someone had handed it to him to hold for a moment, Goldman seems uncomfortable, really uncomfortable. Laker games are clearly not his "thang."

The Lakers call time out. Luce plops down into his seat and turns to Barton.

"I hoped we'd see some quality play here tonight," said Luce. "No such luck. Nothing but bad news here. Reminds me of your recent exploits at SMA."

Barton reacts: "What do you mean by that?"

"You've got to admit," says Luce, "your plans to engage the unions as partners took a hit last week. All that stuff about Ace being a longtime friend and a solid ally looks like nonsense."

"Why would you say that?" says Barton.

"He almost crippled you, man," says Luce.

"I haven't given up," says Barton. "I still think there's potential there. The workers clearly have to be a part of the solution. They have know-how no one else has."

"As if that's your only problem," Luce smirks.

"The board is a mess," interjects Goldman, leaning in, speaking up over the crowd noise. "Governance is not what it needs to be in your company, Jim. Without sound governance, the transformation of SMA will never happen."

Barton nods in grim acknowledgment. "I know. I'm just not sure what to do about it."

"It won't be easy," says Goldman. "But you'll have to tackle it."

"And," adds Luce, "what about your team?"

Barton runs through a list. "Clarke seems trustworthy and talented. Akita's definitely the right choice. Same with Marochek. Most others I've met seem reasonably capable. Kohler might have to go. Maybe Bruun, the HR guy."

"What's wrong with Kohler?" Goldman asks.

"Irreconcilable differences of philosophy," says Barton. "Her reflex is to keep everything secret, avoid engaging with the press. I think that's the wrong approach to communications in a modern firm. Transparency and engagement is better, I think. But she's not going to come around to my perspective."

"Could she be right?" asks Goldman. "You're in a different business now. Military secrets and all."

"No," says Luce, weighing in. "She's living in the past. There are no secrets anymore. It's too easy to forward an e-mail. Everyone blogs, tweets, texts. You'll never lock it down completely."

"There must be some secrets," Goldman says, "or else civilization collapses."

"Civilization?" says Luce.

"Yes," says Goldman.

"I cannot see at all what you mean by that," says Luce. "If you think that, you're going to be in a constant panic nowadays. Things get out. That's mostly a good thing. Civilization persists. Secrecy and panic are surely no way to run a company."

"Some things have to stay secret," says Barton. "We have technology that's proprietary and, as Bob mentioned, military secrets. But I agree with you, Jonathan, that it's damn hard to keep more than a few secrets, and we need to get used to that reality and manage it. We certainly can't keep disgruntled, risk-averse engineers from expressing their opinions about composites to news reporters."

"So Kohler might have to go," says Goldman. "What else?"

"Bruun just has a bad attitude," Barton says. "Again, wrong philosophy, I think. Not sure I'm that comfortable with the new one, but I do think there's something to what Palepu and Akita are saying."

Goldman shook his head. "I think it's nonsense. The world runs on incentives. Incentives will have their say. Assuming otherwise is like assuming water doesn't flow downhill."

"People need a sense of direction," Luce agrees. "But incentives aren't the only way to give that to them. How 'bout you try inspiring them, Jim? Incentives get people's skin in the game, but they don't rally the troops."

Goldman nods. "You have to lead, Jim. They don't need a prophet, but they do need a steady hand showing them the way."

"I don't know how to get people ready for the change that has to come," admits Barton. "It's going to be bigger than they think. They don't realize how much trouble we're in. They don't want a new kind of business. They don't want unfamiliar technologies. Companies usually fail when they try to turn from one core business to another."

"Nothing particularly new about that problem," says Goldman. "Managing change. Hardest thing any leader ever does."

"And I'm struggling with the systems integration model," continues Barton. "It's Ed Frazier's concept. I'm not sure what it means, in practical terms."

"Sounds like outsourcing," says Goldman.

"Yes," Barton says, "but more than that. Relying on partners to do things in your interests that you haven't asked them to do. I'm not sure I know how to set that up."

"Maybe," offers Luce, "you're going to have to learn in progress. Maybe nobody quite knows how to do that yet."

"Or maybe it's a bad idea," says Goldman. "Turning over the keys to your castle to someone who has his own goals and objectives that are not the same as yours."

Barton says nothing. The other two turn their attention to the floor, where the home team is about to inbound the ball. Barton's gaze rises to the ceiling, where the high-definition Jumbotron dazzles with close-up video, animation, and running strings of text. Suddenly, the strings of text looked odd. Streaming across the face of the Jumbotron, the words say:

. . . GET THE TEAM RIGHT . . . NO SECRETS . . . PARTNER RELATIONSHIPS . . .

"Huh?" Barton says out loud. He looks around, then back at the Jumbotron. Were others seeing this? The words continue:

. . . GET KEY CONSTITUENCIES ON YOUR SIDE—THE UNIONS, DUH! . . . RETHINK PEOPLE MANAGEMENT—THE OLD WAY WON'T WORK FOR WHERE YOU NEED TO GO! . . . TIME TO LEAD—YOUR PEOPLE NEED DIRECTION! . . . ADDRESS GOVERNANCE ISSUES—YOUR BOARD IS A MESS! . . .

Barton turns to Luce. "Jonathan, are you seeing . . .?"

Just then, Kobe Bryant steals the ball from a rival guard and the crowd leaps to its feet.

Harder Than I Thought

"Yeah! That's it!" says Luce. "That's what I'm talkin' about, yes sir! Yes sir!" He turns to Barton, slaps him on the back and then notices his perplexed look. Barton repeats, "Did you . . .?"

"Heck, yeah, I saw that! It was awesome!"

"No," Barton corrects, "I mean . . . did you do . . .?"

"Jim, what is it? What are you going on about, man? Get into this! The home team just did good!"

The Jumbotron reverts to prior form. Barton looks over at Goldman, to see if he has seen anything odd. Goldman continues to sit in his seat, holding the popcorn, looking bored.

Then, without warning, Goldman turns to Barton and speaks.

"Start with the board, Jim. Nothing else will be possible before you handle the governance issues."

Barton nods, sighs, and turns his attention to the game. "The hardest part," he mutters.

CHAPTER 8

Rallying the Team

Friday, December 4, 12:35 p.m. . . .

Barton took a deep breath, trying to calm his jitters. He stood at the window of a now-empty meeting room in the historic Seattle Edgewater Hotel, where he'd sought refuge to gather his wits. Through the window, the sun broke through a cloud and reflected from the waters of Elliott Bay: a good omen, he hoped. The rain clouds that had descended earlier that week had suddenly dissipated.

It surprised Barton that he felt so nervous. But a lot rode on how he'd handle the next few minutes. His anxiety combined in a volatile mix with excitement. He'd flown his entire senior team to Seattle for two and a half days of meetings. It had gone very well. But how he would end it—that would be very important. He would enter the large meeting room where he'd deliver final remarks to thirty-four senior executives. They constituted the team that would have to deliver on the vision they'd unfolded in the past two-plus days. They waited only for Barton to give them their final charge and to send them forth—on to greatness.

He hoped he was up to the challenge.

The event had been carefully staged. Barton wanted it in Seattle, for symbolic linkage to the history of the aerospace industry. He wanted to align SMA with the kind of bold twenty-first-century transition that industry giant Boeing had enacted just next door, at the Bell Harbor Conference Center, when it ditched its old "surprise and delight" approach to customer relations and instead recognized customers as "partners," empowering them to vote their product preference into the design: "speed" (the Sonic Cruiser) or "efficiency" (the 787). The Edgewater Hotel, where the Beatles stayed during their 1964 US tour, also sounded the right notes for fortuitous beginnings. In effect, he was relaunching the new cargo jet airliner.

The two days had included many highlights.

"We have a daunting task ahead of us, but one that *is* possible," Barton had told them on the first day. "It's a task that will define each of us. The opportunity is to innovate, to achieve a new kind of twenty-first-century leadership. Although the way is not clear, the direction is. It's going to be about real-time information, new kinds of relationships, capturing new sources of value. New ways of building and doing things. About learning from others.

"Many companies in the computer industry have shown that you don't have to be a fully vertically integrated company, the owner of all the layers of the business that add value, to be an industry leader; you can be virtually integrated, capturing value instead from strategic partnerships.

"Apple showed us how success could come from sustained innovation above and beyond cost improvement, that customers will pay a premium to buy exceptional products and services, and that investors will follow. Closer to our own industry, Boeing, even as we speak, provides a proof point: the 787. The 787 has more innovation incorporated into it than any other commercial airplane; it also has been built and designed collaboratively by a global, virtually integrated, IT-enabled network organization of strategic partners. Are there issues? You bet. You're reading about them in the news, and so am I. But do any of you doubt that Boeing can deliver this plane to customers? I know I don't.

"We, too, have an opportunity to lead, in a new industry segment. The segment is predicted to grow more than 6 percent per year over the next twenty years. That means more than twenty-three hundred air cargo planes will enter the market. More than 70 percent are projected to be conversions of aged passenger airliners. Ours won't be one of those. SMA will redefine the air cargo segment by building a plane optimized to carry cargo. We will sell directly to air cargo operators and maintain detailed knowledge about the needs of air cargo customers to ensure that our commercial cargo planes meet their needs.

"We embark now upon a journey. Our job during these three days is to question everything. To debate the issues and begin to create solutions. To begin to develop a scenario to execute the vision that we will present to our board of directors for their approval. You'll be working, as you know, in six teams. As you work on these big issues, I ask each of you to wear two hats: your functional expertise hat and your SMA general management hat. Good luck. We'll need it. But we can do it. Let's get to work."

The six teams had gone to work on the specifics of what SMA needed to have and do to become a "systems integrator," working hand in glove with global strategic partners to design, build, and service specialized cargo jetliners. The ground rules: each team would develop and present its analysis, draft recommendations, and the key aspects of its action plans. At the presentations, each thirty minutes long on the morning of the final day, groups would entertain clarifying questions only; there'd be no questions about alternatives or risks. Those would come later, after the meeting, after the base scenario had been fully laid out.

That morning, Friday, Barton had read satisfied body language from team members. This contrasted dramatically with what he'd seen on Wednesday evening, after a first day of difficult discussions in groups. That night, in what had seemed like a foreboding sign, the weather had turned to freezing rain. Nevertheless, early Thursday, a group of about seven of his execs, avid runners all, braved the elements and returned to the hotel exhilarated, if soaked, after a run along the Seattle waterfront and uphill to the Seattle Art Museum Sculpture Park, a treacherous journey in the prevailing conditions. Somehow they'd brought enthusiasm back into the meetings with them, a "damn the elements, let's do this anyway" spirit. The group looked pathetic, wet, and cold, but their wretched appearance just magnified their defiant exuberance. It was, Barton thought, a turning point. Several others had said something to him along those same lines.

When the presentations commenced, Susan Akita went first:

"As I know you've all been aware, because I've been quite vocal about it, I've thought all along that we could do better than the airplane we'd designed. We have the aeronautical design capabilities to go further than we did. In arriving at our design, we didn't fully grasp the technological capabilities that exist today, especially new alloys and other new materials. Faced with an opportunity to be bold, we were timid.

"Now discussions that broaden the SMA vision to include the supply chain have led us to a need for more robust design requirements. We're going to be forced to revisit the design, to realize our broader objectives. Our innovation 'jam' and other crowdsourcing initiatives give us important new ways of doing the revisiting. We know from our analyses that existing air cargo airplanes are too expensive to operate, that they haven't taken advantage of opportunities to better serve customers. Customers express concerns about their needs to be able to serve more airports and to have more efficient containerization for air cargo.

"Research tells us that carbon composites are the way forward." A few people in the room groaned at this statement. "I know, it's not what we know best. It's not what we've worked with in the past. But you know they're about equal to metal alloys in strength per pound now, and that metal alloys have reached a limit. It's getting harder and harder—more expensive—to make further advances with metal alloys. In contrast, carbon composites are at the beginning of their potential as major structural materials for commercial aircraft. I know many of you feel uncertain about these new materials, but we need to face the future. We need to master these new ways.

"By using carbon composites in our cargo airplane, we would be first. Commercial airplane manufacturers continue to focus on passenger airplanes. They've been slow to seize the opportunities in the growing air-cargo market segment. We can gain a sustainable first-mover advantage from the operating efficiencies of a lighter, carbon composite airplane. While our first carbon composite airplanes would be about equal in weight to the lightest metal alloy airplanes, our engineers should be able to considerably lighten up the airframes during certification and continue with additional advances in carbon composites research.

"The operating efficiencies of a lighter airplane are important, but there's another exciting aspect of carbon composites. You've all probably noticed that Boeing's 787 *looks* different from any other commercial airplane; it's aeronautically sculptured. Carbon composites open up possibilities for aeronautical designs that have not been possible before.

A whole host of new wing and fuselage designs are being wind-tunnel tested here, in Seattle at the University of Washington and Boeing, as we speak. The results are encouraging and exciting in a tremendous variety of ways.

"Throughout the history of our industry, companies have succeeded and failed based on their willingness to break free of old paradigms. In the late 1940s, British companies could have easily adopted the strut mountings for jet engines that proved a breakthrough on the Boeing Dash 80. But propeller airliner engines had been mounted in line with the wings, so that's where the British engineers mounted them by default. When they saw what Boeing was doing, they dismissed the 'beastly podded engines!'* And it cost them their industry leadership. Boeing, not the leading company then, seized industry leadership. We must see with the same clear vision—and do the same."

Akita's presentation reached its climax: "Our team recommends that we design and build our new air cargo plane using carbon composites as the primary structural material." Applause broke out spontaneously and overwhelmed the uncomfortable squirming and head shaking of a few in the room. Although much remained to be figured out, everyone had the feeling something had just been decided. People asked clarifying questions. But the tone shifted to a "maybe this could work" sensibility. Energetic discussion continued through the coffee break, until Barton called the group back to order and turned the podium over to Paul Marochek's manufacturing team.

"Our team followed Susan's team closely," began Marochek, "so we expected carbon composites would be a major part of our new plane. And, while we've incorporated carbon composites in the leading edges of our wings and stabilizers, we have no manufacturing experience in using them for major components.

"So, as a team, we've concluded that the only way that we can success-fully build a composite plane within the time frame and costs that we need to, is to bring in strategic partners with the experience and know-how we don't have. These would include Japanese "heavies" like Mitsubishi,

*J. Sutter with J. Spenser, *747: Creating the World's First Jumbo Jet and Other Adventures from a Life in Aviation* (New York: HarperCollins, 2006), 60.

currently manufacturing the 787 wing, and Spirit, the Wichita factory that Boeing sold to Onex Corporation. Spirit builds composite fuselage sections for the 787. We also might want to investigate the Airbus factory now coming online built for composite manufacturing for the new Airbus 350. Then there's Italy's Alenia, now building composite fuselage sections. In addition, we're likely to want to have discussions with the Chinese aerospace companies." There was more squirming and head shaking at this point. Marochek pushed on. "The Chinese players have come a long way. They're building high-quality commercial airplane components for Boeing, Airbus, and others. Airbus recently built a final assembly factory in China. We all know that China continues to grow economically, and it's now the most active market for commercial passenger airline sales. There's a commercial cargo airline fleet to be built there, a big one. This is Danielle's area, really, but it matters, too, that we know China's state-owned airline may be interested in being our launch customer for advance purchase of our proposed air cargo airplane." Murmurs swept through the room. Some people sat forward in their chairs.

"Same as we'll need to enlist strategic partners in the design and engineering of our new plane, we'll need to enlist strategic partners in its manufacturing. This will mean transforming our manufacturing operations into a network of strategic partners. It'll mean doing less internally, but we can't compromise at all on quality. It's going to be hard. We'll have trouble. But sharing the investment is the only way to make it doable. And if we're going to be a global player, we're going to have to access the global talent pool for the know-how and skills we don't have. We've got to have the best know-how, wherever it is. We can grow some of the capability we need internally, but not all of it. We just don't have the time or money to do that.

"The vision here is that we become a 'systems integrator.' We focus on what we can be really good at, better than anyone else. We resist doing things that others can do just as good or better, unless there's a competitive or, in some cases, a quality or performance reason that we have to undertake the activity. We've been really good at airplane manufacturing, but now others can do it as well. With the emergence of composites, now we have to question whether we can be as good as others, especially with the new investment demands required.

"As you all know, we've never been able to run our factory at near capacity for manufacturing our own airplane. If we were to allow our factory to compete and manufacture parts for other airplane manufacturing, the factory would be able to enjoy more favorable economics, and the price or cost to us would be lower, too. So our team recommends that we should investigate selling our factory, allowing it to become an independent manufacturer, similar to Boeing's past sale of its Wichita factory." More consternation erupted at this point. "Our team also suggests that we then contract with our factory along with other strategic partners for manufacturing. With this approach, we'd be able to knock down the investment requirements that we're facing, enjoy a better cost structure for our new plane, and focus more on what we need to be good at.

"These are big moves, and they're risky. We're talking about moving from being a twentieth-century, vertically integrated defense contractor to a twenty-first-century, virtually integrated commercial systems integrator. We'll have to learn to work with a network of strategic partners that we don't own or control directly. We've done this with jet engines, but the scale we're talking about here makes this a whole new ball game."

"You can say that again," came a voice from the back of the room. The comment elicited laughter, but excited, not cynical.

"I will," said Marochek. "You're going to get tired of hearing it." These words produced another round of laughs.

The discussion that followed and the tone of it encouraged Barton. People stuck to the ground rules, but a few more excellent points came out in the conversation.

The sort of systems integration network that SMA had begun discussing would present a management challenge of a completely different kind from management of traditional, vertically integrated supply operations. The change would require a shift from "owner control" processes to "partner coordination" processes, raising issues, for example, of how best to build trust and design contracts with partners that engender shared risk taking, shared motivation and commitment, and incentives to share knowledge across organizational boundaries.

Also, information technology would be extremely important to managing a global supply network; for a few minutes, Marochek turned over the floor to Jennifer Sharp, SMA's extremely capable CIO, who described the IT improvements they'd have to make. This part alone posed daunting challenges. SMA had well-developed computer-aided design and manufacturing capabilities; Sharp and her people had worked hard on the interfaces between the systems of internal groups, so that data would flow smoothly from one to another. "But now," she showed them, with a presentation slide that exploded with complexity, "we'll need to use all that experience and learning to do something very similar externally, with our strategic partners." Barton, a former CIO, shook his head. The challenges appeared several orders of magnitude greater than anything he had faced in his old job at IVK.* "We'll need to do some hiring," Sharp said, looking directly at Barton. "We'll need expertise in cloud computing, other technologies, to do this properly. And we'll need strategic partners here, too, to provide expertise that we don't have. For us in IT, this won't be any less daunting than the proposal to make greater use of composites is for the engineers. This is a big deal." Again, she looked directly at Barton, and he nodded in acknowledgment.

Based partly on preliminary work they'd done before the meeting, in anticipation of the direction it would take, another team presented analysis of cases: Toyota, Airbus, and Boeing, in particular the 787 project.† Toyota provided models for lean manufacturing and strategic supplier network management, both of which SMA would emulate (it was already shifting to lean manufacturing). The Airbus case offered lessons about how to coordinate the activities of Tier-1 strategic partners that spanned geographies, languages, and cultures; it had had trouble with digital specification systems among partners.

Boeing's 787 project expanded the scope of the virtual supply chain to global partners and innovated by increasing the speed of the overall

---

*To read about Barton's (fictional) experiences as a CIO, see Robert D. Austin, Richard L. Nolan, and Shannon O'Donnell, *The Adventures of an IT Leader* (Boston: Harvard Business School Press, 2009).

†See, for example, Jeffrey Liker, *The Toyota Way: 14 Management Principles from the World's Greatest Manufacturer* (New York: McGraw-Hill, 2004); Ananth Raman, William Schmidt, and Vishal Gaur, "Airbus A380—Turbulence Ahead," Case 9-609-041 (Boston: Harvard Business School, 2010); and Richard L. Nolan and Suresh Kotha, "Boeing 787: The Dreamliner," Case 9-305-101 (Boston: Harvard Business School, 2005).

supply chain, using specially designed air cargo 747s to move large components to a geographically distant final assembly site. When one considered the complexity of the final product, the size and complexity of the components systems being integrated, and the geographic distance across which the network reached to achieve the best combination of know-how and cost for each component, the whole thing seemed unprecedented. Boeing had experienced unexpected difficulties in getting this vast supply network to operate as designed, and this had already cost it billions of dollars in delivery penalty costs. A grand vision, an operational challenge (some might have said "nightmare"), and quite possibly the way of all future business. If SMA went in that direction also, it would try hard to learn from Boeing's difficulties, but any way you sliced it, it'd be a big, big bet SMA would be placing and trying to convince others to place with it.

When Gardner, the CFO, took the podium, he reinforced that reality.

"I know that you all have been waiting with baited breath for me to get up here and engage you in the pure ecstasy of accounting drama and our financials." This drew the expected smiles and laughter. "The good news is that we are relatively healthy, financially speaking. We have good cash flow; we have a relatively healthy balance sheet for a defense contractor company. The bad news is that we have a relatively healthy balance sheet *for a defense contractor company*. That is not good enough for what we want to be: a successful commercial cargo plane manufacturer.

"If we can execute on the things that we have been discussing—figuring out what we can build to serve the emerging air cargo market—if we can sell it to real air cargo customers and secure a first-mover strategic advantage, we can win. I don't intend today to go into the gory details of what our financials have to look like, because the financials provide the rearview mirror perspective, the post result of execution, not the prior creative strategy, inspiration, and leadership necessary to make the execution happen." Gardner continued a bit longer, but everyone knew the major message behind his story: SMA would need more investment.

Danielle Schoenfeld, the head of marketing and sales, stepped to the front of the room toward the end of the morning. Though her voice was sharp and clear, Barton noticed that her hands trembled, an unusual occurrence given her talent for communication. "Though we've discussed many formidable challenges today," she began, "in many ways, marketing and sales might be our biggest challenge. We're a defense contractor; we sell to the Air Force and Department of Defense. A few others too, but defense has been our focus, our obsession really. Now we've decided to become a commercial company selling to the airlines and air cargo carriers. We have little experience in this, so we have to build from scratch. And we need to do it fast. Securing investment funding for our transition is crucially dependent on selling a first tranche of new airplanes to a launch customer.

"Now I realize that it's not a popular message, but I think you all know it, and if you have any doubts, let me just say it: based on our careful analysis of the market, we believe that the earlier design for our commercial cargo airplane is 'dead on arrival.' It's too expensive and too much a military derivative; it has not been vetted with any real potential buyers. We don't think it will displace the current practice of converting old passenger liners to cargo service. We agree with Susan's group that we must *revisit* the design. So, from our perspective, what does that mean?

"It means vetting design alternatives with potential buyers. It means developing alternative conceptual designs and validating their attractiveness to real customers. If we can do this, we'll be 'in the ball game,' so to speak. Though we'll still be a long way from winning. We'll still have to secure the investments required, figure out a way to build the airplane, certify it, and sell it to real, paying customers. Of course, we've just been talking, all of us, about how hard that will be, so I won't go any further on that point. Let's just say we've got our hands full going forward.

"One more thing: our team has been working with Jim and others to conduct a search for a new sales and marketing leader. It won't be me; I don't have the skill set, though I'll be there in full support. We've interviewed two strong candidates to date. This will be a pivotal hire, and we want to do as much work as possible to ensure that the new person hits the ground running."

Barton worried that Schoenfeld had closed the last presentation of the morning on something of a down note. The room remained unusually quiet after she retook her seat. The group dispersed for a scheduled coffee break, and Barton had retired to a quiet room to gather his thoughts and make sure his plan for how to close the meeting would be the right way to go.

As Barton stood in the room alone looking out through the picture window over Elliott Bay, he spotted a Boeing 787, wheels down in its landing pattern on approach to Boeing Field, with its signature, sculptured carbon composite skin gleaming. A Boeing 787 in flight. It represented the reality that Barton would hang his hopes on at SMA. When Krishnan knocked, signaling the end of the break, Barton gathered his notes and walked toward the meeting room where the others waited.

Friday, December 4, 12:45 p.m. . . .

Barton moved to the podium and spread his notes out in front of him. He intended to summarize the proceedings and to remind everyone of key realities and challenges facing SMA. He could feel tension in the air, but it was interlaced with another energy: expectation, perhaps, or excitement waiting for release. Hope. The emotions of the group hung in a balance. Barton could see the anxieties in each of the faces, reflections of the thoughts and questions in their minds.

Maybe we can do this . . .

Is this really happening?

The opportunity of a lifetime . . .

Am I up to the challenge?

Do my colleagues think I'm up to the job?

Can he handle this?

Will he lead us in the right direction?

Barton studied the faces, trying to make eye contact with each person in the room before he began to speak.

He began to summarize, recounting what he'd seen over the past two and a half days. A sense of normalcy began to return to the room, a feeling of business as usual. He was causing it, he realized, but it wasn't, he realized just as quickly, the mood he wanted. Suddenly, a voice leaped into his head, bellowing at maximum decibel, though he alone could hear it:

Shut up! the voice said. *Just shut up! When you've made the sale, then shut the f___ up!*

In midsentence, Barton stopped. He faltered and started to say something else.

The inner voice roared: *"SHUT UP!"*

They all looked at him. The silence grew long and became uncomfortable. Had Barton lost his train of thought? Was something wrong with him? The tension in the room that had started to abate returned; it shot upward, reaching higher than it had been before, far higher. As the silence elongated, the needle on the group's anxiety meter swung hard over to bury itself in the red zone.

Barton let it happen, let it keep happening. He walked slowly back to the podium, from which he'd wandered as he talked. Slowly, he turned to face them.

"No," he said. "No, no, no . . ."

He picked up the papers before him, stacked them together, and tapped them into alignment against the edge of the podium. Then he stepped across the room to a wastebasket, crumpled the papers into a ball, and threw them in forcefully, before turning back to the group.

Barton spoke: "I won't make this seem normal. Nothing we've talked about here is business as usual." He paused for a long moment, again looking into each face in the room, and then continued in a low tone, almost a whisper: "Everything that needed to be said has been said. We're going to do this. Now, you, each of you, have to decide: do you want to be a part of it?" He looked at them and saw hard-edged resolve materializing on each individual face. "Do you?" said Barton, louder this time.

"Meeting adjourned," he said. Then he abruptly exited the room. Almost immediately, and in near unison, every other person in the room stood and followed him out.

Reflection

What do you think of Barton's leadership of this meeting?

What is your assessment of the execution plan for the new SMA strategy, as proposed in this meeting? Is the leadership team on the right path?

Consider the list of points that came up in discussion of Marochek's proposal: (1) What will be some of the critical decisions SMA leadership needs to make in terms of how it uses IT to manage the new global supply network? (2) How does the challenge of managing a systems integration network differ from managing vertically integrated supply operations?

What new benefits and challenges arise when an organization shifts from "owner control" processes to "partner coordination" processes? How are those challenges best addressed?

Where do you think Barton is in his journey in striving to become SMA's successful twenty-first-century CEO leader?

CHAPTER 9

Restructuring the Board

Thursday, December 10, 9:12 a.m. . . .

Clarke Gardner poked his head into Barton's office and rapped on the door frame. "Krish said you wanted me for something, Jim?"

Barton, at his desk, looked up from what he'd been reading.

"Oh, hi, Clarke. Come in for a minute."

Gardner came in and sat down on the couch. Barton got up and closed the door, which prompted a quizzical expression from the CFO. Barton settled into a chair across from Gardner, attempting nonchalance, with modest success.

"I'm meeting with Ron Haas later to go over some board matters," Barton explained. "I need you to get me some information."

"Sure, no problem," said Gardner, opening a notebook, unsheathing a pen. "What do you need?"

"I need to know," said Barton, "the SMA stockholdings for each of our board members, the number of stock options, vested and nonvested."

"Okay," Gardiner said. "May I ask what's up?"

Barton nodded. "Sure. But I don't want the information to leave this room." Gardner nodded. Barton continued: "We're thinking about making some changes in the membership of our board."

Barton watched Gardner's reaction. The CFO offered a guarded, muted response. "I've never been involved in anything like that before."

"Are you surprised?" Barton asked.

Gardner didn't quite answer the question. "Based on that last meeting, I can see why you might think about that," he said. "And I read that article in the *So-Cal Times* last week. I must say, I wondered at the time if the two things were related. Weird coincidence, how that meeting went, then that article popped up like that."

Barton didn't comment. Perez had gone ahead with her article on sculpting boards for governance and change. As she'd promised, the focus of the article was general, but she'd used SMA as an example toward the end, asking whether a board that worked well for a defense contractor could work well for a commercial firm, or whether some change might be needed. In context, it seemed more like a harmless "for instance" than a targeted critique of the SMA board. But raising the question had planted a seed.

At the same time, the series of articles casting doubt on composites continued. They ran in different papers and mostly focused on problems Boeing had been having, but SMA came up sometimes. Barton had asked his communications staff to think of ways to influence the conversation without inadvertently turning up the volume on what had remained, so far, journalistic background noise. Barton knew reporters did this sometimes as a way of fishing, trying out different concerns and issues in hopes that they might flush out a real problem from undercover. Perez had nothing to do with this series of articles, as far as Barton could tell, though a few were picked up by the *So-Cal Times*.

"Can you get me these figures before ten?" asked Barton, sticking to the point. "I'm having lunch with Ron in Seattle, and I've got to fly up there."

Gardner stood, understanding that Barton was in a hurry and didn't want to say more. "Right away," he said. "I'll have the information on your desk in just a few minutes."

"Thanks, Clarke."

Gardner left. Barton knew that he was taking a chance mentioning this to his CFO, confiding in him so early in such a sensitive matter. But Barton had made a decision in his first week at SMA that he was going to trust Gardner. Disclosing this intention to Gardner would be a strong test of that decision. Gardner still had relationships with other board members, especially Ed Frazier, the former SMA CEO. Barton thought he might as well find out sooner, rather than later, if his CFO lacked the ambidexterity to work closely and effectively with the CEO and the board. Barton hoped Gardner would pass the test. If word got back to Frazier or another board member, it would complicate things. And besides, Barton realized, he liked Gardner and wanted him in place for the challenges to come.

Thursday, December 10, 1:22 p.m....

Barton sat with Ron Haas, SMA board chairman, in a private dining room at the Washington Athletic Club (or the "WAC" as people called it) in Seattle. They'd placed an order already and knew they would not be disturbed until the food arrived.

"Ron," Barton began, "I know, because we talked briefly about it then, that you were as discouraged as I was after our last board meeting. Too many of our board members simply were not engaged during the meeting or seemed overwhelmed with the prospect of transforming SMA. The discussion was disjointed and chaotic, which might also be due to the size of the board. We need to have a strong board, as well as a strong management team, if we are going to pull off transforming SMA. So I am here today to begin a discussion about what we need to do to strengthen our board."

Haas didn't answer right away. Barton expected that he and Haas had similar thoughts in this matter, but couldn't be sure. The longer Haas waited, the more worried Barton got. Finally, Haas nodded.

"Yes. It occurred to me that we might need to slim down the board so meaningful discussions can occur. That we might need to restructure to make sure we have the right skills on the board to take this company where it has to go."

Barton felt a wave of relief and pressed on.

"In today's world, a board must contain a wide range of skills—accounting, organization, compensation, technology, risk management, and general governance. Board members need to be able to provide oversight and key advice on strategic issues and corporate performance. They also need to be engaged. They need to have the time and bandwidth to devote to the job. They can't be overextended, working on too many boards or in other distracting activities."

Haas nodded again. "And you think our board is not stacking up very well by those measures."

"What do you think?" asked Barton.

Again, Haas paused, but again nodded in agreement.

"I had a long conversation last night with Bob Goldman about this," Barton said. "He's had quite a bit of experience recruiting and restructuring boards."

"I haven't done much of that, myself," said Haas. "What I have done was extremely sensitive and delicate. Really difficult. And high risk. Not something to take on lightly."

"That's what Goldman said, too," said Barton. "When it comes to the people who we don't want to continue as board members, it's important that they leave the board in an appropriate way."

"If they resign in a huff," agreed Haas, "we have to explain it to the public in a SEC disclosure statement."

"Right," said Barton. "We'd like to avoid that. So we need them to go quietly, ideally by removing themselves from consideration for reelection at the annual meeting."

"Okay," said Haas. "I see your reasoning. And I'm listening. How do you propose to make it happen?"

"Technically," said Barton, "*you* as chairman, in conjunction with the chair of the governance committee, need to make it happen."

Haas looked confused. "But that—"

"That's right," Barton interrupted, "that *was* me. The governance chair is vacant at the moment. Shepard and Elliot are the remaining members of that committee."

Shaking his head, Haas said, "Shepard is sharp, but young and probably not very experienced in these matters . . ."

"And I'm not sure we want Elliot to do it," said Barton, picking up the thread. "He has a history of taking positions others on the board dislike. I'm not sure the others have enough confidence in him for him to carry off a board restructuring."

"Sounds like that leaves the whole thing in my court," said Haas. "Not sure I like that. Not sure I'm the man to do it."

"I think you could do it," Barton said, "but I agree that it would be nice to get someone in the governance chair role to help and to take on a lot of that delicate work. Someone experienced in such matters."

"So," said Haas, "you have someone in mind?"

A waiter knocked lightly at the door, then entered with drinks. As the door was softly closed again, Barton dropped a slice of lemon into his iced tea, took a sip, and smiled at Haas.

"I suggest we recruit Bob Goldman onto the board. He takes on chairing governance. He helps you with the restructuring." Barton waited for a reaction from Haas. Barton thought he'd probably seen that coming.

"But Goldman has no past relationships with SMA board members," noted Haas. "He doesn't know them. How's he going to convince them to leave?"

"That's not completely accurate," said Barton. "He knows some of them, Smithson, for example, very well. But you are essentially correct: he has no relationships with any current SMA board members as an SMA board member himself. That's true, but I think Goldman's stature in the business community might make it work. He's widely respected, even revered. It might work better, in fact, if he comes in from the outside, with his reputation and seniority, but without the baggage of past SMA board interactions and relationships. That could position him very well to facilitate changes."

"Interesting," said Haas. "That just might work." Barton could see that Haas liked the idea that Goldman would take on some of the restructuring load. Haas appeared relieved, and his enthusiasm for the idea kicked up a notch. "He'll be good at those delicate conversations," Haas offered.

Barton nodded. "And he'll have a strong incentive at his disposal. He can offer to accelerate vesting of stock options for those who leave quietly. A significant incentive. I asked Gardner to pull together information on stock and stock options that our board members hold. In general, those that we ask to leave have a choice of leaving quietly with considerable monies at stake, or noisily with much smaller monies."

"That won't necessarily sway some board members," said Haas, doubtful again. "Most of them have plenty of money in the bank. The conversations will still be delicate. We might not be able to execute the plan perfectly. Some people we'd like to see leave might not."

Barton leaned toward Haas, pressing ahead. "People will assume—rightly, by the way—that Goldman comes onto the board to help us deal with our financing challenges. He'll be seen as the guy who can pull together the investments we need for our corporate transformation and to develop our new airplane. Just this will give him sway. It'll make people less likely to oppose him."

Haas nodded. "Okay. Getting Goldman on board and elected chair of governance is step one," he said. "What's step two?"

"We need to propose who to jettison and who to keep. In fact," said Barton, "I thought we might start down that path today. Try to get a first cut at that list."

"You've been thinking a lot about this," said Haas.

Barton smiled. He reached below the table and extracted from his leather satchel the latest SMA annual report with a paper clip inserted to mark a page. Turning to that page, which listed members of the SMA board of directors, Barton pushed it across the table toward Haas, who scanned the names: Ronald L. Haas, James Barton, John T. Elliot III, Edward G. Frazier, William Ford, Chris J. Harden, Charlotte T. Owens, Russell E. Rigby, Patricia B. Shanahan, Philip M. Shepard, Bobbi Ann Smithson, and Martin Van Busin.

"Twelve people. Some are obvious keepers," said Barton. "Smithson. Shepard. I think we'll have trouble getting rid of Elliot, and I do think he adds value, even when I don't agree with him."

"Twelve people, plus Goldman, will make thirteen," said Haas. "What number do you want to get to?"

"Not sure," said Barton. "But eight or so sounds about right. Smaller group, more efficient decision making, no dead wood."

"You named obvious keepers," said Haas. "Are there board members you think it's obvious we should *not* keep?"

Barton didn't hesitate. "Harden. Van Busin. Maybe Owens and Shanahan. Nice people all. But in my time on the SMA board, I'm not sure I've seen them add a lot of value."

Haas smiled. "Yes. Harden. The general. His background works much better on the board of a defense company."

"Right. His heart's in the right place, but he lacks the expertise he needs to be effective on the board of a new kind of company. He's been out of his depth in most conversations of late. I think he knows it and would be easy to move off the board."

"He plays golf with Bill Ford," said Haas.

"Ford, himself, is an interesting case," said Barton. "He's been a pretty half-hearted participant for a while now. Could be tremendously helpful to us, but too often seems not to give a damn."

"He's got a long history with this company. Might not go easy."

"Or maybe he will. Hard to say. In any case, I don't think he'll spend too much capital defending Harden, especially if Harden is willing to go."

"Frazier might have a problem with jettisoning Ford," suggested Haas. "The whole mentor thing, you know."

"Maybe," said Barton, "but have you noticed how often they've butted heads lately? Ford used to be Frazier's mentor, but I think that just makes him more upset with the way Ford is mailing it in. Also, Ford comes across as being a little bit too interested in a big payday sometimes, and I've noticed that this particularly annoys Frazier."

"I've noticed that, too," said Haas. He looked back at the list. "Shanahan often seems overwhelmed."

"Yes," said Barton. "And Owens, more often than not, arrives unprepared. I don't think she'd prepared at all for the last meeting."

"You blindsided her with that round-robin thing."

"We spelled it out clearly in the agenda that we'd do that. She *shouldn't* have been blindsided."

"Oh, yeah," said Haas. "Entirely fair. She had no reasonable defense. Elliot in particular seemed annoyed with her."

Barton nodded. "Disgusted, I'd say."

"She opposed Frazier's stock buybacks," Haas reminded Barton. "Though she didn't stop them."

Barton sighed. "Neither did Bobbi Smithson," he said. "And neither did I, for that matter. That's not why. I just think we need more of her attention than she's willing or able to give us."

"Van Busin?" said Haas.

"Mostly adds comic relief," said Barton. "I can't remember the last time he said anything substantively useful. When I try to recall his contributions in recent meetings, my memory mostly retrieves jokes and misunderstandings."

"Funny jokes," Haas said.

"Some of them," conceded Barton. "But he often misunderstands details and takes us off on tangents."

Haas chuckled. "If you jettison Owens and Van Busin, that'll take out all the academic types."

"And how could that be a bad idea?"

The two men shared a laugh.

"Let's see," said Haas, "who have we forgotten?"

"Rigby," said Barton. "I'd lean toward asking him to leave."

"He has tons of helpful contacts in California."

"Yes, well, I'm not sure. Maybe he stays."

"He rarely says much."

"That's why I was thinking he goes," said Barton. "But I'm not set on that. He does come with a different tool set than any of the rest of us."

"So, let's see. Where are we?" Hass tore out the page of the annual report. He wrote "Robert Goldman" at the bottom of the list of directors and then went through adding checks and Xs:

Ronald L. Haas   √

James Barton   √

John T. Elliot III   √

Edward G. Frazier   √

William Ford   X

Chris J. Harden   X

Charlotte T. Owens   X

Russell E. Rigby   X

Patricia B. Shanahan   X

Philip M. Shepard   √

Bobbi Ann Smithson   √

Martin Van Busin   X

Robert Goldman   √

"That brings us down to seven," said Haas.

"Lean and mean," said Barton.

"But a lot of delicate conversations," said Haas.

"It's a first cut," said Barton. "Maybe we add Rigby back. Maybe someone won't go. Or maybe someone who we've kept won't want someone else to go."

"When should we start?" asked Haas. "We can't wait to get Goldman elected to the board before we start this if we want to change the board as of the next annual meeting. That's in March, just three months from now."

"Like you said," quipped Barton, "Step one, then step two. First we get agreement from the members that Goldman will come on board. You make those calls. Everyone should agree because they'll see Goldman as bringing essential investment savvy skills to our board. They know my connection to Goldman, so it won't exactly come as a surprise. Hopefully, that part will go easily."

"And once everyone is agreed," Haas said, "Goldman can begin to operate, even though he won't be formally elected until March."

"Right. He and you can start the next round of calls, the delicate ones."

"Then Goldman will be elected in March and the others who we're asking to leave won't be elected at the same time."

"Right," Barton repeated. "Then in April, we'll hold a meeting of the new board, and I'll present the transformation plan. By then, we'll hope to have our investment strategy in place. Or at least, nearly in place."

Barton held up the marked-up page of the annual report they'd been talking about. "Best not to leave this kind of thing lying around." He tore it into several pieces and disposed of it in a nearby waste basket.

"No e-mails," said Haas.

"Only phone calls," said Barton.

Haas nodded.

Their food arrived. As the two men tucked into their lunches, both very hungry as if they'd done a lot of work, Barton thought to himself: *got to keep this totally quiet at home. Too many reporters hanging around there. Hope I don't talk in my sleep.*

Harder Than I Thought

Friday, December 11, 4:15 p.m. . . .

"You needed my help with something, sir?"

Barton removed his glasses and put down the sheaf of papers he'd been reading. Angel Crow, his personal IT support person, stood in the doorway to his office.

"Great!" exclaimed Barton. "I thought you might be gone for the weekend."

"Not me, sir. I stay late."

"Come in," said Barton.

She stepped into his office, wearing a black leather jacket and boots, her usual gear. She stood about as tall as he was sitting. Barton thought he detected something changed about her nose ring, but he couldn't quite figure out what, so he didn't comment.

"And cut the 'Sir' crap," Barton said.

"Yes, sir—I mean, okay."

"That thing I asked you to set up, the prototype from the company Jonathan Luce has going . . ."

"The simulated senior executive experience role-play."

"If that's what you call it . . ."

She shrugged. "It's what *they* call it."

"Fine," said Barton. "We need to make sure it's fully upgraded. We're entering into a crucial period over the next few weeks. I've been using it, but we need to make sure it's set up as well as it can be. Luce promised a newer version, one that would automatically search for new info. I need you to load it up with all the latest inputs."

"You want an upgraded version?" asked Crow.

"If there is one," answered Barton. "But I also want to make sure all the characters I need are there. I've got some names. Confidential, of course." He handed Crow a list. Bob Goldman's name topped it, followed by the names of all the SMA board members, and some others, mostly prospective financing sources. "I'd like you to set up a thorough search in the press, anywhere else, for anything and everything that's been said or done by any of these people, and make sure all of the most current info is getting uploaded. Videos, interviews, club memberships, favorite recipes, all of it."

"You want to mine *all* the data we can find on these people, sir?"

Barton looked up to assess whether or not she meant what he thought she meant. He wasn't going to make her say it, and as long as she didn't say it, he didn't have to draw the boundary at "legal" sources of data.

"Whatever you think needs to be uploaded to the . . . the thing."

"We can just call it the SSEER, if you want, sir—I mean, Mr. Barton."

Barton sighed. "Crow, you make me feel old."

"You are old, sir. As your taste in music clearly shows."

Barton smiled. "That was funny. So I'll forgive you the 'sir.' That's all for now. Call Luce if you need to."

"Will do." She turned to leave.

"And Crow," Barton said. "One more thing."

"Yeah?"

"The Bamboos. You know them?"

"Australian band?"

"That's the one. What do you think?"

"They rock. Especially that number with King Merc doing the vocals."

"That's a good one. But my latest obsession is the one with Megan Washington. A cover of a Kings of Leon tune. The original is good, too."

"I'll take a look. Have a good weekend."

"You too, Crow. Let me know what you think about the video."

"Will do, sir."

Saturday, December 12, 2:09 p.m. . . .

"When dividing perennials," said Clara, "timing and technique are important." She knelt at the edge of a flower bed near the boundary of her yard. Barton leaned over so that he could see past her shoulder. He sipped dandelion coffee and listened.

"You can rejuvenate even the oldest residents of a garden by dividing them," she said. "By moving them to a new location and giving them some more room."

"Sounds like a good principle to use within an organization," Barton noted.

"Yes, well, I guess you're not completely thick," she answered. "But you have to do it correctly. Don't wait too long, until you have to do it because things have gone bad. If I left this—"she pointed to a plant off to her left that had begun to look crowded and shaggy—"for another two weeks, we'd see the center leaves starting to look smaller, to have fewer flowers, to look weaker."

Well, Barton thought, *I've waited too long with the board. But probably not with the SMA organization.*

"You don't want to sever the roots. You move the plant with as much of its roots intact as possible."

"It needs to maintain connections," postulated Barton, "to its sustaining resources."

"So it can begin to grow in its new location, given more room, as soon as possible. You have to be careful and patient.

"You also want to do the dividing in the correct conditions. I like to divide plants in cool weather. If the plant is under stress, it'll have a harder time with the additional stress you're adding by dividing it."

Another mistake I made, thought Barton.

"You also want to tend to the roots," continued Clara, "during the move. Sometimes there's a transition period, between unclumping and replanting. You have to keep the roots cool and moist during this time. The uncertainty of being unplanted weighs on plants, so you have to do what you can to help the plant deal with the uncertainty. Damp newspaper wrapped around the roots is a good idea."

Barton imagined wrapping a wet newspaper around Martin Van Busin, which made him smile.

"You have to restore the soils where you've dug things up, also. Put some new organic material back into the site. You don't want to the next thing planted there to have to contend with depleted soil.

"It's also good to start with the parts of plants that look the most vigorous. Move the more resilient plants first. It's best not to divide when a plant is blooming, but if you must, take extra care. And if you see a part of the plant that looks unhealthy—a dead center, or something that has succumbed to pest problems—if you notice anything like that while you're moving things, don't replant those. Toss them out."

Hmmmm, Barton thought. *Maybe that's another reason to move things around. To better reveal the unhealthy parts.*

"Can I try?" said Barton.

"Sure," said Clara. "If you want to."

Barton got down on the ground next to his mentor and reached for a small shovel that she'd been using.

"Go ahead," she said. "Be careful. You *can* do it. I'll show you."

Barton worked, Clara occasionally guiding his hands, taking his in hers.

"It's good thinking work," she said to him after a few minutes. "I was doing exactly this when I decided not to stay on my company's board."

Barton said nothing. She didn't seem quite finished: "I'm not sure what you think, Jimmy boy, but thinking about weaknesses and power, roots and separation, helped me think through many things. Our board could not provide real oversight of the CEO. People were too clumped. My successor's pay package was out of this world. I tried to do some separating, but it didn't really work."

That's all she seemed to want to say about it, and Barton didn't pursue it. She'd set his mind running on his own company and its situation . . .

Sunday, December 13, 4:46 p.m. . . .

"Yes!" shouted Jackson and Barton in unison. They leaped to their feet and gave each other high fives. Jackson did a little victory dance.

The Raiders had just defeated the San Diego Chargers in overtime with a fifty-two-yard field goal that had literally bounced on the crossbar and through the uprights. Oakland had pulled to within one with a seven-yard pass to the back right corner of the end zone with just three seconds remaining in the game, and tied it with the extra point. Barton thought they should have gone for two, win or lose right there, but Jackson disagreed and turned out to be right. The Raiders won the toss in overtime and converted their first possession into victory.

The two men had watched football and drunk beer together for two Sundays in a row now. Both times, Barton had tried to talk SMA business with Jackson. Both times, the attempt failed. Jackson refused to go there.

Barton thought important conversation about work might yet be possible. Their football talk continued, unaffected by Barton's efforts to talk shop. But he did not doubt that Jackson had meant it when he'd warned Barton not to force a choice between their friendship and the people at SMA who Jackson thought depended on him. Barton had no doubts about how that choice would play out.

He hoped, however, to come up with a better set of choices . . .

Reflection

Do you agree with Barton and Haas's plans for restructuring the board? What other difficulties might they face? Is bringing in Goldman to lead the process a good idea?

How can Barton apply the gardening metaphor of unclumping to the plan to spin off the SMA factory? To what other areas of the organization might this metaphorical approach to management apply?

CHAPTER 10

Consulting with a Peer

"Well, Jim," said Phil Condit, former CEO of the Boeing Company, "to be honest, I'm not sure I can tell you anything that will help you."[*]

Trying to decide what Condit meant by this and unsure how to respond, Barton sipped from his water glass and smoothed the linen napkin on his lap. Condit moved a fork aside to clear space for his glass of iced tea.

Meeting with Condit had been the main reason Barton had flown to Colorado. They'd never met before, but Barton had reached out to Condit through a network of mutual acquaintances. Now he hoped it hadn't been a wasted effort.

The two of them had spent the first ten minutes of their lunch at a Denver hotel restaurant in small talk, mostly about the weather and the local football team, which had just been eliminated from the playoffs by a New York team. Condit explained that he'd come to Denver to teach an executive leadership class (which Barton knew already) and that he'd just finished that morning. Barton reminded Condit why he'd wanted to talk: as a rookie CEO fresh out of the financial services industry, Barton was learning the ropes, working on becoming an aerospace company CEO,

---

[*]This chapter is inspired by material from Philip M. Condit, interview by Richard L. Nolan, Skype video recording, March 1, 2010.

and he wanted to tap into the wisdom of one of the most prominent CEOs in the business. Condit had led a transformation at Boeing, and Barton wanted to learn from him.

"I want to learn from you, Phil," Barton said, opting for a straightforward and honest approach, "and from your experiences at Boeing."

Condit had an easy manner and gazed cooperatively though wire-rimmed glasses. He was a big guy, with a broad, beefy face and the unmistakable appearance of an engineer (which he had been).

"Any thoughts you might have would be of great interest," added Barton. He joked: "Going from COO at a financial services company like Erlington to CEO of an aerospace company like SMA is a bit like being a shooting forward in the NBA who decides to become a defensive end in the NFL."

Condit laughed. "Sounds like a good way to get killed." Barton laughed too, uncertain. Condit fixed Barton with a stare and then seemed to decide something.

"From what I've heard about you," Condit said, "I have few doubts that you can succeed. But the road to transformation must be traveled differently by each company and each management team. So what I can tell you may be of limited use. I'll try. I'll share what I can with you."

He paused for a moment for another sip of tea and then continued:

"I never made the midcareer industry leap you just did. I began my career at Boeing in 1965, and I stayed there up to my retirement in 2004. When I took over as CEO in 1996, I got some excellent advice from the CEO of a board I was on, which I never forgot. This person said that once you start a company transformation, it's like a stampede. If you try to lead from the front, you get trampled; if you try to lead from the back, you have no impact. Best to lead from the sides by carefully nudging and turning the stampede to avoid everyone going over the cliff."

Barton laughed. "Wow, Phil. That nugget alone is worth my trip out here."

Condit shrugged. "Just another way to get killed, Jim: in a stampede." He grinned. "Seriously, though, without a good vision and strategy in place, a target ahead that the herd in the stampede is chasing, I don't think there's much chance of success for a company trying to transform itself. The strategy provides the foundational direction for just about everything that the people in the company do, as well as providing guidance for strategic partners."

Barton was reflecting on the stampede metaphor as he listened, trying to conjure an image of the new SMA strategy ahead. Would it be static, like a neon sign? Moving, like a hot-air balloon? Barton envisioned SMA's many partners, from suppliers to key customers, streaming from all corners of the globe into a herd, as the group gathered overwhelming mass. He still had to ride alongside. He almost winced.

Condit continued: "The first question that you have to answer, for yourself and your company, is 'why transform?' The simple answer is that you have to. For survival. But 'why me?' And 'why now?' Those are important follow-up questions.

"I learned the answers to these questions as chief engineer for Boeing's last new airplane—the Boeing 777. We made a decision to go to full digital product definition. The 777 was the first all digitally designed and manufactured commercial jet airliner. We put our future in the hands of our CAD/CAM vendors, IBM and Desault. If we failed there, we were going to die. But this critical strategic decision allowed a whole bunch of things that we couldn't have done otherwise. We set up a design bureau in Moscow, for example. That could not have happened without digital definition. If we'd had to send paper drawings back and forth, it would not have worked. The whole idea of global outsourcing and a virtual supply chain would not have worked without digital product definition. If you are going to integrate across geographical space and do it precisely, you have to embrace digitization, digital product and service definition. Whenever there is precision required, there is no other choice. If we wanted a part of our jet engines developed somewhere other than at the engine manufacturer, we had to move physical tooling around, gauges, and fixtures, and these things had to fit with each other. Digital specifications for physical interfaces had to be shared across geographical space. Digitization became the enabler to new virtual global organizational structures.

"What became apparent to me was that the very nature of time had—and has—dramatically changed due to IT. Digitization enabled computers to transmit complex airplane drawings with perfect precision at nearly the speed of light. I did not have to look too far to see the impact of this everywhere."

The waitress arrived to take their food order, which they quickly placed.

Barton took the opportunity to ask, "That's definitely a reason to transform. What I'm still thinking about here, Phil, is that stampede. How do I communicate with all those people? How does a CEO communicate with an organization of a hundred thousand or more? Even more problematic: How do the CEO and his senior management team learn what is going on with a hundred thousand employees in the company?"

Condit smiled, "When you are engaged as the CEO, you think about a lot of things, and none of them for very long. I thought about the problem of communication of vision and strategy a lot, but I didn't realize how the functional, hierarchical structure we'd borrowed from the military made communication in large organizations possible. Thinking a lot more about it since, I think that the military model—the foundation of the industrial, functional, hierarchical organization structure—is a communication-driven model. How did I as a CEO talk to the hundred thousand Boeing people? First, I led the development of our vision and strategy, along with my senior management team. They each, in turn, communicated to their direct reports, ten to thirteen of them; incidentally, but perhaps not surprisingly, this is the same size as a Roman military unit or an army military squad. And that action was repeated downward, again and again, until all had been communicated with. In a similar manner, the budget process worked from the top down and then the bottom up to successively aggregate low-level performance right up to the top, where we finally concluded whether we were making any money or not—that is, whether we were 'winning or losing.'

"But, boy, Jim! Did IT ever change this! Because of IT networks, I didn't have to rely on the hierarchy and the rather slow communications relay by each level of management to the next lowest level, nor did I have to wait for the slow process of upward communication back up through the chain of command to find out whether we were winning or losing.

"Henry Ford built this big assembly line on the Rouge River and moved car manufacturing from cottage industry to mass production. How did Ford get cars built in this new way? Well, he built a military-type functional hierarchy that drove instructions down into the masses and then collected data and aggregated it back up through the hierarchy to control the process. That functional hierarchy was designed to accomplish the communication challenges of the time. I believed as Boeing CEO and still do

154

that IT changes the game. It means we can change the way we communicate, so we can revisit that functional—and in Ford's case, completely integrated—hierarchy and remake it."

"So the possibilities for something new were there," Barton said. "The tools to remake the company. How did you go about it?"

Condit nodded. "That's the hard part. In the beginning of my time as CEO, there were a number of people telling me that we needed a strategy. I resisted. What I'd seen in a lot of companies were either overly simplistic strategy statements or overly complex strategy statements. Either a strategy that said, 'We do good things,' which doesn't provide any guidance at all, or a strategy that was so very detailed that it didn't leave room for what you really wanted, which was creativity and innovation. I wanted to come up with something in the middle, but I wasn't finding a straightforward way to do that. Nevertheless, we set out to find something in the middle that would be meaningful and provide the direction that we were seeking.

"Right before I formally took over as CEO, I was able to start with my senior management team to begin our strategy formulation process. I remember it like it was yesterday. I made my introductory remarks about competition and the need to figure out a strategy that would maintain our commercial airplane leadership into the twenty-first century—we picked a twenty-year time horizon—2016. I asked everybody to identify our core competencies. We ended up with just about everything we did written down on those flip charts! This got us nowhere, and it caused me to step back and ask what was going on. Everything we did couldn't all be our core competencies!

"So we went back to the basics; we looked at what we had tried to be and what of that worked and what didn't work. This discussion was pretty much focused around the classic question, 'What business are we in?' Our successes had been in defense, commercial aviation, and NASA space programs. We also observed a synergy across these three areas: important aviation research breakthroughs in space, such as the use of composite materials, led to know-how important in building military airplanes and high returns from learning how to mass-produce safe and reliable commercial airplanes. When we looked at our thirty-three ventures outside the aerospace industry, we were rather startled to find that we were batting zero for thirty-three. We had thirty-three ventures going, none of them sustainable. It was clear to all of us: 'we are an aerospace company, and we are not anything else.'

"Having made progress on who we were and who we weren't, we revisited the core competency question. We began this discussion by focusing on our Auburn facility for machining parts: 'Is machining commercial airplane parts a core competency for us?'

"The Auburn group felt they were as good, or better, than anybody in the world at doing what they were doing. And, of course, you want that to be the case. On the other hand, when you look at the fabricated parts and machines, there clearly *are* people in India and China and other places who have every bit as much skill, can do the task, and are willing to do it for a fraction of what it cost us to do it. We could make just about anything. We had the capability. We reformed the question to: 'What can we do that others *cannot* do?'

"We had a pivotal discussion about wings. The wing is one of the most important components of a commercial airplane. We had always manufactured our own wings. But when we took a close look, we discovered that we had only about a 4 percent efficiency advantage over our competitors when it came to wings. If you look similarly at all the systems that together make up an airplane, this was a comparatively small advantage. Others could manufacture wings as well as us, almost as well anyway. And, the original reason that we'd manufactured wings was because they were so big, and at the time we didn't have a way of transporting them. The argument that building wings was a core competency didn't hold up when we limited our core capabilities to the three, maybe four, for which we had a big advantage over competitors. Plus, we noted this: the logic that the wings were a most important part of the plane led us to say that the engines also were a most important part of the airplane. But we had not manufactured our own engines since 1934."

"Do you mind telling me," asked Barton, "what core competencies you identified?"

"The one core competency we could all agree on, the one thing that we did better than anyone in the world, was large-scale systems integration. A commercial airplane involves hundreds of systems, all of which must be integrated into one perfectly working system. Boeing knew how to put an air-conditioning system, electronic systems, landing-gear hydraulics, and a lot of other things together better than anyone in the world.

"Another core competency that we thought met the test was the detailed knowledge we had about our products and their performance, and especially about our customers.

"We had a service network out there telling us what was working and what was not working. We had an airplane-on-the-ground service where we flew a SWAT team to wherever an airplane was on the ground for whatever reason to analyze why and to get it flying. All this gave us information about our products, and we used this information to create an untouchably low failure rate for our airplanes, one in a billion, and to create great new products, like the 707, 747, 777, and now the 787.

"Then there's the knowledge we had about our customers. We were in everyday contact with customers everywhere in the world. Our maintenance tracking of all planes we've built, for instance, was continuous. This customer knowledge gave us an advantage over our biggest competitor. Because of the relationships between European governments and our biggest competitor, European airlines had a louder voice inside Airbus than other airlines did. And so their products had historically been biased by the views of European airlines.

"This had serious implications. For example, the A310 had way too short a range, when compared to the 757, because European airlines said, 'We don't need to go very far. It isn't very far from the southern tip of Italy to the northern tip of Norway.' Given our Boeing world market, we had people in China and Japan and India and the US and Europe all talking to us. That gave us an advantage in the world market. Even other companies outside Europe didn't have the dense customer network and understanding that we did. The Chinese companies didn't have it, and neither did the Japanese companies.

"The last core competency we identified was a little different from the others. We decided that if we were going to manufacture things, it needed to be 'lean.' We were not going to win because we had the lowest-cost production. But we *could lose* in the twenty-first century if the cost to make our products was too high. We learned this with the manufacture of our 737 airplane. In response to concerns about costs, we implemented a moving 737 line. Lean concepts leveraged the value of IT and helped us reduce unproductive time in our plants and the supply chain. So in everything we did, we wanted to become a lean enterprise.

"Those were the three core competencies our senior management team identified. I spoke about them at our 1996 management meeting, and that speech became the basis for Boeing's 2016 vision and strategy, which still stands and continues to unfold today."

"How did you deal with the objection that lean means fewer workers?"

"People do worry. Everybody says, 'Well, pretty soon there's not going to be anything at all to do.' If one person will do the job formerly done by two, people think, one of those two is out of a job. But that's where lean and efficient comes in. There's a lot to do. There's a whole bunch to be done—many of them are information functions, things that you and I might have, in an earlier terminology, called 'audit functions.' I had to be cognizant of what was going on, where all the pieces were, and that they were all arriving in the right place, at the right time, in the right configuration. That took real skill. It took people using and communicating information to manage flows. It might not be the same way of working we had or thought we had before, but we got to be really good at that, and that made for more jobs, even if we got more efficient at specific manufacturing tasks."

The food arrived. The two men took a moment to start eating. After a short silence, Barton made a request.

"Phil, if you don't mind, put yourself in my shoes for a minute: How would you relate your Boeing vision and strategy to my challenge at SMA?"

"The amount I know about SMA is, of course, limited," said Condit. Barton thought for a moment that his question wouldn't be a productive one, but then Condit charged ahead anyway. "Last week in my leadership class, we had a discussion around a question about the generality of strategies. First off, we concluded that a company's strategy had to 'fit' the uniqueness of the company. Second, upon researching strategies in various industries, we noted that, actually, they were pretty much the same. So if you read about the strategies of companies in the aerospace industry, they pretty much all include customer intimacy and lean, for example. The larger competitors also often include systems integration. I think that we're partly seeing the effects of the IT revolution. Companies can access information about their competitor's strategies and then copy them. 'Good' strategies are pretty much known throughout an industry, and companies adopt them as their own. You have to have a good strategy, but no one can win with *just* a good strategy. So winning involves, first, a good strategy, and second, execution.

"Now how you go about it—execution—is really, really hard. It involves business transformation, cultural change, and a different kind of CEO and senior management leadership than we have experienced in the past century. How do you execute? It's such a simple question, but, unfortunately, it has no simple answer. So given that reality, let me share with you a bit of experience that may or may not be helpful to you and your team.

"Our senior management team initially focused the execution of our strategy on becoming a more balanced aerospace company. Until 1996, Boeing grew organically, and our commercial airplane business was dominant in size compared to our space and defense businesses. We decided that the only way we could become a more balanced aerospace company in a timely manner was through acquisitions. That led us to buy the aerospace part of Rockwell. It led to the Hughes acquisition. Then we made our biggest acquisition ever: McDonnell Douglas. What happened was that McDonnell Douglas lost the bid to be one of two finalists on what became the joint strike fighter. So Douglas's stock went down, Boeing's went up. Our currency was more valuable. McDonnell Douglas was clearly going to do something. And either we were going to carry out the strategy that we had laid out, and now would be the time, or that opportunity was going to pass. We seized it. McDonnell Douglas was about $16 or $17 billion in revenue; we were about $35 or $36 billion. Combined, we became a $52 billion company overnight.

"Our acquisition was seen as the 'merger of the century,' and our stock reached a high of $107 per share. When we came to 2001 and 9/11, though, the commercial business just absolutely collapsed. The value of having that balance was apparent then: we had good, strong, cash-producing businesses without which we would have been in serious trouble in those days. If you go back to the 1970 meltdown in the commercial airplane world, when Boeing came close to bankruptcy, it was that singular dependence on the commercial business that caused that problem.

"After 2001, we continued to restructure by setting up decentralized business units with presidents for each. We moved our headquarters out of Seattle to Chicago, to further establish an executive-level leadership team for the newly restructured company. So, from a purely business standpoint, our strategy was right on.

"In hindsight, our vision and strategy was right and it still is. I would do the same restructuring and acquisitions again. Execution is always hard, very hard, and it still is. But if I could do one thing over, I would have put more emphasis on getting the company cultures to come together after the merger. It's just so incredibly important.

"The biggest difficulty was integrating the Boeing and McDonnell Douglas cultures. Both evolved from twentieth-century organization cultures that were centered on discipline and our factories—highly influenced by our World War II defense work when we scaled to multibillion-dollar-revenue companies. The discipline was often referred to pejoratively as the 'kick-ass and take names' approach to getting things done. Boeing's culture continued to evolve to a culture of meritocracy and, above all, doing what you said you would do. Meeting your commitments. We understood the importance of technology in our products and, most of all, safety and reliability. Budgets got missed if we miscalculated the integration of technology, but safety was never compromised. Schedules were rarely missed.

"McDonnell Douglas had suffered through a series of difficult acquisitions. Its business was primarily defense, which was why we were acquiring the company. The defense business was highly contractual and financial, resulting in a senior management team with a lot of financial background. Getting to the top required strong financial backgrounds. So the twentieth-century factory and financial emphasis of the McDonnell Douglas culture was different from that at Boeing. That's a clash that might mean something to you, Jim! And, of course, with the size of McDonnell Douglas being one-third or so of Boeing at the time, both John McDonnell (who was a major shareholder from the founding family) and the McDonnell Douglas CEO were invited to join the Boeing board of directors.

"Indeed, we did take actions to integrate the cultures into one company. We leveraged McDonnell Douglas's executive education campus in St. Louis that had been modeled after the successful GE program to bring

Boeing and McDonnell Douglas management and workers together to discuss 'being one company.' We began to interchange management among business units. We relocated our headquarters; Chicago was a neutral place between Seattle and St. Louis. We set up business units by line of business and established presidents for each business unit.

"But here is the main lesson that I learned about company cultures: a company culture is a learned thing that becomes embodied in your autonomous nervous system. It's 'how we do things around here.' You don't really think about it; you just do it. The company culture is learned through a million things, the most important of which is what people do, not just what they say. In Boeing, our company culture had remnants that went all the way back to Bill Boeing about 'letting no airplane technology pass us by,' which was emblazoned in rock above the entrance to our Boeing development center. It had to do with safety: no airplane flew until the chief engineer said it was ready to fly. People in the company learned the culture by watching the feet of the leaders, not just what they said.

"We weren't the only ones who didn't fully appreciate the importance of a company's culture and managing culture change during the restructuring and transformation of a company. Lou Gerstner returned to the Harvard Business School to comment on an HBS case about IBM's transformation in the late 1990s and told the MBA class there that only after understanding the existing IBM culture did his management team begin to make progress in transforming IBM from a successful twentieth-century company to a successful twenty-first-century company.[*]

"Like Gerstner, I had to learn about the importance of understanding and managing company cultural change the hard way—through experience. I know that 'knowledge can't be told,' but I would tell you that not only is managing the cultural change to transform SMA important, it is likely the *most* important thing you do."

With this pronouncement, Condit stopped, and turned to focus on his sandwich. Barton had been eating, but Condit, doing most of the talking, hadn't had a chance to. Barton let him eat and used the time to reflect on all he'd just heard. After a while, Condit started to talk football again, and

---

[*]Robert D. Austin and Richard L. Nolan, "IBM Corporation Turnaround," Case 9-600-098 (Boston: Harvard Business School, 2000).

Barton joined in. Throughout the rest of the lunch, the topic turned occasionally back to the airplane business. At one point, Condit came out with a gem, Barton thought, an assertion that, as Condit had discovered at Boeing, an organization could really only deal with five major technological changes in a new airplane program at once. When they'd gone beyond that at Boeing, all hell had broken loose, Condit said. You needed organizational slack to cope with issues that you did not or could not fully anticipate.

"Phil, I know that I have taken more of your time today than we agreed on. I can't thank you enough. I'm much indebted to you. Still, I'm going to ask if I might get in touch with you again later."

"Sure," said Condit. "Give me a call, Jim. I wish you the best of luck. I'll be following your progress."

Barton thought about that. That was the price, he guessed, of drawing on Condit's advice. Now the great man would be looking over his shoulder.

That's a good thing, Jim, Barton thought to himself. *A good thing . . .*

Reflection

What do you think are the implications of Condit's stampede metaphor for leadership? What are the benefits and risks of leading change this way?

Do you agree that "winning" strategies have become widely known and can be applied generally across firms in the same industry? How is competitive advantage best gained, in that case?

Do you agree with Condit's assertion that managing cultural change at SMA, as it transforms into a virtually integrated company, is likely to be the most important thing Barton does? What challenges do you see ahead for Barton in terms of cultural change at SMA?

How valuable is it for Barton to seek out peers, fellow CEOs, for advice? What would be your advice to Barton about translating such learning to his own role and experience?

CHAPTER 11

Implementation

Barton and Akita moved to the back of the engineering building cafeteria with their food trays. Very few people lingered at other tables. The cafeteria would close soon. Workers had started to wipe down tables and sweep floors.

A late lunch had been the only time that worked in both their calendars, and by this hour Barton and Akita were hungry. They got a brief start on eating before Barton came directly to the point:

"Why haven't I received the report I expected yesterday? I scheduled this meeting for today so we could discuss it."

Barton said this in a calm, even tone. Akita studied his face, trying to decide whether he was angry.

"Truth is," Akita answered, "we're having problems."

Barton had suspected something like that. "How bad is it?" he asked.

"Disappointing but surmountable," said Akita, still eating but with eyes steadfast on Barton's. "I'm having trouble getting my engineers behind the idea of working with composites. They thought if they put it off, it would go away. Now it's not going away and they're having trouble."

"What kind of trouble?"

"They have limited experience with composites. They've designed composites for leading edges of wings and stabilizers, but now we are asking them to design major structural components and the entire skin

163

of the airplane. They're accustomed to being the experts in what they're designing with. Now they need to call on vendors, pull in outside experts, share internal knowledge, even share design documents with people who don't work for SMA. Some of them are not taking to it very well. Partners have always been people *we* told what to do. *We've* always been the experts. Things are upside down."

"How'd this cause you to miss your report deadline?"

"We couldn't reach agreement on the contents of the report. It got heated. Colleagues accused other colleagues of being willing to compromise inviolate safety—heavy stuff for engineers. I called a truce. People needed to cool off, get some distance, and remember they're still on the same team and like each other. I did send you an e-mail notifying you there'd be a delay."

"Yes," said Barton. "I got that." He reached for his glass of water, took a sip, and replaced it on the table. "I'm disappointed," he said.

Akita said nothing but looked wounded. For an instant, her usually stoic face twisted and reddened, displaying some combination of anger, embarrassment, and resentment. Just as quickly, she pulled it together and resumed her usual appearance. But she remained quiet.

"Can you get us back on track?" asked Barton.

"I can," she said, voice saturated with resolve. "You'll get that report Friday."

"I don't have to remind you how important it is to get to a solid conceptual design that the board can approve, that we can use as a basis for early sales. Our financing of the transformation depends on being able to show investors those early sales, which are dependent on completion of the conceptual design."

"I know that—," said Akita, but Barton interrupted her: "Which requires that your engineers get over themselves and get on with it."

Akita nodded grimly.

"It's an ominous start," Barton said. "We can't afford delays."

"You'll have the report by Friday."

"Do you need any help from me?"

"No," said Akita. "You'll get your report Friday."

The two finished their meal in silence. Akita was, Barton knew, angry. *That's okay,* he thought. *I'm a little bit angry myself. It's not my job to keep everybody happy all the time . . . This is a business.*

Wednesday, January 27, 9:47 a.m....

Barton had just finished signing some papers when Krishnan buzzed his office.

"Ron Haas is on two."

"Ron?" said Barton. "That's not on the schedule, is it?"

"No, sir. I told him you're available."

"Of course I am. Put him through."

Barton started to put the call on speaker, then had second thoughts and picked up the handset.

"Hi, Ron, what's up?"

"Am I on speaker?" asked the SMA chairman of the board.

"No," said Barton. This had to be about the board. Haas came to the point.

"We're having a problem with Owens. When we broached the topic of her removing herself from reelection consideration, she got into a huff and offered to resign. A few minutes later, I received a fax of her letter of resignation from the board. Effective immediately."

"Hmmm," said Barton. "You tried to reason with her? To explain?"

"I tried," said Haas. "I intend to try again in a few minutes. Maybe she's cooled off. Goldman will try also, if necessary. We figure he's the one who should bring up the options issue."

"That offer that's also a threat."

"The dispassionate explanation of what she will be foregoing in her stock options. If she resigns now, the board will not vote to vest her unvested options. By simply staying on our board but not putting her name up for reelection, we would vote to vest her remaining stock options, which represent a significant financial gain. We'd like her to attend the February board meeting too, at least by phone. But we could give on that if we had to. It would mean we would have to disclose her nonattendance."

"Doesn't sound hopeless," Barton noted.

"Not unless she vents to the press or something. The monies here are significant, and I think we should be able to talk her down. Just wanted you to know, just in case she does something stupid, or in case she calls you in the meantime."

"Appreciate that," said Barton. "How's it going with the others?"

"So far, so good," said Haas. "Van Busin was funny, as usual. As soon as he caught on to what we were suggesting, he blurted out, 'Oh, thank God!' He's been feeling out of his depth."

"Perceptive of him."

"Yes. Pat Shanahan was pissed, told us in no uncertain terms what we could go do with ourselves, but she's going to play ball. Harden heard us out. Agreed with our logic, asked what he could do to help make it as smooth as possible."

"A class act."

"No kidding. Made me have second thoughts."

"Excellent progress, on the whole."

"I think so. I'll call you when we know what's going to happen with Owens."

"Thanks," Barton said. "I'll let you know if she calls here."

Friday, February 5, 11:18 a.m. . . .

"We're delighted you're here, Jose," said Barton, shaking hands with SMA's new senior vice president of sales. The guy had huge hands and massive shoulders, and he towered over Barton. *He's going to look gigantic in the Far East,* Barton thought.

The two had met for just half an hour. Jose Montero had only a short time to spare with his new CEO before dashing off to the airport for his first sales trip to China. In that short time, Montero had inspired confidence in Barton, great confidence.

"You get me a conceptual design," Montero had said, "and I'll get you the sales you need to secure financing."

He'd mentioned only one caveat: substantial portions of those sales could come, he said, from China. "You'll have to run interference on the political fallout and any critical press. I can't be drawn into that. I'll be busy closing deals."

Barton had agreed to these terms, not knowing what real, if any, leverage he had. But Montero had had more to say on the topic. He'd been burned before, he told Barton. "It's the reason I left my last position," he said.

"I'm here because I'm good at what I do. I make sales. I close deals. You put me in a position where I can do my thing, and you *will* win. But I can't do what I'm good at if there are sideshows back at headquarters undermining me. It drives me crazy when a sale unravels because somebody somewhere else in the company can't do his or her own job. That starts happening, I'm out of here."

"I get it," said Barton, hoping silently that he and the SMA organization could hold up their end of the deal.

After a few more pleasantries, Montero went on his way and Barton returned to his desk, feeling good on the whole. *That's a major piece of the puzzle in place,* he thought. *Now, what else do we need to line up?*

Sunday, February 21, 4:22 p.m. . . .

"Jim, I will never, ever agree to that."

Ace Jackson picked up a beer can, tipped it against his lips, and found it empty. He shook it twice, as if to confirm that it was really empty, then flung it sideways into the dining room wall without looking in that direction. It struck noisily and fell, rattling, onto the floor, rolling to a halt in the corner. Jackson reached toward the center of the table, submerged his hand into the tub of now nearly melted ice, pulled out a new beer, cracked that one open, and drank from it. Though he sounded annoyed, and the beer can flinging could hardly be interpreted as a friendly gesture, he didn't storm out of the room or even stand up. He simply sat there, drinking and thinking. Barton took notice of this.

Barton had been talking with Jackson about possible futures for SMA. They'd started out watching college basketball, in their usual pattern, and Barton had tried, as he did often, to start a conversation about SMA. Usually this didn't work. But this time, on this day, Jackson engaged. They'd bounced around some ideas and eventually Jackson had stood, agitated. Which Barton took as a sign that he'd gone too far, that the conversation, as promising as it had been, had come to an end. But no, Jackson just relocated to a seat at the table. Barton followed him and they continued talking.

Barton had been making the case that spinning off some of the company's manufacturing operations, or selling them to a private equity firm, could be good for all involved parties, especially the workforce. The manufacturing capacity of the plants could be more fully utilized if the plants were free to work for other customers as well as SMA. With more demand for their services, there would be less risk of forced layoffs than in a declining military cargo plane company. "More work, more overtime, more money," Barton had said, trying to persuade Jackson. "You know," Barton said, "that the current situation is untenable. You know that."

Jackson didn't disagree. But he was having none of Barton's suggested spin-off or sale. "I will never, ever agree to that, Jim," Jackson repeated. "Private equity firms are cost-cutting bastards. We're not stupid you know."

Barton opened a beer and sighed. He nodded. "I know that," he said. "We need to find a way to get it to work for everybody."

"That's right," said Jackson. "And you realize," he added, "that for my guys, you're a real problem there."

"What do you mean?" said Barton, genuinely puzzled.

"Come on, Jim," said Jackson. "Where's your skin in this game?"

Taken aback, almost offended, Barton protested: "I'm all in, Ace. You know that. You know me."

"Yeah, well, maybe I do. But my guys, far as they're concerned, we've got our necks stuck out and you're all safe and protected. What's going to happen to you, Jim—and I mean really what's going to happen—if this whole thing goes south? We're going to lose our jobs. What will you lose?"

"A lot," said Barton. "My reputation. That means a lot to me."

"But I'm guessing you'd get some parting gift that makes you feel a lot better about it, right? Tell me it's not true, Jim. I dare you to deny it. If things go south and all of us get laid off, you're still going to be cushy fine, with a big fat pay parachute unfolding. Aren't you?"

Barton sipped his beer and thought about it. "You're right," he admitted. "It's in my contract."

"So my point—on behalf of my guys," said Jackson, "is pretty simple: There's something wrong here. Things go bad, we lose everything, but you get a payday. Not to mention that your pay, compared to ours, is already out of whack. I bet you make at least a hundred times what my starting guys do. At least."

"Maybe not a hundred," said Barton, "but I get your point. Especially the skin-in-the-game thing. Let me think about that."

Jackson shrugged. "I'm just sayin' . . ."

"We'll find a way to get it all to work," Barton said. "We're in this together. It's not tenable for any of us in the long run."

Jackson said nothing. But he didn't leave. *We're not there,* thought Barton, *but we're talking. And that's progress . . .*

Wednesday, March 10, 10:16 a.m. . . .

"Ron Haas on the phone," said Krishnan over the intercom.

"Put him through," Barton said, and picked up the handset. "Hi Ron, what's up?"

"Progress. We're just about there."

"That's great. Sounds like there's a "but" coming, though."

"Yes, well, we have hit a little bump."

"Owens?"

"No, that's all put to bed. It's Ford."

"Ford. So is Frazier fighting it after all?"

"It's Elliot who's fighting it."

"That's weird. Why?"

"Elliot and Ford have more history than we thought. Worked together on some government project together way back. Could also be that Ford is the only one who's supportive of the liquidation option."

"Hmmm," said Barton. "So where do we go from here?"

Haas waited a beat on the other end of the line and then posed a question: "How strongly do you feel that Ford has to go?"

Barton thought about it. "Not that strongly. Especially if we've accomplished most of the rest of what we planned."

"That's where Bob and I are coming out," said Haas. "Choose your battles. This doesn't look like a battle to fight. Maybe we just keep Ford. He's not hard to manage, and we've got the numbers well down."

"Okay," said Barton.

"Well, I think we're there then," said Haas.

"Who's gone?"

"Harden, Shanahan, Van Busin, Owens, Rigby."

"How'd it go with Rigby?"

"Like a dream."

"Who stays?"

"You, me, Smithson, Frazier, Shepard, Elliot, Ford."

"Plus Goldman."

"Plus Goldman. Eight in all."

"That sounds good," said Barton. "Kind of wish it was an odd number, but okay. How're you feeling about it?"

"It works for me," said Haas. "I think that's a strong group. We should work well together."

"Another important piece of the puzzle in place," said Barton. "Thanks for working so hard on it, Ron."

"My pleasure, Jim. Still a lot of challenges ahead."

"It's coming, though," said Barton. "It's coming . . ."

Monday, March 15, 10:33 a.m. . . .

"There's one more thing I want to ask you about," Barton said.

He and Clarke Gardner had been meeting in Barton's office to discuss pro forma financials generated from the latest iteration of the conceptual design. As the engineers made choices, Barton wanted to quickly identify their financial implications. Gardner was proving very good at staying on top of the engineering process. They'd been meeting weekly on this, and Gardner had placed numerous members of his staff into engineering teams as full-time residents.

Gardner set aside the binder he'd been working from and flipped to a new page in his notepad. Barton stood and moved to the window.

"I don't think you'll need to write anything down," Barton said. He turned back to Gardner. "In fact, I'd prefer that you didn't."

"Okay," said Gardner.

"As you know, as I think I've mentioned to you, we've been working on restructuring the board."

"Yes, you did say something about that. How's it going?"

"Well," said Barton, "I'm not the one doing it, but I think it's going fine."

Barton thought of his earlier reservations about mentioning the board restructuring to Gardner. Barton had wondered whether Gardner might tip off Frazier, the former SMA CEO, about it. Gardner had passed that test with flying colors, apparently keeping the confidential information confidential, at least as far as Barton could tell. This pleased Barton. The guy was a very, very good CFO and was demonstrating real CEO potential. Barton needed him.

"Now," continued Barton, "I'm thinking about whether I need to do something similar with the senior management team."

Gardner nodded, processing this statement. He'd be trying, Barton knew, to decide whether he was about to be consulted or fired. But he'd come down on "consulted," Barton knew, because you don't follow an intense conversation with your CFO about the conceptual design and the ongoing evolution of resulting financials only to turn around and fire him.

"How can I help?" asked Gardner.

Barton noted the confidence in his voice.

"Where," asked Barton, "would you say our weak points are?"

Gardner whistled. "Sure you want to ask me? I hardly have any exposure to some of them."

"Oh, come on. You've been here long enough to know the strengths and weaknesses of everyone. I'm asking you because I trust your judgment."

"Okay," Gardner said. He leaned forward in his chair, propping his elbows on his knees, clasping and unclasping his hands together as he thought.

"HR. Jack Bruun is pretty old school for what we need. I suspect we need a fresh approach when it comes to managing talent. His strength is managing workforce reductions."

"That's not irrelevant."

"No, but I suspect he'd do it differently than we'd want to as we transform this organization. He'd make mistakes. We'd lose key talent."

Barton sat down again, mirroring Gardner's body language. "I agree with you. Who else?"

"Well," said Gardner. "To be honest, I think you've got a problem in PR and communications. Linda Kohler, for whatever reason, doesn't like you. Goes back to before you even started."

"Not entirely her fault," said Barton. "I kind of blew it by taking on an interview before I arrived without clearing it with her."

"Agreed," said Gardner. "But nevertheless, she's never gotten past that, and it hurts her effectiveness."

"She's pretty old school too, wouldn't you say?"

"Yes, I would," Gardner agreed.

"I think we're going to have to adopt a much more open approach and culture going forward. We're going to have to be less guarded. It's a trade-off, of course, determining the extent to which a company should open up in the way it manages information. But the situation has changed, in my judgment. The benefits of openness have increased, and the benefits of controlling everything as if it might need to be secret have decreased. We still need to be smart, of course, but I think we need a more open approach."

"You'll never get that from Linda. Though, for the type of creature she is, she's a pro, one of the best. You might miss her. Maybe you want to line up a replacement before you pull the trigger. Pretty important to have someone in that role."

Barton nodded. "Others? Akita? Marochek? Or how about the CIO, Jen Sharp?"

"Or for that matter," said Gardner, "how about the CFO, Gardner?"

Barton smiled. "No, we've already had that conversation. You're in. For now," he added, winking.

Gardner laughed and continued. "Akita and Marochek are rocks. They're critical to us, to what we're trying to do. No way we could do any better."

"And Sharp?" asked Barton. "She has a very big role in the new transition. Maybe one of the biggest in the company."

Gardner nodded. "Yes, but she's good. She's up to it, I think. Also, I just can't imagine how we'd find a better choice out there. Better to make sure she gets all the help she needs, I think. There's lots of tech talent in this area, in San Fran, and in Seattle. We'll need more of it."

"Agreed," said Barton. "Anyone else?"

"No one else I'd suggest at the moment," said Gardner. "Keep an eye on Montero. He talks big, but can he deliver?"

"I get a good vibe," said Barton.

"It'll take more than vibes," said Gardner.

Barton laughed. "Yes," he said, "it will. Thanks for your thoughts, Clarke."

Gardner seemed energized as he stood up, collected his things, and departed from Barton's office.

Friday, March 19, 2:11 p.m. . . .

"Linda, there's no point in soft-pedaling this. I think you'd probably agree that it hasn't worked very well between you and me."

Linda Kohler leaned forward across the conference table, drawing nearer to Barton, her eyes widening. She said nothing, but her unblinking eyes burned into his. He waited to give her a little more time to reply, then went on: "I'm thinking it might be in your best interests and ours if you moved on to the next stage of your career. You'll have a generous package, of course. I'm sure you'll have no trouble—"

"Are you *really* firing me?" Kohler said, interrupting Barton. "Are you—are you *really* firing me? Haven't you provided enough evidence of your poor judgment?"

Barton frowned. *So this is how it's going to be,* he thought. *Very well. Makes it easier, in some ways.*

"Yes," he said. "I'm firing you. Effective immediately. You'll find an envelope waiting for you on your desk that describes the details. If you have any questions, there's a number in the envelope you can call. Please return to your office, gather your things, and let us know if you need any help with transportation."

He paused to give her a chance to respond. She said nothing.

"You've given tremendous service to this company, and I want you to know that I recognize and appreciate that, as do many others. I don't intend to take anything away from that. But the company has turned in a different direction now, and changes must be made. As you know, we've had to make some other changes this week also. Nevertheless I'm sorry, I truly am."

"What makes you think you can run an aerospace company?"

Barton stood. "That's not the subject we're discussing here. Is there anything unclear in what I have said?"

"*This,*" hissed Kohler, "is because you're sleeping with that *journalist*—isn't it?"

Her question struck Barton hard, but he said nothing and remained expressionless. It was all he could do to avoid displaying his astonishment.

"You think I don't know about that?" said Kohler. "You think others don't?"

"I don't think that makes—" Barton began weakly, but Kohler interrupted:

"It makes *all kinds* of difference, smart guy. I've had conflicts with her for a long time. Everybody knows that. Now you start sleeping with her, and I get fired. Do you honestly think *that* won't come home to roost?"

Kohler stood and slammed both fists down on the table. "You, Jim Barton, had better call your best lawyer friend, because I intend to file a wrongful dismissal suit. And I bet I've got a damn good case. Even if I don't, we'll see how this plays in the newspapers. That sweet little tart of a journalist might know some people in the business, but she can't stop this story. Hell, she might want in on something this sensational herself." Kohler laughed maniacally. "You have really done it this time, Barton," she said. "Cooked your own goose. Hah! Cooked your own goose! You think you're so smart, but you're dumber than a rock!"

She lifted her fists high into the air as if to slam them down again on the table, but instead she stopped, whirled, and exited the room, leaving incongruous calm in her wake.

Barton stood still, forcing himself to breathe. Then he dropped back into his chair. *She's got no case,* he thought. Then: *How does she know?* Then: *Who else knows?*

Barton sat in the conference room alone for a long time, long enough to miss the beginning of his next meeting.

Saturday, March 27, 9:08 a.m. . . .

Barton had finally gotten around to transferring a huge and growing pile of filled trash bags accumulating in his Venice bungalow kitchen to the garage, where they would wait for Tuesday garbage-collection day, when he spotted his neighbor, Clara, across the backyard, already at work in her garden. She saw him also.

"Hey there, Jimmy boy," she shouted lyrically, standing and moving closer, propping her elbows on the fence between their two yards. "How does your garden grow?"

Barton thought about this. He put down his trash bags beside the garage door and leaned against the side of the garage.

"Well," he said. "we've had to pull some weeds. There are some plants here and there that look a little sickly. We've done a little new planting. And we're beginning to see a bud or two."

"Hmmm," said Clara. "I see." She frowned and turned away.

Barton shouted after her: "Hey! What? I meant that as good news!"

Clara shouted without turning back toward him: "So far, so good, Jimmy," she said. "But the hard work is still ahead of you." She looked back at him: "Don't kid yourself. Those buds don't mean a thing yet. You've got to get the fundamentals sorted out. The structural things. The soil. Exposure to the sun. How you'll organize your watering and other cultivation activities. Only when you're getting these things right can you trust that the buds will grow and spread. A few buds can pop up anywhere. Bad gardeners let themselves believe that means things are going well. Bad gardeners use the appearance of a few buds to put off confronting the hard work." Then she turned again, walking away.

Barton nodded. He bent down and picked up the garbage bags and went back to toting trash.

Clara noticed. "That's the spirit, Jimmy," she said, now kneeling in the dirt. "Success in the garden is not glamorous."

Barton stepped into the garage and stuffed the plastic trash bags into a big plastic barrel. When he came back out, Clara shouted to him: "Come over a bit later, Jimmy. We'll have some dandelion wine."

"Coffee," shouted Barton back. "It'll have to be coffee. Too much work to do."

"Thatta boy," Clara called back across the yard. "You'll get there . . ."

Barton turned toward the house to get some more garbage.

Reflection

Was Akita's explanation for the delay in meeting the new airplane design report deadline reasonable? Since R&D is leading in the process of organizational transformation, what might Barton learn from its challenges, and how might he (and the senior leadership team) apply that learning to leading the transition in other areas of SMA?

What do you think of the way Haas and Barton handled the board restructuring?

What's at stake for Barton if Linda Kohler follows through on her threat to file a wrongful dismissal suit? Is there any action he should take now?

Barton has now cleared his critical first one hundred days as CEO. Given the objectives he set for himself on his first day on the job, how well is he performing? How well do you think the transformation is progressing so far? Is Barton making the right moves? What should he prioritize next?

CHAPTER 12

Test Drive

Barton, still at his desk, finished reading a document prepared for him by Angel Crow, then set it aside and looked up. Light from the window faded; late afternoon was becoming evening. *Time,* he thought, *to try out the new version of the SSEER.*

Following Crow's instructions, Barton removed from his bottom desk drawer a head cover made of lightweight, almost skin-like silver fabric, with attached thick-framed, dark wraparound glasses attached. As he slid the cover down over his head like a ski mask, the visor came to life. Three LEDs lit amber, and two of them started to blink. One turned green, and then the rest did.

Barton adjusted the form-fitting garment against his head, positioning it so that his ears rested against soft headphone cushions, and his eyes took in the shapes forming on the interior surface of the glasses. Just as it had in its prior form, the SSEER first displayed a test pattern. A voice told him to speak the command, "Stop," when the test pattern was in focus. It oscillated through a cycle, from fuzzy to clear, to fuzzy, back and forth, until he stopped it. He calibrated the headphone's sound level in a similar manner, with another voice command. The test pattern disappeared, replaced temporarily by a message hovering in a dark space before his eyes: "You are entering the SSEER environment. What scenario do you wish to engage?"

Barton said: "Engage file BARTON BIZ-STRAT."

For a moment, the words "SIM ACTIVE" flashed before his eyes; then they dissipated like a cloud. Barton stood at one end of what looked to be a very, very long room. Its walls were covered with rich, dark wood panels. Behind him, he noticed a door, large with decorative moldings, made of the same dark wood. Attached to the door, handwritten in an amateurish scrawl, a sign said:

> Path to a gracious early exit.
> Recommend you leave through
> this door now.

"Very funny, Jonathan," Barton said quietly.

Squinting toward the opposite end of the room, he could see that the wall panels vanished almost to a point in the distance. But at the far opposite end of the very long room he thought he could make out images of people, some of them moving.

He started toward them.

He approached what looked like a courtroom, although the furniture appeared overly large and too vividly colored, almost cartoonish. Most prominent: a huge, purplish mahogany judge's bench that towered over everything else. A solemn Bob Goldman sat behind this, square-jawed and suitably large in proportion to his immense seat. His hand gripped a large wooden gavel. Goldman nodded to Barton, but said nothing. Off to one side, a jury composed of the other SMA board members, satirically depicted (long faces made longer, stout figures made stouter, unfortunate quirks made quirkier), sat quietly in wooden chairs behind a rail, looking in Barton's direction, waiting. Some of them also nodded. Beside the judge's bench stood a suit-clad Jonathan Luce, holding a legal pad. He fluffed his silk pocket handkerchief and looked toward Barton with a sinister smirk on his face.

He did not look right in a suit.

Barton heard murmuring behind him and turned his head to see a spectators' gallery, just materialized. SMA employees, customers, financial analysts, and journalists populated the gallery. He recognized many, but not all, of them. He scanned quickly for Perez, his heartbeat quickening, but didn't see her. They all looked toward Barton expectantly, but none of them nodded or attempted to communicate with him. They spoke softly with each other, and the noise they generated gained volume.

Luce took a few resonant steps across the marble floor. Sounds from the gallery decreased.

"How nice of you to finally join us, Mr. Barton," said Luce, voice dripping with sarcasm. "So glad that you could . . . find the time."

The crowd grew silent.

"Nothing," said Barton, "could be more important for me than to be here, with all of you—" He gestured toward the jury and the gallery, and nodded warmly to Goldman. His voice echoed, "—to be here for this purpose."

"And yet you took your time getting here," said Luce.

"I've had a long way to come," said Barton, tipping his head in the direction from which he had arrived.

"Yes. Indeed," said Luce, "And you are not there yet, are you?"

"No," Barton admitted. "I'm not."

The crowd of spectators clamored to life, mostly murmuring, but Barton thought he also heard a few gasps. Goldman pounded the gavel. "Quiet!" he commanded. "Quiet, I said! We will have order."

The crowd stilled. Goldman extended his great torso forward across the judge's bench, coming eye to eye with Barton, and spoke: "Mr. Barton, are you prepared to present your case?"

"I am," said Barton.

"Bailiff!" shouted Goldman. From behind the bench, Krishnan emerged like a windup toy set loose. In a gratingly high-pitched voice, he called out, "Docket number 4592, James Barton presents the plan for transition of Santa Monica Aerospace from a declining military cargo plane provider to a modern commercial aircraft company. Said plan to be tried by a jury of fellow board members. Jonathan Luce, Esquire, will serve as opposing counsel." Luce bowed. Krishnan continued: "Hear ye, hear ye, all come prepared to hear this case!"

Goldman struck with the gavel once, loud and hard. "Over to you, Mr. Barton."

Barton smiled. The creators of the SSEER were clearly having some fun with this scenario. But it seemed likely, Barton thought, to serve well enough for his intended purpose: to try out the arguments he'd use at the real board meeting later in the week.

So he set about making his case. Luce smirked from time to time, but did not interrupt Barton, who discovered that he could call up the charts and graphs he'd prepared on his computer, and some that he had not, whenever he needed them. He had only to lift a hand and whatever file name he called up appeared in space, floating high on a wall opposite the jury box. Barton noticed that whatever he displayed seemed visible to all, from any angle. Freed from concerns about presentation logistics, he pressed ahead with his arguments.

He began with an impressive visual display prepared by Susan Akita's engineering department: SMA would design and build a state-of-the-art commercial cargo airplane that used carbon-fiber composites for structural components and the airplane skin; this would be a radical departure from the design of past planes. The plane literally looked different from every angle, exotic, elongated, with swooping, rounded surfaces. It elicited "oooohs" and "ahhhs" from the crowded gallery. The visuals hammered home the point: building such a thing would require that the company move to the frontier of material science and manufacturing, with the help of strategic partners.

This last detail fed seamlessly into his second point: development of such a composite-based plane would require reliance on a network of global strategic partners, for design and manufacturing expertise. No longer would the company be the authority in all details of its business, with its "how to build an airplane" manual locked away in the company's proprietary safe. In the future, SMA would not always swoop in to save its suppliers with its greater expertise. In this new approach, sometimes suppliers would have to do the swooping, to help SMA. The company would become a collaborative systems integrator at the center of a network of value creation. Barton displayed a clever three-dimensional graphic designed by Angel Crow to illustrate this. The spectators traded interested, hushed whispers.

His third point: SMA would need to restructure, to address questions of control and value capture separately from questions of ownership. This would probably mean selling off some of its manufacturing facilities, which would then work for competitors and, thereby, operate at fuller capacity and be able to realize economies that could be passed along as lower prices to SMA. The idea was that the independent companies would benefit from greater management and engineering focus on their specific system components. Barton did not give details, but asserted, as he met with agitation from the gallery of spectators, that this would be the best direction for everyone. Further, he believed (imagining that "Ace" up his sleeve) that he could communicate the benefits to the unions and, eventually, reach an agreement with them.

Financing for this transition, he continued, would be achieved by approving the conceptual design for the new plane, a draft of which had already been conveyed to board members, and, on the basis of this design, securing advance sales of the plane. Probably, the biggest advance sales would be in China, which could have political repercussions that needed to be managed (defense contractor selling advance commercial technology in China, and all that). A high-profile sales VP, Barton noted, had already been recruited and had begun to work, primarily in the Far East.

Barton called up a dandelion-patterned slide and smiled at the undisclosed metaphor. HR policy would need to evolve, he explained, from incentive- and cost-based to retention of key integration resources, and putting top-notch talent into conditions in which they could achieve "outlier" performance. This might seem like coddling employees to some old-school managers. But Barton claimed this was the way to achieve exceptional outcomes. He noted, also, that he had already fired the old HR manager and was seeking a new one experienced in managing high-performance aeronautical and software engineers.

Organizational processes would be revised with an emphasis on creating cheap and rapid experimentation, iteration, and feedback cycles; when in doubt, the company reflex should be "trystorming," quickly coming up with and trying out, through 3-D simulation and prototyping, new concepts. Barton played a few engaging, short video clips to give the "jury" a better understanding of the exciting potential of this approach, given new technologies.

The transition, argued Barton as he turned to engage more directly with the vast gallery of diverse stakeholders, would require substantial changes to the culture of the company. First, engineers would have to give up their historical inclinations toward controlling all information involved in the design and manufacture of a plane. Second, the entire company would have to shift toward a more open approach to communication; more ideas would come from outside the company, SMA would have fewer secrets, and more would be gained from information flowing across organizational boundaries than from preventing such flows (to protect SMA proprietary knowledge). Barton noted that the new communication director SMA hired would need to advocate, or at least be comfortable with, a more open philosophy. Third, within the company, supervisory practices would change and become more collaborative and consultative. There'd be more management by walking around and talking to people, less reliance on formal incentives that too often gave people reasons to conceal problems in order to stay on schedule or avoid being the reason something cost too much. Bonuses for all, including execs, would be scaled back, and when they were employed, they'd be linked to joint achievements, not individual ones. Finally, the company as a whole had to stop believing in silver bullets, like incentives or proprietary secrets, and instead adapt to a rapidly evolving problem-solving and integration orientation. In the future, how fast something could improve would matter much more than how well it was done at the outset.

Barton, imagining the galley members quite moved by the new vision at this point, next emphasized the need to lead ethically—to do the right thing by all the company's stakeholders, and to seek to diffuse past tendencies toward adversarial attitudes. Going forward, Barton said, "We'll seek to balance as best we can the interests of all parties," as that would, Barton said, be the best way to enduring (though possibly not short-term) financial success. SMA would need to continue to make adjustments to its team, but it would always treat people with dignity and respect, even when it had to make a change.

As Barton finished, he sensed that his presentation had impressed those present. The gallery kept quiet, respectfully, but seemed to breathe as one. He noticed, however, that Luce, whom the SSEER had set up as a skeptic, seemed worried and uncertain.

"Is that all, Mr. Barton?" asked Goldman, acting in his judge's role.

"For now," said Barton, a bit startled by the perfunctory question, but still confident in the effect of his presentation. "I'll respond to concerns, of course," he said.

Goldman nodded, looked at Luce: "Mr. Luce?"

Luce paused as if thinking for a moment, as if considering what path to take. Then, rather than starting out on the attack, as Barton had expected he might do in the beginning, Luce turned to the jury.

"Yes," said Luce, in a strong, even voice, no longer sarcastic. "Well, I suspect this plan, although obviously interesting, raises concerns for the members of this board." This, Barton thought, was a change in strategy. No longer relying on ridicule, Luce sounded reasonable. Barton sensed danger in this change.

At first, no one on the jury said anything. Then:

"Too radical," said Frazier, his broad, flat head satirically flatter. "We should adopt a more modest plan, one that we're more likely to be able to successfully carry out."

Elliot, his head perched on a near-ostrich-length neck, nodded: "It's too risky. Why wouldn't we just sell off some pieces, and get private-equity investors in here to generate value from the rest?"

Frazier squirmed, his narrow eyes narrowing: "That's not what I meant."

"Same diagnosis," said Elliot. "Different prescribed cure."

"I think," said Goldman from his judge's seat, jutting forward his thick jaw, "that it makes some rather rosy assumptions about our abilities to shed adversarial attitudes and work with the unions. What makes you so sure they'll go along with selling off the plants?"

Luce, Barton noticed, had materialized a flip chart from thin air and had written down each of these objections in shorthand notation. Now he spoke what he'd written aloud: "Too radical, too risky, too rosy." He looked out to the gallery. "These seem like pretty valid concerns."

The gallery of spectators rumbled. Many in the audience nodded in agreement, especially, Barton realized, the SMA engineers in the crowd. Customers appeared concerned. Journalists jotted in their notebooks. A few of them stood and moved to the back of the room, whispering into cell phones.

Luce seized the initiative. He began to point to the core competencies that had, he argued, allowed SMA to succeed in the past. Detailed knowledge of the technologies used in previous generations of the SMA cargo plane: planning; quality assurance; compliance with safety standards; proprietary knowledge, carefully protected, about how to build a cargo plane; tough negotiation with unions; and incentive-based compensation. He made his points forcefully: there was almost no overlap between what Barton had proposed to do with the company and what had made it successful in the past. As he made these points, supporters in the gallery shouted their approval. Goldman looked at them with annoyance, but did not interrupt Luce. Finally, he finished with a flourish: "We all wonder," he said, "why you so badly want us to be something that we've never been." The approval from certain corners of the gallery grew deafening.

"Perhaps," said Luce, "it's because you were not part of what we have been, our past successes. Not even," he said, "a part of our industry. We are proud of what we have done. What makes you think you—a newcomer, an outsider—can just ride into town with a better idea? Perhaps it is time," said Luce, "for you to sit down and do your homework. Time for you to 'get real.'" This provoked applause from many in the gallery. Customers looked uncertain. More journalists spoke into phones, and Barton could hear some of them now.

"We'll go with the headline 'Too Radical.'"

"'Too risky,' that's our theme. We want to say that over and over."

"'Too rosy,' and sprinkle in the word *naive* a lot . . ."

Barton paused, listening to the momentum slip away from him, before reclaiming it dramatically.

"WE CANNOT," he said, raising his voice above the racket, nearly shouting, "CONTINUE TO LIVE IN THE PAST!"

Barton paused. The gallery grew quiet; that sea of bobbling heads stopped bobbling.

"We're in trouble, folks," Barton said, softly. "We can't take half measures. We can't go back to a past where we could make a good living selling a cargo plane to the Air Force. That past is gone, so we need to stop clinging to it. We need to stop looking back to it. We need to live in the future. A future that works."

"But that's the problem exactly, isn't it," said Luce. "That the people here—" he gestured to the jury, then swept his arm across to indicate the gallery as well. "These people don't believe what you've proposed *will* work."

Again, a furor erupted from the gallery. Heated arguments seemed to be breaking out in the crowd. People shouted at each other. Goldman pounded the gavel. "Order!" he shouted. "Order!"

When things settled down, Goldman looked at Luce.

"Do you have anything more to present?"

"No, sir," said Luce. "I recommend we vote."

"Mr. Barton?" Goldman asked.

"Fine with me," said Barton.

"Very well, then. Members of the jury, please rise."

The six people seated behind the rail stood.

"Mr. Elliot," Goldman said. "Concerning Jim Barton's plan for transforming Santa Monica Aerospace, how do you vote?"

"I'm against it," he said, and sat down. Goldman tallied the vote on a piece of paper.

"Mr. Frazier," said Goldman.

"Also opposed, your honor," said Frazier, settling his squat form back down. Goldman tallied that vote also.

Barton did the math. Six jury members. He'd need four in addition to himself to avoid splitting the board. Two had already gone against. He assumed Goldman would vote with him. If so, he'd still need three of the remaining four.

"Mr. Haas?"

"I'm in favor," Ron Haas said, despite worry lines that overwhelmed his forehead.

About time, Barton thought. He had suspected he could rely on Haas.

"Okay," said Goldman, tallying this vote also.

"Mr. Ford?"

"I'm against it, sir," said Ford, his broad mouth opening like a frog's.

"Okay," said Goldman. "I've got three against, one in favor."

The rest will all need to be in favor, Barton thought.

"Mr. Shepherd?"

Shepherd's low-hanging mustache fluttered. "In favor."

Goldman tallied.

"And Ms. Smithson?"

"In favor, your honor," she said, her eyebrows arching emphatically.

Goldman tallied. "And I presume," he said, "that you, Mr. Barton, will support your own plan."

"Yes," said Barton.

"That makes it four votes in favor, three against. And I," he looked up at Barton. "I'm not so sure about this plan, but I'll give it the benefit of the doubt. I've known you a long time, and you have a tendency to be right about these things. So, despite reservations, I'm in favor. Which makes it five to three in favor. Mr. Barton, that's a little closer than one would like for a company facing such challenges."

"I agree," said Barton. "But I hope even those who don't completely agree can support us in the plan on which we've decided."

"Let us hope so," said Goldman. Then: "This court is adjourned!" He pounded the gavel. The room and the people in it began to fade to black. A message appeared in the black space in front of Barton: "SIM COMPLETE."

"Exit," said Barton. He took off the head cover.

So, he thought to himself. *If the SSEER is any good, I ought to win over five of eight board members.* He'd hoped for more, but this outcome aligned with his most honest expectations. It *was* too close for comfort. *But change,* he thought, *is hard and often not a matter of wide margins or ideal arrangements.*

Barton took a few deep breaths to slow his heart rate. He realized that Luce's challenge of his motives for becoming SMA's CEO and his lack of industry experience had set off his temper. He had responded by reacting in a loud voice, and while he'd caught himself and corrected his approach, he had to be sure he didn't lose his temper in the real board meeting. He also felt now that he'd barreled through his points a bit, without properly taking in questions or concerns. He'd felt he needed to proceed confidently at this stage, unwaveringly. He was acting on Goldman's early advice, advice given before he'd even accepted the job: "You'll have to hold onto convictions while others, including board members, get cold feet." He had made it his responsibility to get them and keep them on track. But he also wanted to be careful that he was truly listening to the concerns of others and demonstrating that he took criticism and other viewpoints into careful consideration.

Triggered by these thoughts, he picked up the book on his desk, *Legend & Legacy,* and flipped it open to an earmarked page, where he had been reading about Boeing's fourth CEO, Bill Allen.* Allen, a lawyer, had been the first Boeing Company CEO without a formal background in aerospace engineering. Yet he and his senior management team led Boeing into the jet age, its first billion-dollar-revenue year, and lasting industry leadership retained throughout the last half of the twentieth century.

Right after accepting the CEO position, Allen had listed what he believed he had to do to be an effective Boeing CEO. Barton reread the list:

Must keep temper always—never get mad.

Be considerate of my associates' views.

Don't talk too much—let others talk.

Don't be afraid to admit that you don't know.

Don't get immersed in detail—concentrate on the big objectives.

Make contacts with other people in the industry—and keep them!

Make a sincere effort to understand labor's viewpoint.

Be definite; don't vacillate.

Act—get things done—move forward.

Develop a postwar future for Boeing.

Try hard, but don't let obstacles get you down. Take things in stride.

Above all else be human—keep your sense of humor—learn to relax.

Be just, straightforward; invite criticism and learn to take it.

Be confident. Having once made the move, make the most of it.

---

*Robert J. Serling, *Legend & Legacy: The Story of Boeing and Its People,* 1st ed. (New York: St. Martin's Press, 1991).

Bring to task great enthusiasm, unlimited energy.

Make Boeing even greater than it is . . .[*]

Allen was grappling, it seemed to Barton, with similar tensions, between making a decisive move and being open. Barton genuinely believed many of the challenges facing SMA were new, twenty-first-century problems, but there were fundamentals in terms of human behavior. Allen's list was relevant to leadership today. He tore out the page of the book and tucked it into the folder that held his tablet.

Reflection

What are the benefits and dangers of "rehearsing" or imaginatively playing through important upcoming presentations, debates, or decisions such as this?

Is the courtroom scenario the right metaphor for this exchange? Does it make sense to conceive of the CEO's presentation of the company strategy as a hearing, in which the board members sit as jury to determine the company or CEO's fate? What other scenarios might be used?

Would you vote in favor of Barton's proposed strategy for SMA? Why?

What do you think of Allen's list for effective CEO leadership? Which seem most relevant or least relevant today? What would you add to the list? How does a list like this serve a CEO?

---

*The original source of this list is Harold Mansfield, *Vision: A Saga of the Sky* (New York: Duell, Sloan and Pearce, 1956), 150–151.

CHAPTER 13

The Agony of Defeat

Wednesday, April 7, 3:18 p.m. . . .

"There's no way," said John Elliot, craning his long neck forward to catch every eye, "that any investor we might interest in buying these plants would ever agree to provide work guarantees to the unions."

"I understand that," said Barton. "But what if we were willing to discount the selling price a little, to offset the buyer's exposure—?"

"You're dreaming, Jim," Elliot interjected. "If the plan depends on this element, it's dead on arrival." He folded his arms, shook his head, and looked around the table.

"Obviously, it doesn't depend on that specific detail. It's an example. An idea." *A detail I should not have mentioned,* thought Barton. "The end result," Barton tried, "would be a lower cost basis for SMA . . ."

"Buyers will never go for it," said Elliot. "It's DOA."

"We need to do something for the unions, or *they* won't go for it," Barton said. "What do you suggest?"

Barton did not restrain his frustration. Constructive criticism was welcome, but Elliot's skepticism didn't seem constructive.

When Elliot didn't respond, a silence fell over the room. As intended, the gleaming model of the new SMA airplane at the front of the room had elicited awe at the meeting's outset. Now, however, it seemed to mock the proceedings. *Would it ever be built?* Barton thought, *or would Elliot's liquidation fantasy prevail?* He looked around the room to assess support for Elliot's position, instinctively looking first to Bill Ford, who had supported Elliot in the past.

Turning to Ford, Barton mostly expected to see the usual expression of bored acquiescence on the former CEO's face. But today something else was going on with Ford. The older man stared at the model of the new plane, lost in thought. Barton thought he detected a hint of excitement but couldn't imagine what that might mean.

Nothing about this first meeting of the newly reconstituted board had gone as planned. Unlike the sim, where the board had let him present his entire plan before starting to ask questions, in this real meeting, the questioning had started early. Ed Frazier jumped in on the use of composites on the new plane. Elliot weighed in repeatedly to renew his call to simply sell the company in pieces. The pattern of interruptions, once set into motion, persisted.

From the second PowerPoint slide in Barton's presentation, Frazier had hammered him about the idea of basing the new plane on composite technologies. Very quickly it became apparent that disgruntled members of the SMA engineering group—a subset of people with a deep and abiding commitment to the way it used to be and unwilling to come to grips with the new reality—had been feeding concerns to Frazier, a sympathetic ear because of his engineering background and the decisions he'd made as the past CEO *not* to move in the direction of the new technology. The anticomposite crowd had, Barton began to realize, decided to use this meeting and Frazier's help to make their last stand against use of the new materials.

Safety emerged as a central theme in Frazier's comments.

"This plane will be completely fly-by-wire? No hydraulics?" asked Frazier.

"Electrical and electronic systems replace hydraulics, yes. That's the idea," Barton responded.

"What about electric overloads and fire concerns? Composites burn. We'd have to be sure there'd be no potential for electrical fires."

"Yes, we would," said Barton.

"I'm not sure," said Frazier, playing the engineering expertise trump card, "that you understand the nature of electrical load factors and how difficult it is to replace the hydraulics on an airplane."

"I'm sure," said Barton, "that you have a deeper appreciation of that than I do, Ed. But Susan Akita assures me this is a solvable problem."

"All her people agree with that?"

"I don't know if *all* of them do," said Barton. "But she's our expert on this, and we have to trust our experts here, don't you think?"

"We have to be sure. *That* is what I think," said Frazier. "Maybe she just knows how much you want her to say that it's solvable."

Barton felt his temper and his voice rising: "Ed, you know Susan well—have you ever known her to tell you want you wanted to hear if she believed otherwise?"

Frazier backed down: "I just think we need to be sure. Really sure."

Whenever anything related to risk in the SMA transformation arose, Elliot weighed in to say, "With all this risk, I think our shareholders are better off with a cut-and-run liquidation." Elliot's objections always produced squirms from the others, but they had grown tired of engaging with him on this point. The good news, from Barton's perspective, was that the content of Elliot's comments didn't lead the naysayer contingents to join forces. Frazier was among those most adamantly opposed to Elliot's plan of action, so there was no way they were going to gang up on Barton, not on the same points anyway. They remained separate attackers. The bad news, however: although the board was newly reconstituted, it seemed to be, Barton thought, in these early stages of its operation, as dysfunctional as its predecessor.

"I don't think we have the expertise to build a composite plane," Frazier said, taking up a new tack.

"Not in-house," admitted Barton. "We'll have to rely on strategic partnerships. As you'll see on the next slide, that's an important part of the plan."

"So what will be our competitive advantage, then?" said Frazier. "We've always maintained our proprietary expertise. You're saying we'll go elsewhere for that?"

"Not all of it," Barton answered calmly, controlling his temper. "And anyway, just because we don't bring a particular technical expertise to the party doesn't mean we have no defensible competitive advantage. We'll be the unique player who is able to *integrate* all these disparate kinds of expertise. You're right about part of it, though: we *will* need a different mind-set. The future of this company is not about keeping our proprietary 'how to build an airplane' manual locked in a safe. Going forward, there's more to be gained from openness than from closedness."

Frazier shook his head. Barton knew that Frazier would probably never be able to get on board with that idea, philosophically. But Barton wasn't looking for agreement from Frazier on this point, and everyone in the room knew that. In making the statement, Barton, in effect, asserted his right as the current CEO to take a different path, to have a different philosophy. It amounted to an escalation, addressing such a direct point of divergence directly to the past CEO, but Barton thought the risk was worth it. Engineering expertise might be Frazier's trump card, but being the board's current choice of CEO was one of Barton's.

"I'm just worried," said Frazier, retreating, "that we'll end up with nothing. Our supposed global strategic partners will be telling *us* what to do, because they have all the expertise and own the intellectual property that goes with it."

Frazier fell silent and no one picked up his point to argue it further. Elliot took the opportunity to weigh in with his usual suggestion.

When Barton came to the part in his presentation about selling off some manufacturing facilities, maybe striking a deal with the buyer to ensure some cash flow in the short term, Elliot engaged.

"What will happen to the workers?" Elliot asked.

"There could be some reductions, probably would be," said Barton, prepared for this discussion. "But we could help control the severity of the adjustment by guaranteeing some early orders. The plant would likely enjoy more business in the long run, because it would be free to take work from other companies."

"Including our competitors," said Frazier.

"Yes, possibly including our competitors," said Barton. "As a major customer, we could influence that decision, of course. But we'd no longer be able to order the plant to not take a particular order. Laid-off workers would probably be rehired pretty quickly."

"How will the unions react to this proposal?" Elliot asked.

"It's a good question," said Barton. He explained that he'd been in informal discussions with the head of the mechanics union about this for some time. "They can see the writing on the wall, too," said Barton.

"They know all too well that the days of the past are numbered, and that they have to adapt to global competition just as we do."

"Why the mechanics union?" asked Bobbi Smithson.

"Good place to start," said Barton. "If they agree, the others will likely fall in line." He looked at Frazier, who nodded for a change. The others noticed. "Also," Barton continued, "I know the guy heading the mechanics union. Went to school with him. In fact, we both had summer jobs in our factory between high school and college."

Bob Goldman spoke, for the first time: "You went to high school with the head of the mechanics union?"

Barton nodded. "Yes." Barton had forgotten for a moment that only the simulated version of Goldman knew this. "You all know I am from this part of the world. He's not the only SMA employee I went to school with."

A little later in the discussion, Barton again mentioned the idea of possibly sweetening the deal somehow to help the unions agree to the plan. "I don't know," Barton said, when asked *how* the deal might be sweetened, "maybe short-term work guarantees."

That's when Elliot launched his objections that included pronouncing the plan DOA.

Board members raised no issues with the organizational culture and process changes Barton had explained. But those few minutes of his presentation turned out to be the eye of the storm. Ill winds resumed on the other side of it.

"China is playing a pretty prominent role here," Goldman observed.

Barton agreed. "It's the main area for commercial airline and air cargo growth for the rest of this decade and probably into the next one."

"Kind of weird for a US defense contractor to get that cozy with Chinese companies," Elliot observed. "Especially if we're going to put such advanced technologies on the plane. Are we sure this won't queer the situation with the Air Force or Congress for the remaining defense sales?"

"We can't be completely sure," said Barton, "not where politicians are involved. But we have considered that and talked with some key people about it. Our major hedge scenario is the one that I already mentioned: sell our current factory that is manufacturing the last production run of our military cargo airplanes to a private equity firm."

"The Japanese 'heavy manufacturing' company that will probably work closely with us on the advanced composite technology for our commercial cargo airplane actually manufactures in China. So we won't be taking them any technology they don't already have access to. And, we all know our US economy is highly dependent on trade with China. If we have any hope of selling our new cargo airplane to Chinese airlines, we will have to demonstrate that a significant value-added manufacturing activity of the airplane resides in China."

"All it will take is one grandstanding congressman to make this an issue," said Elliot. "It could blow up on us."

"Our Washington people are on it, and they say it's a manageable risk," said Barton. "If we were talking about a jet fighter, that would be different. But this is a commercial cargo plane. It doesn't sound high-tech enough to capture the public's imagination, so it's not a good platform for grandstanding. That's the opinion of our experts in these matters, anyway."

"To get the advance sales," said Frazier, "you need us to approve the conceptual design today." He gestured toward the model at the side of the room. "Right?"

"That would allow us to run ahead with an aggressive time frame," Barton agreed. "Montero has laid the groundwork for some high-profile sales already. He's somewhere in the Far East now, awaiting word on the outcome of this meeting."

"Where in the Far East?" asked Ron Haas. He hadn't said much so far.

Barton wasn't sure he understood the question. "You mean where is Montero today?" Haas nodded. "I think he's in Malaysia."

"Malaysia," said Haas. "Huh. How'd a guy named 'Montero' get so good at sales in the Far East?"

Barton laughed. "I think he's just good at sales, period. Just happens that the big buyers are in the Far East these days."

"That's certainly true in our business," said Phil Shepherd, also speaking up for the first time in this meeting.

Haas was trying to lighten and broaden the discussion, Barton realized. He appreciated the help. But Frazier brought things right back to the previous topic.

"You're kind of holding our feet to the fire, then," said Frazier. "Making us decide without a lot of time to consider things."

"The urgency," said Barton, "is not artificial, and it's not of my making. The longer we wait, the more potential that our finances will degrade before we can turn the corner. It's a real concern."

Haas and Smithson seconded this.

"I still don't like it," said Frazier. "Being forced to move this fast. Feels like we're not taking the time to do due diligence. I'm worried there's something we're missing that we're going to trip over later. Especially with all this new technology involved."

Barton acknowledged, as he felt he had to, the validity of this concern. "It's a trade-off," he said.

Discussion of sales in China went quite well, however, compared to what happened when Barton mentioned the possibility of moving SMA headquarters to the Seattle area. Judging from the immediate reaction, almost nobody liked this idea. Only Goldman appeared indifferent.

Barton made the case that the strategic restructuring would involve hiring new engineers and that Puget Sound is the aeronautical commons, the place where people have the needed talent and know-how. They could work with the University of Washington aeronautical engineering department on wind-tunnel and carbon-fiber tests. Consultation with Boeing's developmental center would be important to understand tooling design for spinning the carbon fiber into large airplane components. Akita had explained all of this to Barton, and now he explained it to the others.

No one seemed to buy into the arguments though.

"It's too much," summarized Frazier. "Too much change, too fast. And on top of all of it, a move. Uprooting people. It's just piling on."

Others indicated unspoken agreement. "Your plan," said Frazier, with a transparent tone implying his experience as the former CEO of SMA, "is too radical, too sharp a departure from the past. I don't think it will work."

This cued Elliot to bolt back into the discussion with his "sell everything" recommendation once again.

Then there was silence.

Barton could tell that his proposal was in dire straits. He could also tell that the others knew that, and that everyone was wondering where that left them.

In a gesture he'd later regret, Barton decided at that moment to finish with a little speech about the need to lead ethically and to take into account the interests of all stakeholders in whatever they decided. No one disagreed, but he could tell that even Goldman thought the speech poorly timed. The timing made it seem to imply that it would be unethical to oppose Barton. No one really thought Barton intended that. But everyone detected the awkwardness of the moment. A bad time, Barton realized, to put his foot in the wrong place.

Clarke Gardner presented some supporting financials, filling in some blanks. A bit more lackluster discussion wandered and circled around some of the former points.

Barton concluded by going for it, laying it all on the line. Trying to turn the tide.

"This plan," he said, "is what you hired me to produce. If you don't want to go with my plan—" he paused dramatically, then continued "—then you need to reconsider whether I'm the right person to lead the company."

Laying it out like that made the point explicit, but the content of this conclusion had hung over the meeting regardless. The board hired a CEO. The CEO produced a plan. If the board couldn't get with the CEO's plan, then the CEO was probably not the right guy. *Quod erat demonstrandum.*

Barton looked around the room, trying to make eye contact with everyone, trying to read their positions, their readiness to say yes. Goldman didn't look back but instead stared down at the table. An unsettling impression, a sense of sudden realization, flashed in Barton's mind: Goldman looked very much like a schoolteacher disappointed and embarrassed that a star pupil hadn't done his homework.

Haas took control of the meeting.

"We need to know where people stand," he said. "Shall we go around the table? No secret ballot on this one, folks."

"I'll start," said Elliot.

Smithson laughed. "You think we should sell off the company in pieces to a private equity firm."

"Well," said Elliot. "Yes. Doesn't have to be a private equity firm. But that's the general idea. Had I mentioned this already?"

The half-hearted joke produced a few strained chuckles.

"That makes you against the plan—right?" asked Haas.

"I'm against it," said Elliot. "I vote no."

Haas turned to Frazier, who sat next to Elliot: "Ed?"

"I vote no, too," he said. "But I also disagree with Elliot. I don't think we should chop up the company and sell it. We need a more realistic plan than the one we've seen presented here today."

"Okay," said Haas, making marks in his notebook. "That's two against. Bobbi?"

Smithson sat forward, hands folded, elbows propped on the table. She unwound her fingers and sat back in the chair, rocking back and forth. Barton knew this was a vital moment. If Smithson didn't say yes, no one would.

"I'm willing to go along with it," she said. "It looks hard, but that doesn't mean we can't do it. I think we have to do something bold. Incremental won't get it done."

Haas nodded: "Two against, one in favor."

Haas himself was next in line, so he continued: "I'm going to vote with Bobbi. I'm not ready to shoot this down, and time's awastin,'" he said. "So that's two to two."

He turned to Shepherd. "Phil?"

Shepherd didn't hesitate. "I vote in favor."

Haas made a mark in his book. "That's three to two in favor." He turned to Barton. "I assume you're in favor of your own plan, Jim?"

"If I'm allowed to vote," said Barton.

"Let's include your vote for now," said Haas. "That's four to two in favor. Bill?"

Ford, if he voted no, would likely be the last no vote, Barton thought. Goldman would vote with Barton, and the final vote would be five to three in favor, or four to three even if Barton's vote wasn't included. Not ideal, but acceptable and expected, Barton thought. It'd be good enough.

Again, Barton noted some difference in Ford. His eyes lingered on the model of the new conceptual design. But then his expression hardened and he returned his attention to the center of the room, speaking with a tinge, Barton thought, of regret: "I vote no," he said. "I like some of what I've seen and heard here today. I like the idea of designing a new plane and that—" he gestured toward the model, "is a thing of beauty. Susan and her people have done a marvelous job.

"But let's face it, this is not really an airplane company anymore. We haven't even tried to design anything like this for a couple of decades. I'm sad to say it, but I just don't think we can do it. We've lost too much since our glory days."

Frazier reacted with a sudden movement, but said nothing.

Ford noticed. "I'm sorry, Ed. You know my appreciation for you and the work you've done, and my interest in your career. But we got away from what we were good at. And we don't have it to go back to now.

"So I'm with Elliot. Let's sell off the damn thing, make some money, and get on with our golf games."

Ford's pronouncement left an expansive, stunned silence in its wake. After a suitable period, Haas interrupted it.

"Four to three in favor," said Haas. "Bob? What think you?"

It was clear that the entire room assumed that Goldman, Barton's long-time mentor, would vote in favor of the plan, which would give Barton a victory, if a hollow one, after Ford's damaging comments. Barton wondered how he could overcome the feeling in the room that Ford had brought to life. He didn't notice how long Goldman was taking to answer.

What Goldman said, after a long delay, surprised all of them.

"I'm trying to go along with this," he said. "I'd really like to. But it feels a little too much like a house of cards."

Barton looked at Goldman, startled. Would he really vote against? Had Ford's comments turned the tide?

"I'm especially worried about the talk about the financial restructuring by selling off the plants. I don't think it's realistic that we'll get the unions to cooperate. And I don't think we'll get as much for them as you've projected, because any buyer will be quite shy of the uncooperative workforce."

"Bob, honestly, I think I can pull this off," said Barton, suddenly in a two-way conversation with his longtime mentor.

The two men looked at each other. The others watched, rapt, as the drama unfolded. Barton couldn't figure out what was happening. Had he embarrassed Goldman? Failed to consult him adequately? Had he threatened to eclipse his mentor, and now Barton was seeing a side of the older man he'd never before seen, an envious side?

Goldman turned away to finish his thoughts: "No, I can't go along with this. I have to vote no."

A stunned silence fell over the room. Haas broke it. "That's four to four, counting your vote, Jim. As chairman, I'd have to say I don't think that's enough to approve the plan. Anyone object to that conclusion?"

No one did. No one said anything, so Haas continued: "Jim, I for one would not like to see you resign over this. But I think this means we need an alternative plan. Unless you're prepared to present one today, we'll have to handle it at the next meeting. We can schedule an extraordinary meeting if we need to, but I think it will really depend on how long it takes you to arrive at an alternative."

Barton nodded, his lips drawn into a tight line. "I need time to think this over. But not long. I'll get right back to you."

Haas nodded. "Thanks," he said. "Other business?"

The group discussed a few more minor items and then adjourned early. It was the first board meeting Barton had ever participated in at SMA that finished early. The meaning was clear: nothing else could really move forward until they had a viable plan, including making advanced sales of the new airplane without first obtaining board approval of the conceptual engineering design. Barton needed to either get out of the way or get on it.

As the meeting broke up, Barton sidled up to Goldman and spoke to him quietly.

"Bob, what can I say to change your mind?"

Goldman's reaction startled Barton. The older man stepped back and raised his voice, breaking free from Barton's presumption of confidential communication: "I'm sorry, Jim. I'm now a part of this company's board, with a fiduciary obligation to do what I think is right for the shareholders. That obligation overrules any considerations of friendship and personal loyalty. I don't agree with your plan, nor do I think you have the ability to pull it off. So there's really nothing you can say that would change my mind."

Goldman turned and left the room.

Barton stood, dumbfounded, as the others filed past him.

Reflection

What is your assessment of what went wrong in this meeting? Did the failure lie in the proposed plan, the presentational approach, or the board members' views?

In hindsight, how else might Barton have navigated this difficult meeting?

What should Barton do next?

CHAPTER 14

Wild Card

Wednesday, April 7, 7:38 p.m. . . .

Brash, percussive music. Montage of images: stock market listings, corporate jets flying, factory machines operating. Overlaying all, austere letters:

BUSINESS NEWS NIGHT
with Lisa Jessup

Fanfare resolves. A male voice booms: "You're watching TTC's Business News Night, with Lisa Jessup." Cut to Camera 1: Lisa Jessup, smartly dressed and coiffed, seated behind a news desk. Suspended above her right shoulder, the words "Trouble at SMA" are imprinted over an unflattering snapshot of Jim Barton with his mouth gaping open.

Jessup: "There are reports tonight that Jim Barton, the chief executive officer of Santa Monica Aerospace, appointed by the company less than six months ago, might be in trouble. Big trouble."

Cut to Camera 2; Jessup looks left.

"According to anonymous sources within the company, today's meeting of the board of directors ended in turmoil, with the board refusing to approve Barton's plans for the future of the company.

No word from SMA on what this means, for the company or its CEO. We go now to Hans Kreitzer who is on the scene at SMA."

Cut to Kreitzer standing in a dark, deserted parking lot outside a tall glass and steel building. A "Santa Monica Aerospace HQ" sign is visible behind him.

Kreitzer: "Hi, Lisa. I'm standing outside the corporate headquarters of SMA, in Santa Monica, where it's pretty quiet at the moment. According to some people, however, what happened earlier today up there ..."

The image pans up the side of the building to its distant top, which is dimly lit against the night sky.

"...on the top floor of this building ..."

Camera drops to Kreitzer, who looks back down at it.

"... was anything *but* quiet. We've heard accounts of a shouting match, perhaps even a fistfight, during the meeting. One person told us they thought an ambulance had been called, though our subsequent investigations suggest that the ambulance *might* have been on-site for another purpose. The truth is, we don't know nearly as much tonight as we'd like to about this important new development. The company has been unwilling to comment. As a result, this tranquil community—"

The camera swings out to show homes, lights in the windows, off in the distance.

"—waits anxiously for some indication of what's going on. The only thing that's clear: this could have very, very grave consequences for our local and surrounding economy."

Split screen, Jessup on right, Kreitzer on left.

Jessup: "Any sense for the nature of the disagreement, Hans?"

Kreitzer: "Yes, Lisa, we've heard it from multiple sources now that CEO Jim Barton proposed moving the whole company from Santa Monica to Seattle, and that several board members vehemently objected. We haven't managed to reach any board members, but we tracked down a member of the Santa Monica City Council earlier tonight, and here's what he had to say about that idea."

Cut over to a man in a ball cap and T-shirt, clearly taking time from a softball game, with a microphone jammed into his face.

City council member: "I'd like to know more, but my first reaction is that it's a bad idea. Bad for the company, bad for Santa Monica. Bad all around. I'd certainly oppose it. We've got great people, great talent in this area, and government officials have over the years, as you know, granted that company various concessions. To hear now that they're considering turning their backs on us . . . well, that's just outrageous."

Cut to Kreitzer.

Kreitzer: "There you have it, Lisa. The alleged proposal to move SMA to Seattle is 'Outrageous.'"

Cut back to Jessup.

Jessup: "Thanks, Hans. Stand by, if you would. We have a report coming in from Charlie Lee, who's been comparing notes with colleagues at the *So-Cal Times*.

Cut to Lee standing at the entrance to a nondescript building.

Lee: "Hello there, Lisa, I'm here the offices of the *So-Cal Times* where they're apparently working on a story about Robert Goldman, the newest member of the SMA board, and a longtime colleague, friend, some would even say 'mentor,' to Jim Barton. We're hearing that it may have been Goldman himself who cast the deciding vote *against* Barton's plan today—a betrayal, you might say, of their longtime friendship."

Split screen with Jessup and Lee.

Jessup: "Wow. Betrayal, outrage—this just keeps getting scarier."

Lee: "It sure does, Lisa. In fact, we're hearing that Goldman has expressed a lack of confidence in SMA's leadership, perhaps to the reporters working on this story."

Jessup: "He's gone on record with that?"

Lee: "That's what we're hearing, Lisa."

Cut back to Jessup, who looks into the camera, shakes her head.

Jessup: "Lack of confidence in the leadership of SMA. Betrayal, Outrage. Hans . . . ?"

Split screen, Jessup and Kreitzer.

Kreitzer: "Yes, Lisa."

Jessup: "Hans, what might be the outcome here?"

Kreitzer: "Well, Lisa, it's pretty hard for a CEO to survive something like this. I think most would place their bets on Barton submitting his resignation."

Jessup: "Won't that leave the company pretty much where it was six months ago? With no good plan, and no one willing to take the CEO job?"

Kreitzer: "That's the way it looks from here, Lisa. It'll be a real setback for a company that's had too many of those already. But what can Barton do? Goldman's opinion is extremely influential. That's one of the reasons Barton brought him onto the board in the first place—for his connections. The idea was that those connections would help the company raise financing for its new plane, and for an organizational transformation and modernization. This now appears to have backfired. With Goldman going public like this, the sources of financing are sure to dry up—until and unless the company can get someone new at the helm."

Jessup: "Thanks, Hans."

Kreitzer: "My pleasure, Lisa."

Cut back to Jessup alone.

Jessup: "A grim day for Barton and SMA, and likely for Santa Monica as well. We'll bring you more updates as this story develops."

She turns to face the first camera again. Now, hanging over her left shoulder is an image of a white rabbit, with the words "Bunny Business" imprinted over it.

Jessup: "Our next story this evening features—believe it or not— a rabbit with entrepreneurial tendencies. Inspired by a pet bunny named "Fluffy," brought to their attention by a nine-year-old girl, researchers at SCU have discovered a thing or two about bunny behavior that are making scientists revisit what they thought they knew about carrots and sticks. What can you learn about how to manage your employees from rabbits and other pets? Stay tuned to find out!"

Fanfare crescendos quickly. Cut to commercial.

Thursday, April 8, 9:42 a.m. . . .

The phone on Barton's desk buzzed. Sitting on the couch, feet propped on the low table, he'd been talking with Clarke Gardner, who sat in an armchair, looking nervous. Krishnan's voice came through the intercom. "Susan Akita on line 2, Mr. Barton. *Wall Street Journal* still holding on line 1. Another call coming in on line 3."

"I told you," said Barton impatiently, "to hold all calls!"

"I just thought you might want to take the call from Susan, very sorry, sir—"

"All calls!"

"Yes, sir!" Krishnan signed off.

"So what do you think I should do, Clarke?"

Gardner looked as if he'd feared this question. He tried an evasive gambit: "I think maybe you should talk to Susan . . ."

Barton laughed. "No, I mean about the overall situation."

Gardner shook his head slowly. "I honestly don't know, Jim. Haas said he hoped you wouldn't resign. Everybody I've heard comment on it seems to assume that you will."

"Who have you heard comment on it?"

"Just the talking heads on TV. Nobody, really."

"Nobody here?"

"Nobody here," Gardner lied. Barton knew he was lying and decided not to hold it against him. After all, Gardner was just trying to be merciful. Like one of those guys in the cop shows on television who holds his bleeding partner in his arms and says, "Don't worry, buddy, you're going to make it," knowing full well the guy's a goner.

"So resign is obviously one option. What's another?"

Gardner shrugged. "You could *not* resign, I guess. Develop another plan to take back to the board."

"Something more incremental."

Gardner nodded. "That's the read I got. They didn't like how big your plan seemed to them."

"Why?" Barton asked.

"Different reasons, maybe," said Gardner. "For some of them, like Ed Frazier, it's kind of a reproach. The more radical, the more it changes the way he left the company, the more it seems to him like disapproval of his leadership."

Barton cursed under his breath.

"For others, maybe they just think the company can't carry it out, that it's too much change at once. For others, maybe they just don't like certain aspects of the plan. Maybe that's the way to go at it. To ask, 'what can we change that will swing another vote?' You just needed one more vote."

Barton placed his feet on the floor and sat forward on the couch. "So what single, noncrucial aspect of the plan could we change?"

"The move to Seattle was controversial. I'd say there was disproportionate furor around that part of the plan."

"I feel that's an important part of the plan."

Gardner shrugged. "Maybe you could explain that better to someone for whom that was a determining factor. How about Ford? His comments certainly turned the tide in the meeting."

"I couldn't get a read on him," said Barton. "He kept looking at the model like it reawakened something inside him. He looked almost excited at times."

"Absolutely," Gardner agreed. "I noticed that, too. But in the end, his comments were negative. And, unfortunately, influential. It's possible he turned Goldman. But there was something going on with him that I hadn't seen before."

Barton nodded. "I can't put my finger on why, but I think I agree."

"He's usually not very passionate, goes with the flow," said Gardner.

"He mails it in," said Barton.

Gardner nodded. "Sometimes."

Barton stood and walked to the window. "It's almost like we got him excited, then he got angry with us for getting his hopes up. Like he thought the plan was based on false promises."

"Promises he might *want* to believe but won't let himself . . ." said Gardner, following Barton's train of thought. "That bit about the glory days."

"I'll call him," said Barton. "Maybe we can awaken those hopes and keep them alive. Help them flourish. Maybe I can convince him that we won't betray him."

"He's an old-school chief engineer. That kind of makes sense," observed Gardner.

"Who's been disillusioned for far too long," added Barton.

"You really don't want to resign," Gardner said. It was a statement, not a question, and though it seemed like a change of subject, it wasn't really, and both men knew it.

Barton answered: "I sure as hell don't. Never in my life have I left anything this unfinished. I'd rather not start now."

Barton stood looking out the window. Slowly, as he contemplated the open sky, the corners of his mouth turned up into the beginning of a smile.

"Yes," he said. "I'll give Ford a call. It's worth a shot."

Thursday, April 8, 11:45 a.m. . . .

Barton's optimism had passed. Before he'd been able to reach Ford, bankers had begun to call, one after another. They called to tell Barton that they'd need to reconsider their financial support for SMA's new initiatives, in view of recent reports. In a period of thirty-five minutes, Barton watched 40 percent of the financing for SMA's transformation evaporate. And they'd only arranged 83 percent of it so far. So that was damn near half.

Sitting at his desk, his face buried in his hands, Barton had concluded that he would have to resign after all. He opened a Word document and began to type the letter. Then the phone buzzed again.

"Another banker calling to pull funding," Barton speculated to himself.

But Krishnan surprised him. "It's Robert Goldman on the phone, Mr. Barton."

Barton snatched up the phone, punched the blinking light, and said, "Jim Barton."

"Jim?"

"Bob?"

"Jim, I just wanted to tell you . . . The news reports are wrong. I'm mortified. I would never say to the press I've lost confidence in the SMA management. It's nonsense, pure invention. I'm not sure where it's coming from."

"Well, thanks for calling me to say that, Bob," Barton said. "Think there's anyway you could get that word out? Our financing has been drying up all morning. I'm going to have to resign, I think, to have any chance of getting any of it back. I can't be the reason this company doesn't recover."

There was a silence at the other end of the phone for a moment. "That's just the kind of reasoning I'd expect from you, Jim. I'm proud."

A wave of gratification washed over Barton. Quickly, he recovered from that and pressed Goldman: "Does that mean you'll change your vote, Bob?"

Again, there was a long silence at the other end. "No, Jim, I can't do that. I don't like your plan. I think your relationship with that union guy, your old friend, has colored your judgment. I'm sorry, but that's the way it looks to me, and my ethics require that I place the dictates of my conscience above loyalties to individuals. No matter how fond I am of the person in question. And I am, indeed, very fond of the person in question here."

Now it was Barton's turn to remain silent. He felt angry and didn't really want to accept what Goldman probably intended as a sort of peace offering. Finally, Barton spoke: "Fine. But if you could do something to kill that rumor, that you've got no confidence in us, that'd be a great help."

"I'm already doing that, Jim. I've issued a press release, and I'll meet with some trusted members of the press in about forty-five minutes. We'll kill that story."

"Maybe some of our financing will come back."

"Probably not all of it," said Goldman. "Maybe not much of it. I'm sorry. I'm just being realistic."

"I know, Bob," said Barton. "Whatever you can do. Thanks."

Goldman disconnected without saying anything else.

When Barton looked up, Clarke Gardner stood in his doorway.

"Goldman?" asked Gardner.

Barton nodded. "He didn't say that stuff the press says he said. He's going to try to fix it."

"I doubt he can fix enough of it," said Gardner.

"I know," nodded Barton. "I probably still need to resign."

"What about Ford?" asked Gardner.

"Haven't been able to reach him," said Barton. "Been taking calls from bankers since you and I spoke this morning. All of them pulling funding . . ."

"That had to happen," said Gardner.

Barton nodded.

"Unless you're going to resign in the next half hour or so," said Gardner, "you need to start taking calls from your direct reports. This organization is paralyzed. No one knows what the plan is, what they should be doing. They're screaming for information. For guidance. For leadership."

"I've been handling everything I can, Clarke. Too much is happening at once."

"I know, Jim. But you might need to turn some of your focus inward. Your organization needs you."

"My organization?" He laughed.

"Your organization, Jim."

Barton looked hard at Clarke. "I'm not going to resign, am I, Clarke?"

Gardner smiled. "I don't think so. Call Susan Akita back. Give her the job of telling others what course we're on. Then try to reach Ford."

"Thanks, Clarke."

"We can still do this," Gardner said.

"I hope you're right," Barton said, though he doubted it.

Harder Than I Thought

Thursday, April 8, 1:14 p.m. . . .

For what seemed like the nine-hundredth time that day, Barton's phone buzzed.

"Jose Montero, calling from Indonesia," said Krishnan.

Barton sighed, knowing he'd have to take this call. He picked up the phone and pushed the button.

"Jim Bar—"

"Jim," Montero interrupted, "what the bloody hell're you doing?! I told you about this. I told you! I told you this is the one thing, the one thing, I would not put up with. I'm out here working my ass off, and you can't keep it together back at the home base—"

"I know, I know," said Barton. "We're working on getting it under control."

"Well, you sure as hell better," Montero said, "or you can kiss my tushy goodbye. I told you, I'm an artist—*an artist*—at what I do. I can bring you the sales you need. I'm the rainmaker, man. I can make it rain. I can make you and me a lot of money. But you have to keep it together there. I've had three deals fouled in the last two hours. People calling me. Some of them just leaving messages on my voice mail. Freaking cowards! I can get them back. I can still reel them in. But only—only—if you get your damn act together back in Santa Monica. You've got to rein in that crap. *Comprende*?"

"I hear you."

"You still got that broad in PR? What's her name?"

"Linda Kohler. No, I fired her."

"So who you got to replace her? I want to give them a call. I need some messaging. I've got strategy I know will work . . ."

"The position's vacant right now," said Barton.

"Vacant!?" said Montero. "Vacant!? You fired your PR director right before this? That wasn't very good planning, was it?"

"No, it wasn't," admitted Barton.

"You people are amateurs," said Montero, now more or less screaming into the phone. "Total freakin' amateurs! You've got forty-eight hours to calm this thing down, or I'm off to the highest bidder. That's the way I work. Nothing personal. But that's the way it's going to be. You got that?"

"Hang with us," said Barton weakly. "It'll be worth it. I promise."

"Your promise," said Montero, "isn't worth the air you just puffed out to say it. From what I hear, you might not be around in forty-eight hours to make good on that promise."

"I might not be," said Barton. And then summoning a stronger voice, he said: "Or then again, I might. How about you do your job, I'll do mine. Deal?"

Montero paused and then exploded with laughter. He laughed long and loud. Barton held the phone away from his ear and rolled his eyes.

"Hot dang, Barton," said Montero when he'd finished laughing, "that's the first thing you've said that made any sense at all."

"Deal?" repeated Barton.

"Deal!" said Montero. "Forty-eight hours."

"And you know what," said Barton, suddenly livid. "You're a jerk. A total jerk. Next time you're here, I might just kick your butt."

"You and what army? You bet I'm a jerk," said Montero. "But I'm a damn good sales guy. And you need me. Bad."

"You do your job and I'll do mine," repeated Barton.

"Deal!" repeated Montero. "So go f—"

Barton slammed down the phone and gestured rudely toward it.

"I'll do my job," he said to the now quiet phone. "My job," he repeated.

Thursday, April 8, 8:05 p.m. . . .

Barton arrived home late, to an empty house. Perez had been there, but was no longer. She'd left some things, a file or two, on the kitchen table, like she'd left in a hurry. Barton checked his voice mails (several waited, he hadn't caught up with all of those either), and one was from her.

"Hey there, Jim. If you're home now, I'm not there. Sorry I had to dash. You know how it is. I've got three places to be tonight. And . . . to be honest, when I heard the news reports, I thought the press might be on your doorstep any second, and I didn't want them to find me there. Would have created another aggravation you don't need. Give me a ring when you can. Let's see if we can arrange a meeting soonest, somewhere

211

away from the press." An ironic laugh escaped her lips. "Okay?" A pause, then: "I'm very sorry how this seems to be playing out."

What she'd done made sense, Barton had to admit, but it bothered him. He'd rather hoped to take refuge in his home, with her. Just one of the many things today that had not unfolded as expected.

Barton went to the window to look for reporters. No one yet. Maybe no one would come. Maybe the story would not take flight.

He went to the refrigerator and looked in, not sure what he wanted. A bottle of orange juice drew his attention. He emerged with it and, without bothering to use a glass, opened it and took a deep gulp. Sitting down at the table, he reached for the folders that Perez had left behind.

The first contained a set of articles about problems with composites in airplane design and construction. Notes in Perez's handwriting framed the page. Squinting closely at them, taking out his glasses, Barton discerned that Perez's scribbles were advice to the writer of the articles about angles to take, what to emphasize, what to play down—how to make the story more sensational.

Not entirely friendly to the interests of SMA, Barton noted.

He pushed that folder aside and opened the second. There, typed neatly in twelve-point Times New Roman, he read the starting words of a fresh feature story:

THE RISE AND FALL OF JAMES BARTON, CEO

by Veronica Perez

This reporter has had unprecedented inside access during the short reign of a modern-day tragic hero . . .

"What the . . ." said Barton out loud, unable to restrain himself.

Within a few sentences, he could see that the story amounted to a career obituary and postmortem for one James Barton, former CEO of Santa Monica Aerospace, with sensational and exclusive details available only to someone close to the source. A journalistic coup, without a doubt.

Had she left it for him intentionally? As a warning? A goodbye letter? A way of pouring salt on his wounds?

The resolution of these speculations came quickly when his phone sounded.

"Jim Barton," he said, answering formally, though he could see that it was Perez calling.

"Jim?"

The voice on the other end of the line sounded uncertain.

"This is Jim Barton," he said.

She wanted him to say more, but he did not. For a few moments, neither of them said anything.

"Jim, I'm sorry I had to dash . . ." she said.

"You did the right thing," he responded.

"Oh. Glad you see it that way. Any press there yet?"

"No," he said. "Not last time I looked."

"So I didn't need to rush out of there quite so soon. I just didn't know, Jim, but I hated to take the chance, to feed them anything else sensational, you know."

"Like I said, you did the right thing."

"But you're angry. You sound angry."

"Not angry," lied Barton. "Just coming to grips with reality. That's been the theme for today."

"I heard about the board meeting," she said. "Must have been horrid. How did it happen? I'm surprised . . ."

He resisted the urge to tell her the story, as much as he wanted to talk to someone about it; it would, he knew, only become a juicy new detail in her exposé.

"Long story," he said. "Look, I've got to go. Still got some calls to make."

"Shall we meet up later?" asked Perez.

"Not sure," he said. "My day's not over yet."

"Okay," she said. "Just ring."

But she didn't hang up. Barton listened to the silence.

"Jim?" she said after a long pause.

"Still here," he said.

"In my hurry to leave, I might have left some papers—"

"They're here," he said, a little too quickly.

Again she fell quiet. Then she whispered: "I thought so. Stupid of me."

"No," said Barton, "stupid of me."

"I'm a journalist. I couldn't help writing it. I haven't decided to publish it."

"You'll publish it," said Barton. "It's what you do. I should have realized that."

"Please, Jim, it has nothing to do with us," she said.

"We'll talk later," he said. Then he toggled the phone to off.

What was I thinking? Barton thought.

What a crazy, reckless thing I've been doing. Playing footsie with the enemy. Swept away by a power trip. Impressed with my own importance. Tempted into stupidity. And played for a fool.

That's all his career obituary and postmortem really needed to say.

Friday, April 9, 7:32 a.m. . . .

Barton was dressed and starting his second cup of coffee before he glanced out the front window of his Venice bungalow and noticed the army of press laying in wait for him.

"Oh, no," he said.

He counted at least seven news vans, two of which had parked across the driveway. There was no way he'd be able to get his car out of the driveway, not without going outside and talking to them, convincing them to move. Exactly as they'd planned it. For the first time, Barton missed having the limo come to take him to work.

This early, there weren't too many people stirring out there. He saw a couple of reporters drinking coffee from Styrofoam cups. But clearly this was a stakeout. If he appeared, the scene would change quickly.

Barton wondered what to do.

Then he heard something. A low sound, muffled and distant, but approaching: engine noise. He thought he recognized the sound, but couldn't quite identify it. Then, suddenly, he knew exactly what it was: a mid-1960s Mustang.

Ace Jackson, in his vintage convertible, skidded to a stop in front of Barton's house. He shifted up into a sitting position atop the driver's seat and motioned toward the house.

Barton wasted no time. He grabbed his briefcase and dashed through the front door. Taken by surprise, reporters and camera crew scrambled, but they were too late. In no time, Barton covered the ground to the waiting car and didn't bother with the door. He half-jumped, half-climbed into the Mustang, landing awkwardly in the front seat, and shouted, "Go, go, go!"

Jackson peeled out, tires screeching and burning, carrying Barton away from his ambushers. Some of them hurried to get into their vans, as if to rush after the Mustang, but it was no use. Barton and Jackson were long gone.

Cruising down the highway, Barton looked over at Jackson.

"Thanks, man," he said.

"You bet," smiled Jackson.

"You picking me up," said Barton. "That'll be the big story today. 'CEO consorts with union boss.' That sort of thing."

Jackson shrugged. "Screw 'em," he said. "I was thinking we might go save ourselves an airplane company. That okay with you?"

Barton nodded, smiled. "Let's do it." Jackson gunned the engine, and Barton felt the wind race through his thinning hair.

Maybe, he thought, *I'm not dead yet.*

Reflection

Should Barton do anything to manage the press situation? Should he prioritize hiring a communications director?

What do you think is the best approach Barton can take with the SMA board, given its vote against his proposed plan? How should he respond?

What action should Barton take with Perez, given the new information? Do you agree he's been reckless in continuing this relationship? What do you think matters most to Perez?

What solution do you imagine Barton and Jackson can come to, to keep SMA alive?

CHAPTER 15

Bluebirds Fly In

Friday, April 9, 8:53 a.m. . . .

After their Mustang convertible getaway, it didn't take long for Barton to realize that Jackson wasn't driving toward SMA headquarters.

"Where're we going?" said Barton, shouting to overcome wind noise from riding with the top down.

"Me and some of my boys," Jackson shouted back, "we're going to need some time to work on you, Barton. Plus, we're still thinking through the ransom amount . . ."

Barton looked sideways at his friend, who kept his eyes straight ahead on the road, face expressionless. Then Jackson grinned broadly and pushed at Barton's shoulder. "Just messin' with you, man. They told me to bring you downtown. Century Park. Avenue of the Stars. Perfect for you bro.'"

"Who's 'they'?" asked Barton.

"Not sure," said Jackson. The money man, Gardner, he called me. I think your friend Luce might be there."

"Jonathan Luce?"

Jackson shrugged. "Jonathan. Paul. George. Ringo. I don't know these guys. Though I have this feeling we're all about to get to know each other a whole lot better. Some of my guys are heading down, too."

Barton left it at that. The wind blowing hard past the open cockpit made conversation difficult, and if Jackson knew more, he didn't seem inclined to admit it.

A few minutes later, they pushed through a mahogany door into a nondescript office suite on the fourteenth floor of Century Park East. Barton was surprised to encounter what appeared to be a copy of the model of the new SMA airplane, right there in the suite lobby. As far as Barton knew, there'd only been one such model made. Then he saw Gardner down a hallway, talking with a group of men Barton didn't know, and guessed this model was probably the same model that'd been in the boardroom two days earlier. Gardner, Barton speculated, had brought it with him.

Jackson entered the suite at Barton's side and gasped when he spotted the model: "What the heck is that?" He broke away to look more closely.

Barton smiled. "It's the concept model," said Barton. "For the new airplane."

Jackson ran his fingers along its sleek shape. "It's gorgeous," he said. "We're going to build that?"

"That," said Barton, "is the key question, Ace."

Gardner noticed them and waved. Jackson looked up, saw Gardner and the other men, and seemed to recognize some of the ones Barton didn't know. The entire group moved up the hallway toward Jackson and Barton. Barton was startled again when one of the men, who he hadn't quite been able to see before, turned out to be Jonathan Luce.

"Jim," said Luce, shaking hands. "It's good to see you in one piece."

"Good to see you too, Jonathan," said Barton, "but looks can be deceiving. I'm not sure I'm in one piece."

"Yeah," Luce said. "I've heard something about that. You might be right."

Jackson had moved off to talk with three others, who Barton now recognized as heads of other SMA unions. Dressed in jeans and casual shirts, they stood out, a study in contrast, from the corporate office surroundings. Luce, as usual, featured his own style, though relatively sedate by his standards, in polo shirt, Dockers, and deck shoes.

Gardner stood between the two groups, acting as a liaison: "I believe you've all met . . ." Everyone shook hands all around; Barton detected no warmth emanating from the union guys.

"We thought it might be easier to do this away from the limelight," Gardner explained, answering a question Barton had been thinking.

"Whose offices are these?" asked Barton.

"They're ours," said Gardner. "We lease them. We used to have an office down here, to work on patents in close proximity to our law firm, but we moved them a few months ago. The lease is good for another two months, but I doubt we'll need the space that long. To be honest, I'd forgotten we had this space. Angel remembered."

Angel Crow emerged from one office and disappeared into another, carrying a piece of equipment. Gardner waved in her direction: "It was her idea. A good one."

A door opened at the other end of the hallway, and a short dark-haired man emerged, barking back into the room: "That's fine! Great! We'll do it your way!" He turned and headed up the hall toward them, snorting and muttering to himself. As he passed Gardner, he cursed, said, "Madam queen bee in there is an unbelievable control freak!" He shook his head and disappeared through another door into the nearest office. Gardner smiled and looked toward Barton, slightly embarrassed.

"Communications consultant," said Gardner. "Hector Sacio. Ms. Jenkins wants you to meet with him later."

"Who? Ms. Jenkins?" stammered Barton.

"Let's go say hello," said Gardner, not quite answering.

"Gentlemen," said Gardner, nodding to the union guys and Luce, before moving down the hallway with Barton following. He stopped at an open doorway on the left and stood aside so that Barton could enter.

Barton recognized the attractive woman behind the desk the moment he saw her: "Maggie!" His longtime, East Coast romantic ex-partner, Maggie Landis, rose and rushed around to embrace Barton, in a gesture that exhibited both formality and familiarity.

"Hi, Jim," she said. "Just thought I'd come see if I could help. Is Ace here?"

Still not over the surprise of seeing her, Barton nodded and pointed. She peered around the edge of the doorway, spotted Jackson, and moved quickly to greet him similarly. Jackson reciprocated warmly and a good deal less professionally. Barton thought Jackson seemed both surprised and emotional.

"What're you doing here, Maggs?" Jackson asked.

"I'm here to help get two of my favorite people in the world to play nice and maybe just do something great," she said mysteriously.

"You mean me and Jim," said Jackson.

She poked him hard with a finger to the chest. "That's it, Ace Jackson."

She turned and took Jackson's arm, leading him down the hallway, reaching her other hand out for Barton's arm. "Let's get you in to see Ms. Jenkins."

"Ms. Jenkins?" said Barton, again. But he followed Landis through the doorway at the end of the hallway. Then, yet another time, Barton's jaw dropped.

"Hello, Jimmy boy," said the woman at the head of the long conference table. Though without her characteristic hat, the person in the seat that commanded the room, around which three people from the SMA finance staff clustered, was none other than Clara Jenkins, Barton's gardening neighbor. She stood and extended a hand past Barton: "Hello, I'm guessing you're Mr. Jackson. I'm Clara Jenkins. I don't believe we've met."

Jackson and Jenkins shook hands then she looked disapprovingly at Barton: "Get your jaw off the floor, Barton," she said. "I told you I used to be a CEO. Is it so surprising to see me without my hat on?"

"But I thought you'd given it all up?"

"Given what all up? I said I didn't stay on my company's board, if that's what you mean. But I still know a few people."

"Ms. Jenkins and Mr. Luce have been very helpful in pulling together some other possibly helpful people," said Landis. "We'll be meeting with them later."

"The first of them," said Jenkins, "arrives in just a few short hours, so there's not much time to iron things out, gentlemen. Have a seat."

Barton and Jackson did as they were told. Jackson spoke: "Maybe everybody else here gets what's going on, but I'm just a lowly worker. Somebody's going to have to clue me in a little better."

Barton nodded, put a supportive hand on Jackson's shoulder. "Me, too. Who's coming? What do you need us to do?"

Jenkins tsked and looked at Landis, who also sat down. "Not the tallest monuments in the hangar, are they?" Jenkins said. "Whatever did you see in them, dear?"

Landis shook her head. "Sometimes I wonder."

Then Jenkins turned all business. "Pay attention, boys. Starting at 3 p.m., I've got some people coming in who might like to get in on what you're trying to do with that company of yours, SMA. These people are *not* philanthropists, however. They're looking to make money. Everyone okay with that?"

Barton shrugged. Jackson nodded: "I'm listening."

"These people will want to look at the numbers Mr. Gardner has assembled, and we will provide those for them. That's what these people are here for." Jenkins gestured to the staff members seated near her, who she'd been talking with before Barton and Jackson arrived. "But there are other things that we need to show them, too. Important things. The first of these is in the lobby. That gorgeous model. That hot rod of a cargo plane. But that's not the biggest thing, not nearly . . ."

She stood, circled the table, and leaned down between Barton and Jackson, talking into their ears. "Do you know what the biggest thing is, gentlemen?"

Barton had an idea, but he kept quiet.

"They need to see the two of you, side by side, talking, cooperating, and agreeing. They need to see agreement between management and the unions on a plan that they believe could save the company."

"We don't have an agreement," said Jackson.

"No," said Jenkins, returning to her seat, "but you *do* have a few hours. A window of opportunity. Get this right, and the people you'll talk with later today and tomorrow might just vie for a chance to get in on what you're doing. Blow it, and . . . well, let's just say that Mr. Elliot will probably get his way. SMA will be ripped apart and sold off in pieces."

"I can't agree to anything without running it by my numbers guys," said Jackson. "And they're not here."

"They're already on their way, Mr. Jackson," said Jenkins. "But we don't have to nail everything down. We need an agreement on the broad principles of a restructuring, starting from plans you've already developed, Jim. The details we can work out later."

"You're forgetting something," Barton protested. "The board shot down my plan. They'll have to approve anything we do, and they've basically said they want something incremental. Without their approval of the conceptual design, we can't make the first sales. Without those, there's no financing scenario that works. I'm sorry to rain on this parade, but it can't work. We're short of votes on the board."

Barton looked around and spotted Gardner in the doorway. "I never reached Ford," Barton said to Gardner. Gardner and Jenkins exchanged looks. She nodded. Gardner stepped back from the doorway and vanished. No one said anything.

"What?" said Barton.

He looked back toward the doorway, caught sight of Gardner returning, and then someone else . . .

Bill Ford.

Ford stepped through the doorway and sat down at the end of the table farthest from Jenkins. "Sorry I'm late," he said. "I was on a call. How's it going, Jim? Ace?" He reached across the table to shake hands with both of them.

"A lot better," said Barton, "if this means what I think it means."

"What's that, Jim?" said Ford.

"You're willing to change your vote," said Barton. It was more statement of a conclusion than a question.

Ford nodded. "It's a terrific airplane, Jim. It looks like greatness. I didn't think we could rise to it. But I'm realizing now that I very much want to think SMA is still capable of greatness. If it was just wanting, that wouldn't be enough, but when I look at what Susan and her staff have come up with, and when I see the great work people like your friend Ace here are doing, well . . . I start to believe. Maybe that makes me a foolish old man. But I like the foolish old man version of me better than I like the cynical old man version of me."

"A sentiment," said Jenkins, turning to Barton and Jackson, "that you two gentlemen will understand better and better as you grow older. And, of course, this leaves things with you two." She nodded toward Barton and Jackson. "We've got a conference room waiting for you. Maggie's going to referee. Jim, we also need to find some time for you to talk with Hector Sacio. As you know, you've created a rather significant PR problem for us, one that has the potential to distract or even derail any progress we might make. Since SMA does not have a communications director at the moment, we've had to call in the cavalry. Sacio is a jerk, but he's good. You're not going to like what he has to say, so start preparing yourself for that now."

Barton sighed. Landis looked sympathetic, though also perturbed with him. The three of them—Barton, Jackson, and Landis—stood and moved toward the other conference room to make their collective future, for better or worse.

Friday, April 9, 10:21 a.m. . . .

"So this is what it's come down to," said Barton, gazing at his old friend across the conference room table.

"This, and some order guarantees as part of the spin-off deal," said Jackson.

"With Ford's vote, we can overrule Elliot on the order guarantees," said Barton. "We can sell off manufacturing and you can be sure of short-term demand."

"Assuming the investors will go along," said Jackson.

"They will, if we have an agreement in place," said Barton. "That's where you need to let me do my job."

"So," said Jackson. "What about it?"

"What about what?" asked Barton. He knew, though.

"The other thing."

Barton was genuinely angry. Jackson was insisting on two things. The first, a pay cut for the CEO, was annoying but not horrific. The unions wanted him to lop off a third, a considerable amount that would leave him at a level lower than the job he'd come from at Erlington. But Barton's needs were simple. He'd long ago reached an income far beyond what he really needed, so his dedication to the mission made this concession doable. He'd give in on this one, he knew, despite his annoyance.

But the second demand was tougher. They wanted him to agree to give up his parachute and institute a pension payment outcome the same as any other worker had if things went bad for SMA. They wanted him to fear the same suffering they did. If he lost his job, there'd be no consolation prize.

Barton tried to explain that he was already invested in the company, that he'd lose a bundle if SMA went bankrupt, more than the amount of his parachute. But they answered, rightly, that much of that investment had been conveyed to him as part of his package, the benefits of his position. That money he stood to lose was money he'd never actually had. Most of it was "on paper," thus not the same as being out on your butt with whatever savings you might have in the bank and maybe a pittance payment from the company, some fraction of your planned-on pension.

Landis, who had carefully positioned herself midway between the two men and had kept silent until now, spoke: "He wants you to have skin in the game, Jim."

"That's it," said Jackson.

"I get it," Barton said. He wasn't ready to give in on this one yet. But he knew that he would . . .

Friday, April 9, 2:09 p.m. . . .

"You screwed up, Barton," said Sacio. "And it's probably going to cost you your job, eventually. That's my assessment."

This sobering statement combined in Barton's head with the concession he'd just made to the unions: no golden parachute if he lost his job.

"You really think it's that bad?" he asked. Grasping. Trying to avoid being dragged under.

Sacio chuckled. "Come on, Jim. You were having a fling with a reporter who was actively working to undermine your company's comeback." Barton held eye contact with Sacio. As uncomfortable as that was, he feared a worse appraisal in the eyes of Landis. Sacio went on. "You fired the communications director who was the reporter's arch nemesis. Now the fired communications director has threatened legal action claiming you fired her to satisfy your reporter girlfriend. Maybe this will never happen. Maybe she'll drop it. But I don't think so. Her lawyers have made their intentions clear. They're just waiting for the right moment. Because Perez is a reporter, the media will proceed carefully at first. But if it comes to court proceedings, it's going to be a mess."

"Are you saying I should go now?"

"Absolutely not. We're going to walk a line, try to keep you as long as we can, use your skills to save the company. But when you become more of a liability than a help—and I believe that day will come—I'll tell you and I'll tell your board that it's time for you to go."

Barton sighed. "I was stupid."

Sacio agreed. "You were stupid." It was his turn to sigh. "But we work with what we have."

Friday, April 9, 3:03 p.m. . . .

A somber group of people in business suits had been escorted into the elegant conference room at the front of the office suite. Barton and Jackson, having reached an in-principle agreement, sat with Landis, Jenkins, and Ford in the back conference room.

"You look good sitting there together," said Jenkins. "Now's the moment of truth. You'll have to go in there and show a unified front. No quibbling about details in front of the investors."

Barton nodded. Jackson looked over and put a hand on Barton's shoulder. "Just like the big wave, man," said Jackson.

"The one that almost killed me?" asked Barton.

"Yeah," said Jackson. "That one. I didn't let you drown."

"No," said Barton, "you didn't."

"Nobody's going to drown this time either," said Jackson.

Saturday, April 10, 9:31 a.m. . . .

This is National Independent Radio. Now for today's business news headlines:

In a striking development, the mechanics union at Santa Monica Aerospace has expressed public support for the company's beleaguered CEO, James Barton, and suggested that it will endorse a plan rejected last week by the company's board of directors. By endorsing the plan, it's believed the union is signaling a willingness to make contractual concessions. Specific concessions have not been disclosed, but an unconfirmed report suggests that the union has expressed new flexibility on its willingness to be part of future restructuring of the company.

Also at this hour, an unconfirmed report suggests that Bill Ford, SMA board member and former SMA CEO, has also expressed support for Barton as current CEO of SMA. Ford expressed support for the plan that was reportedly the subject of last week's rancorous board meeting. It's unclear how this will play out, but some analysts are now arguing that this might turn the tide in favor of Jim Barton and his plans for the company. More on this story as it evolves.

Monday, April 12, 10:17 a.m. . . .

"Okay, Bill," said Haas. "Moment of truth . . ."

On the top floor of SMA headquarters, an emergency board meeting had convened at 9:30 a.m. and gotten immediately down to business: a revote on Barton's plan for the company. Barton had made a brief statement, reporting details from conversations with unions, partners, and investors on Friday and over the weekend. Then Haas had moved things directly to a vote. Half the board members attended by telephone, and Haas simply followed the order in which he'd recorded the votes at the last meeting. The votes up until this point had exactly replicated the pattern from last time. Bill Ford, however, turned the tide.

"I vote yes this time," he said quietly. What sounded like a frustrated sigh came into the room from somewhere out on the phone link. Other than that, however, there was no reaction. Haas, in businesslike fashion, completed the round and announced the result:

"By a narrow margin, we now have support for this plan. Any comments?"

There were none.

"Okay, then, this meeting is adjourned. Thank you for being available on such short notice." He turned to Barton. "Lots of press waiting downstairs. Shall we go down and let them know?"

Barton nodded, but his attention was still on the members of the board. "I'd like to add my thanks to Ron's," he said. "You won't be sorry."

Barton's eyes instinctively sought out Goldman, but he wasn't there; he was one of the members joining by phone.

Smithson, who was present, spoke: "We're behind you, Jim." She looked around at the other board members. "That's the way this works, folks. We voted. We have a result. We get behind it, or we leave the board. Right?"

This met with mumbled agreement.

"Okay then," said Haas. "Let's go see the press corps . . ."

Monday, April 12, 4:01 p.m. . . .

This is National Independent Radio. Now for today's business news headlines:

In a startling sequence of events, the CEO of Santa Monica Aerospace, James Barton, who as recently as last week had heard almost universal calls for his resignation, has seized control of the company's situation. This morning, the company's board of directors narrowly approved his restructuring plan. In a further dramatic move, Robert Goldman, who only recently joined the board, has announced his resignation. We have an unconfirmed report at this hour that his seat will be taken by Clara Jenkins, the former CEO of Welacore Pharmaceuticals. More on this story as it develops.

Wednesday, April 14, 7:46 a.m. . . .

When Krishnan rang the doorbell, Barton was ready. He finished a last sip of coffee and reached for his rolling bag. Leaving and locking the door of his Venice bungalow, he glanced in the direction of his neighbor, dandelion farmer and international corporate power broker. Without spotting her, Barton walked past Krishnan to the waiting car. He found Bill Ford already in the backseat.

"Morning, Bill," said Barton.

"Good morning, Jim," Ford answered. "Ready to close some deals?"

"Ready as can be," said Barton. "Long flight though."

"Yes," said Ford. "Beijing. What is that, in hours?"

"About eighteen, all told," said Krishnan, also climbing in.

"We're meeting Montero there?" asked Ford.

Barton nodded. "In Beijing, yes."

"So by next week," said Ford, "with any luck, our little house of cards might just have a foundation."

"Yes," said Barton. "It's getting a little bit more like cardboard, though, don't you think? Tending toward plywood. And one could say that we already have the makings of a foundation."

"Don't jinx us," said Ford.

"Okay," said Barton. "But my fingers are already growing together from being so often crossed."

"Mine, too," said Ford. "Mine, too."

Reflection

Did Jim Barton make his own luck, or was what happened just a fortuitous event?

A bluebird's arrival at the end of a long winter signifies spring: do you think Barton has reason to expect this turn of events similarly predicts sunny skies ahead for himself and SMA after a stretch of tough times?

In hindsight, did Barton appropriately work with Goldman as a board member? What might he have done differently?

Execute, Execute, Execute

SSEER, a simulated senior executive experience role-play by Simavatar Studios

A deafening roar fills Barton's ears. He gulps for air as he comprehends the precariousness of his perch on a strut nestled under one wing of a high-flying turboprop plane. A landscape stretches wide and far beneath his feet. Seized with acrophobia, he barely notices that someone at his side has locked arms with him.

"Ready, Jim?" Luce shouts in his ear.

Barton realizes that he's wearing a helmet but can't figure out why. *Ready for what?* he thinks, and he's about to speak it when Luce leaps from the strut, pulling Barton off, too.

Free fall.

The wind blows past Barton. The ground rises toward him. Luce loosens his grip on Barton's arm and swings his body outward, turning so that they can face each other. They're both laying out flat against the air whooshing up past them, both looking down, and now Luce interlaces his fingers with Barton's, on both hands, bracing them in a falling formation. They're just a couple of feet from each other, and Luce locks eyes with Barton.

"Okay, boss," says Luce. "Over to you."

"What's that?" says Barton. It's hard to hear and he has to shout over the wind noise to make sure Luce can hear. "What do you mean 'over to me'?"

"You're supposed to take it from here," shouts Luce. "Now, what do we do?"

"*You* pulled *me* off the plane," Barton protests. He doesn't have to remind himself to shout. The adrenalin takes care of that.

"This is what you wanted, isn't it, Jim?" Luce answers. "You wanted a shot at this job. We helped. Now you've got it. And I recommend you get busy. The ground is coming up at us pretty fast."

"*This* is *not* what I signed up for," Barton yells.

"Nonsense," Luce yells back. "It's exactly what you signed up for! Get real, Jim."

"But I don't know what to do," Barton says.

"Oh, now you tell us?" Luce says. "I hope you're a fast learner then, 'cause a lot of people are depending on it."

Composing himself, Barton pats at his vest, looking for a rip cord. The little he knows about skydiving suggests it should be there. But he finds nothing.

"I don't know how to open the parachute," Barton shouts. "Do you know how to do it?"

"You've always gotten it to open before," Luce says. "How'd you do it then?"

It's a metaphor, Barton knows that. He's been in situations he didn't know how to get out of before. Where he didn't know what to do and didn't even know what he didn't know. And somehow he'd managed.

"There's supposed to be a rip cord," Barton shouts. "But there isn't one. I don't know what to do."

"Think, Jim," says Luce, his voice taking on a begging tone. "We need you to figure this out."

Barton grows angry. "This is not helpful. This is a nightmare, not a management sim." He is using a new, portable rig for the SSEER, one that he can take with him on the trip to China. But clearly this new rig is defective. He shouts: "SUSPEND SIMULATION!"

Barton, hovering in midair, can make out buildings and people in the landscape below. For a moment, he ponders what would happen if he crashed into the ground within the SSEER environment. It couldn't hurt him. Could it?

He decides not to chance it: "ENTER NEW SIM!" he shouts.

Instantly, his body rotates to a standing position, and the helmet and gear he'd been wearing vanishes. The wind noise disappears from his ears, replaced by repetitive hissing and beeping.

Barton is clad in surgical scrubs standing over a still form draped in sanitary fabric on an operating table. Between his latex-gloved fingers, he now holds a small pair of forceps and a razor-sharp scalpel, both smeared with blood.

"Geez, that was close," says a voice from nearby. Barton turns a little, sees Luce behind him and to the right, also dressed in scrubs and holding up a tray that contains other surgical instruments. "You almost lost him," Luce adds.

Barton notices several others standing around, also dressed for surgery. Maggie Landis is there, as well Clarke Gardner and Ace Jackson.

"You would've lost him," Jackson says, "if we hadn't stepped in to save your butt. Think you've got it under control now? Or are we going to have to keep riding to your rescue?"

"Hey," Barton says, improvising, "we're a team, right? I need your help. I need all of you." He notices Susan Akita behind Landis. Behind Akita, he spots Rajit Palepu.

Barton notices that all eyes are on him, and their faces express a common sentiment: we thought we could depend on you to save this patient, Jim Barton—but now we're not so sure.

"It's okay, Jimmy boy."

A familiar voice conveys these words. It's Ms. Jenkins, as she'd become known to him recently. She emerges from beyond the other medical forms to take up a position right beside him. Placing a hand on his shoulder, she reassures him: "Steady, Jim. You can do this."

"Okay," he answers. He looks around at the others, their faces still searching his. "Yes, I can do this. I can."

"We're convinced, Jim," she says. "Aren't we?" This last question is addressed to the others, and Jenkins signals the right answer with exaggerated nods of her own, waiting for each of them to also begin bobbing their heads in agreement. "That's right," she says when all have begun nodding.

She turns back to Barton. "From here on out, Jimmy boy, it's execution. You've got to close the deals and grind out the results. You've got to stay on schedule, address the unexpected when it comes up, and press your people to problem solve like crazy. You've got to stay on it, Jimmy. At this point, it's really pretty simple: execute, execute, execute. Okay?"

Barton nods. "Okay," he says. "Execution."

Jenkins gestures. "Now get back in there!"

Barton looks back at the patient, noticing a chart on a nearby table. In the "name" field on the chart it says, "Mr. SM Aerospace." The respirator hisses. The heart monitor beeps. Barton raises his scalpel and positions it for another incision.

CHAPTER 16

Globalization

"Mr. Wu says we would like to assemble the plane here in China," said the translator. Mr. Wu nodded.

Barton was flabbergasted. Though perhaps he should not have been. Montero had warned Barton that this might happen, but he'd discounted it.

It felt like a time warp. Twice before, the negotiation with Mr. Wu had reached this same point. Both times, Barton had politely replied that political concerns in the United States made final assembly in China impossible, but that SMA would be happy to assemble significant components there. Each time, Mr. Wu had nodded and moved on to discussing the size of the potential order from SMA and the price. The numbers of planes in the potential order had grown each time, while the price per unit had declined only somewhat. For SMA, the deal kept getting sweeter and sweeter.

Barton concealed his growing excitement. This deal, if he could close it, would be *the* launch order that made financing of the new plane and the company's transformation possible. It felt tantalizingly close. At the end of every conversation with Mr. Wu, Barton left sure that the deal was practically done and the signing imminent. But the next day Mr. Wu would start the conversation at the beginning again, rewinding and repeating. Barton began to think that one of his answers in this ritual might be wrong. It seemed that they were destined to repeat the ritual until he got that answer right. And he had a suspicion which answer it was.

The "final assembly in China" answer. Barton had always answered with a diplomatic "no, I'm afraid that's not possible." Apparently this needed to change to "yes, of course, we'd love to."

Barton hadn't wanted to be the one negotiating. He'd wanted Montero to do it. But within the social pecking order that prevailed in the minds of these clients, that would not do at all. It would be disrespectful to Mr. Wu to ask him to negotiate with anyone except the highest-ranking person present. According to his title, Wu was a mere VP himself, a rank not nearly as high as some of the other people in the room, so the reverse logic seemed not to apply. Montero had figured out why everyone kept deferring to Mr. Wu.

"Mr. Wu is the ranking party member," Montero whispered in Barton's ear. "He's the real power in the room. You'll have to convince him."

Barton nodded.

Of course. He should have realized.

It had been a humbling several days. Working in the East Coast financial services industry had given Barton little sense of airfoils, lift, or reverse thrusters. But it had provided even less learning about negotiating in other cultures, which he'd now had to do both in China and in Japan.

In Japan, he'd created a minor incident by involving Angel Crow, who turned out to be fluent in Japanese, in the conversation. The Mitsubishi and Fuji engineers he'd interacted with had definite gender issues with Crow. She had tried to warn him that they might, but he hadn't listened. *Not a thing to compromise on,* he'd thought. But it had made the deal with SMA's Japanese partners harder. He'd also brought along Shelly Kranz, SMA's top test pilot, and Susan Akita, of course, the company's top engineer. All women. Montero told Barton he was an idiot, straight out, no sugar coating. "What do you plan to do when we sell to the Saudis?" he asked.

Barton didn't apologize. He had no intention of cutting his top talent out of conversations because of their genders. But he admitted to being blindsided by this and other "cultural issues." He had no idea yet how to square the need to sell SMA planes globally with his convictions about fairness and gender equality.

Having the legendary engineer, Bill Ford, with them on the trip eventually overcame the issues with Crow, Kranz, and Akita, but even then the situation had caught Barton unaware: he'd been surprised how the

Japanese engineers fawned over and deferred to Ford, even in the presence of Barton, the CEO. In seating arrangements at dinners, and in many other ways, it was obvious that Barton's position did not measure up alongside Ford's stature. The Japanese engineers clearly knew Barton was a finance guy and just as clearly didn't think very much of that.

Nevertheless, Barton, with the help of his team, had reinforced and strengthened SMA's partner deals, and broadened the scope of two of them. These partner companies already had big deals with Boeing and Airbus for major airliner components, and it made sense for SMA to leverage that expertise in the construction of its own plane. In some ways, the new SMA plane would push the boundaries beyond what Boeing or Airbus were asking the partners for, but mostly SMA could follow those bigger companies and benefit from what the Japanese engineering companies had already learned. There were still issues within Akita's organization with SMA engineers unwilling to rely on partner expertise. But the expertise was there, in the partner companies, and Akita assured Barton that her staff would adjust. "It's the right way to do it," she said, and he believed her.

The big challenge, however, the make-or-break challenge, remained: Mr. Wu and his ritualistic repetition. After a long pause, Barton adjusted his answer.

"Let me sit down with my team and see what we can do," he said. "Perhaps we can get a bit more creative."

The translator conveyed that to Mr. Wu, who smiled, nodded, and promptly proceeded with the conversation, following the usual outline. Yet again, the numbers in the potential order increased. *Thus increasing his leverage,* Barton thought. *It's kind of like drawing a line under that part of the conversation,* he realized. Or like holding up a small chunk of meat in front of a dog when you're training it. *He's training me to assemble planes in China,* mused Barton, smiling and nodding back at Wu.

Tuesday, April 27, 1:52 p.m....

Barton convened his traveling team in a conference room back at the hotel. Everyone was there: Barton, Ford, Gardner, Akita, Marochek, Kranz, Crow, Krishnan, and Montero. There'd been a flurry of phone calling to prepare for the meeting and checking with various people back in Santa Monica and a few in DC. Now, members of the team, tired but also excited, sat around a table in a nondescript room with no windows.

"The moment of truth has arrived," said Barton.

"Another one," said Akita. Barton stopped, surprised at the interruption, then smiled at the uncharacteristic joke from Akita. They were jetlagged, sleep deprived, and overexcited—riding a travel buzz.

"Yes, another one," said Barton, "with more to come." The others laughed. "We need to decide," Barton continued, suddenly serious, "what we're going to do here." The others stifled their giddiness. "I need to hear what you think. It's pretty clear that we're going round and round in the negotiations.

"The numbers and prices are looking good. If we can close this deal, we'll get the financing we need to build the new plane—to transform SMA." Here he paused to look at Gardner, who nodded confirmation. "This is the infamous 'launch order'—or it can be. *If* we can close the deal.

"The hitch," Barton continued, "is that it seems clear that they consider assembling some airplanes here in China a requirement for closing the deal. Jose, you've been there for all the discussions. Do you agree with that assessment?"

"I do," said Montero. "It's become obvious."

"My question," said Barton, "is simple: What do we do? Assembling in China will generate a raft of issues for us. Some of them have to do with practical things, like can we get that to work? Can we assure quality? Control cost? Manage risk? Other issues have to do with people. The unions won't like it. The engineers won't either. Still other issues will be political. Though it's a decreasing part of our business, we remain a defense contractor, and China is a geopolitical rival of the United States with a powerhouse economy and growing influence in the world. The same factors that bring us to this doorstep in search of our launch order make the idea of doing too much work in China threatening to some. We're a private company. But if provoked, political leaders can make things much harder on us.

"We're going to decide something here, today. Mr. Wu clearly expects an answer before we leave. I don't want to go back home without a clear resolution. Some things are apparent, I think. If we don't do the deal now, it might not be as good next time. It's a bird in the hand, and an excellent bird at that. But we don't quite have a grip on it yet.

"So," Barton finished, "talk to me, people: What are we going to do?"

No one said anything. No one wanted to go first.

Finally, Montero spread his hands, palms up, in a theatrical shrug. "You know what I'm going to say—let's close the damn deal. Choose to move forward. Agree to their terms and then manage the consequences. Nobody said this was supposed to be easy. But we've just about got the major part of what we need to do this thing. I say we grab it."

Barton looked at Akita. She looked unsure. She realized Barton wanted to hear from her. But her comment was noncommittal. "Possibly," she said, "we don't have everyone in the room we need to decide this. All of us want this deal. But maybe we need to pull in some other people before we agree to something like this."

"Other people. Like who?" Barton asked.

"Our DC people?" Akita suggested. "More of my staff? Union reps?" Barton sensed something deeper in Akita's hesitation, but he wasn't sure she knew what it was. He was about to probe to try to surface it when Gardner spoke.

"I had a long talk with the DC folks," he said. "They're saying there *is* political risk. They won't make guarantees. But they think we can manage it. The big guys, like Boeing, Intel, many others, provide cover for us. They're already doing lots in China."

"Airbus is already doing final assembly in China," Akita added. "But it's a considerably smaller and less technologically advanced plane than ours."

Gardner added, "The DC guys think any flak we get for assembling cargo planes in China can be redirected toward semiconductors or something like that. 'Cargo plane' doesn't sound high-tech enough to get people really worried. Of course, that's wrong. They are high-tech enough. An immensely complex integrated system that makes use of some of the world's most advanced technology. But people hear 'cargo plane' and they don't think that."

"That's the political issue," said Kranz. "But maybe we should think about the underlying issue. Regardless of how 'cargo plane' sounds to the public, or how stirred up politicians will likely get, do we—knowing what we know about the new design—think there's a national security issue? Will we be giving away too much to a rival power? If we think so, maybe we should consider that as we try to figure out the right thing to do."

"Susan?" Barton said to Akita.

"There's some very advanced technology in the proposed design," she said. "It's not clear to me, however, that any of it is technology they can't access many other ways. Working with Airbus, for example. Or any of a dozen other companies."

Ford and Montero nodded in excited agreement. Others remained more hesitant, but Barton had the sense that no one in the room really objected to what she'd said. Barton looked back at Kranz, who didn't seem inclined to rejoin on her previous point.

"What about the unions?" Ford said, when it became clear that the question about transferring advanced technology had lost momentum.

Barton nodded. "That will be tricky," he said. "We've pretty much convinced them that selling off some of our manufacturing capability will be good for employment. Now we're turning right around and moving work offshore."

"But we've got order guarantees built into the deal with the unions," said Gardner. "Moving some assembly to China won't hurt them in the short term because of the guarantees. And in the long run, they'll see orders from other companies."

"From our standpoint, is assembly in China inconsistent with the guarantees we've offered the unions?" asked Barton. "Do the guarantees become too expensive if we assemble in China?"

Gardner was shaking his head. "No," he said. "It's different work. The guarantees have to do with subassemblies and components. Assembly has been an area of declining numbers for some time. And we'll still do some of it in North America, right? We're not talking about doing all of the assembly in China, are we?"

"No," said Barton, "that's right."

He looked around the room. "So where are we? Susan, who else do you suggest we pull into the conversation?"

"Some of my staff. But I don't think there's reason to do that, actually. I already know what they'll all say. Some—the same ones who don't like a lot of the new stuff we're proposing—will dislike the idea a lot. Others will say, 'Fine, we'll figure out how to do it.'"

"So we've already heard from the DC folks, we think we can manage the unions, and there's no reason to bring in Susan's naysayers."

No one disagreed with any of this.

"It sounds to me," Barton said, "like we're deciding to do this. To agree to assembly in China."

No one answered.

"Well?" Barton said.

Marochek, who had said nothing so far, cleared his throat. He unfolded his lanky frame from where he'd leaned back in a chair, put his feet firmly on the floor, rested his elbows on the table, and spoke: "I'm sorry. I'm going to have to spit in the punch bowl here." He stopped and looked around. Disapproval radiated from most of the faces around the table. But Marochek pressed on: "I don't think we can do this. Not because of what we've been discussing, but for some of the reasons you mentioned at the start, reasons that we haven't been discussing: Practicality. Quality. Risk management."

Gardner waved a hand dismissively. "With all due respect, Paul, manufacturing always says, 'We can't do it; it's too risky.' That's happened every time we've outsourced anything for as long as I can remember. The finance guys say we can save money doing it; the manufacturing guys say it will be a disaster if we try. In the end, we do it and figure out how to manage the risk."

Marochek shook his head. "I wish you were right, Clarke. I really do. But this is different. This is not just another outsourcing decision. There's a strategic issue here." He looked to Barton with a questioning look, as if wondering whether his comments were welcome.

"Oh, we've got to hear you out now," said Barton, a hint of annoyance in his voice. "Say more."

Marochek looked worried but continued: "Our new cargo airplane's assembly is going to be very different from the 'stick building' of a plane on the assembly line that we've traditionally done. Our new process will involve snapping together Tier-1 components fully stuffed and pretty much completed. This is a new kind of final assembly, one that we don't have experience with—clicking together sophisticated components, much faster and with no monument tools involved. Everything's supposed to be coordinated well enough that when it comes to putting it all together, everything just fits.

"We're planning to do this in Seattle—probably in existing factory space at Boeing's Everett factory. Already, Boeing's fleet of 'Dreamlifters,' 747s converted to transport major components, are flying in and out of that facility, and it is our hope that we will be able to make arrangements with Boeing to use this fleet. This is new, too. Very significantly, the new process will include coordination of engineering change orders throughout an extended supply chain of strategic partners creating sophisticated components that will all snap together at final assembly. We don't yet know how to do this either.

"I've been studying the Boeing 787 case, talking with my peers at Boeing. Like Boeing 787 manufacturing, we are effectively shifting the process of outsourcing from 'build to print' to 'build to performance.' Under the old system, our engineers created all the drawings for every part and major component of the airplane. If a supplier was having problems, we had our own engineering SWAT team standing ready to be parachuted into the outsourcer's facility with engineering drawings in hand to fix the problems. If the supplier did not or could not respond, we exercised our contractual right to break the contract, and award the contract to another supplier.

"With strategic outsourcing partnering, that's not going to be possible. We won't have direct control or the threat of shifting to another outsourcer. We're going to have to choose our outsourcing partners more carefully than ever before and create open and trusting relationships with them, so we can maintain full information transparency in the supply chain. Our partners will be doing design engineering and detailed engineering drawings, including tooling, for major components, like wings and fuselage sections. Our engineers will be working closely with our strategic outsourcing partners, but we won't have the expertise to parachute in and fix problems the way we used to. And with partners so integrated into our processes, it just won't be feasible to shift, in midstream, to a different outsourcer.

"It's natural to imagine that strategic outsourcing, versus tactical outsourcing, still mainly benefits us by yielding a lower overall airplane cost than we could achieve in the old way. But that's not the only benefit, or even the main one. With this new approach, we can tap skills we don't have. We can build a different, better airplane. But it's going to take a lot of hard work to learn to build strategic outsourcing relationships with our new airplane partners.

"I don't think we've spent enough time considering the challenges of managing a different kind of supply chain. I'm worried about it. Our risk here is huge; it's a fundamentally different approach. When the outsourcing process changes from tactical to strategic, managing risk becomes a whole new ball game. Learning to manage this risk with strategic outsourcing partners requires unprecedented levels of trust—relationships that lead to transparency, the visibility into our partner's operations that we must have. Boeing learned all this the hard way. It experienced unprecedented 787 airplane delivery delays and penalty costs that it's still struggling with. We would never survive similar problems.

"The plain fact is that we will be transforming final assembly to a much different way than what Airbus is already doing in China. To try to do all this new stuff in China involves too much risk. We just can't manage it. Our shareholders or prospective investors wouldn't tolerate us taking on this amount of risk. If our investors understand what's at stake, this risk should be a deal breaker. Which means that if we agree to this, and then in due diligence investors reach this same conclusion about the risks, it'll all unravel. This won't be the launch order we need, no matter how big it is."

Marochek finished. No one responded. Contagious disappointment spread through the room as the people who understood Marochek's argument realized he was right, and as those who didn't understand noticed the reactions of those who did. Oxygen seemed to leave the room. Barton, distraught by this sudden development, turned to Akita: "Susan?"

All eyes turned to Akita. She looked down at the table and began to nod.

"Paul is right," she said quietly. "If Jen Sharp were here, she'd agree, too. There would be IT issues. Big ones."

"I agree," said Ford.

"Well, I wish," said Barton, exasperated, "that someone would explain it to me. I don't get it. Why is this harder, this clicking parts together? It sounds easier."

Gardner answered. "Jim, you'll get this if you think it through. Like Paul said, it's a strategic issue."

Barton starred daggers at Gardner. The CFO had changed sides. It felt to Barton like betrayal.

"This is the biggest issue of all," Gardner continued. "We're talking about a new business model for SMA, making the company a large-scale systems integrator. The capabilities associated with this kind of integration, like our ability to manage change orders throughout such a complex network of partners, will be our core competency and our strategic differentiator. We have to protect this. And in creating and protecting this core competency, *place matters*. It's a version of the same argument you've been making about why we need to move our engineers to the Seattle area."

Barton was frustrated. But he began to see what the others meant. For a long time, he sat in silence, thinking, all eyes on him.

Then Barton turned to Marochek: "Thanks, Paul," he said quietly, "for bringing us to our senses. For bringing *me* to my senses. I was letting my desire to close this deal cloud my judgment and divert me from the fundamentals of our strategy. A strategy I've been advocating. You might have just saved this company."

"Or not," said Montero. "What are we going to do? Are we seriously going to pass on this deal?" His tone of voice stretched beyond frustration to annoyance.

But it was a good question. Once again, the room became quiet. As Barton looked from person to person, he realized that no one could see a way out. *Maybe this is it,* he thought. *The end of the road. A dead end we won't be coming back out of . . .*

"Maybe there's a way . . ." a new voice began and then faltered. Everyone turned to look at Angel Crow, the IT support staff person. Generally, she and Krishnan remained quiet during discussions like this one. She cleared her throat and went on. "Maybe," she said, "we can explain this to them."

"Explain what?" asked Akita.

"That we're still learning a new way of building airplanes. That we need to learn it first, before we do it elsewhere. That we'll consider doing it elsewhere once we've got it figured out. Maybe even that they can participate in some of the learning."

"I'm going to convince them of that?" said Barton skeptically.

"No," interjected Marochek. "Not you. No offense, but you're just a finance guy."

Barton smiled, and in the same moment, everyone in the room realized the implication in Marochek's words. Heads turned in unison toward Ford.

"You have to do it, Bill," said Barton. "You're the legendary engineer. It's an engineering argument. Only you have the credibility to make that argument."

"Will he talk to me? Mr. Wu, I mean," Ford asked.

"He will," said Montero. "Mr. Wu's advisers were trained at MIT and the University of Washington. Listening to our conversation here, I'd be surprised if Mr. Wu hasn't already heard this argument about why it will be impossible to assemble in China."

"So," Barton said, "if he knows we're going to say that, it means . . ."

"That he's actually angling for something else," said Gardner, completing the thought. "Maybe a promise to do some assembly in China at a later date?"

Montero nodded. "That sounds right to me. It fits with the way I suspect they'd negotiate. Bill, you're the man to make the argument and offer the assurances of future cooperation. You're the only one of us, other than Jim, that he'll talk to. But I believe he will talk with you happily about this. I suspect he'll be reassured to hear an argument that he's likely already heard from his engineering advisers."

Barton looked at Ford. "Bill?

"Okay," said Ford. "It's worth a try. I say let's try it."

"Susan?"

"I agree. Let's do it."

"Paul?"

Marochek squirmed in his chair, but only for a moment: "We can do it. I say yes. Bill, let's work together to come up with the most convincing arguments."

Excitement had returned to the room.

"Do you want me to schedule another meeting this afternoon with Mr. Wu?" asked Krishnan.

"Why not?" said Barton. "Let's get this thing done."

Reflection

How do you think Barton should manage the conflict between his convictions about gender equality and fairness and clients' cultural preferences?

Has Barton's China team figured out their Chinese potential strategic partners' motivations and what they realistically want? Why? Why not?

If you were in Mr. Wu's shoes, what would be your response to SMA's revised proposal in the negotiations?

If you were Jim Barton going in to pitch the revised proposal, what kinds of contingency planning should you do in advance? For each of the alternatives, what should be your counterargument?

CHAPTER 17

Execution

Tuesday, July 20, 10:26 a.m. . . .

"There's not enough *green* on this dashboard, people," said Barton, his voice conveying rising temper.

Rajit Palepu stood frozen, not saying anything, not continuing his presentation. Barton had interrupted him in midsentence. Silence descended like fog into the large conference room. Akita appeared angry. Marochek looked down at his hands, seemingly embarrassed. The product and manufacturing engineers in the room displayed a range of emotions, from annoyance to disappointment to dismay.

This major review of progress on the new plane had begun promptly at 10 a.m. and would continue throughout the day, with only a short break for lunch. Akita and Marochek had fashioned a status dashboard, a list of major tasks with green-yellow-red coding to show progress and issues. They'd begun by passing out the dashboard and explaining what the colors meant (progress according to plan, plan at risk, serious issue). According to the agenda, each of the groups would then present, to each other and to Barton, moving from an explanation of issues to joint problem solving.

Barton had hoped to see the dashboard in advance of the meeting, but it had not been ready. They'd been working at full speed, so Barton didn't think it was necessarily a bad thing that they were getting things done at the last minute. Moving fast was exactly what he wanted.

But as Palepu began the first presentation, Barton remained stuck, leafing through the multipage dashboard document. He'd expected to see a lot of green, some yellow, maybe two or three reds. But when Akita handed him the sheaf of papers, he saw something very different.

The document was ablaze with yellow and red. More yellow than red, but more of both than he liked. Palepu had moved to his fourth slide, starting with some good news, an area in which they were doing well, when Barton could not contain himself and interrupted.

"And there's *way* too much yellow and red," he added.

No one responded. Akita interrupted the uncomfortable silence: "How do you want to proceed, Jim?" she asked. "Do you want to continue with the agenda, or move through the dashboard in some other way?"

Barton felt his patience slipping away. "Frankly, Susan and Paul, I'm stunned," he said. "Look at all this red! And yellow! The page looks like it's on fire! Why haven't I heard about any of these—?"

"You have heard about many of them!" protested Akita. "Maybe all of them!"

"I thought there'd be a small number of reds, all of which I'd recognize—"

"If you'll let us get into this," said Akita, not backing down, "you'll realize that you *are* familiar with many of the reds—"

"—but just look at this!" said Barton, waving the document though the air, almost shouting.

He glanced around the room, seeking to connect with others as exasperated as he felt, but he did not find the room very friendly. A lot of people stared angrily back at him.

"This is not easy, what you're asking us to do, Jim," said Akita, taking an uncharacteristically candid and casual tack. She spoke calmly, trying to get the meeting back to moving in a productive direction. "There are going to be problems. That doesn't mean we can't solve them."

"I don't think you're right," Barton said, stuck on one of Akita's earlier claims. "I don't think I've heard about a lot of these." He tossed the dashboard down onto the table.

Akita, not bothering to conceal her irritation, confronted him: "Show me one," she challenged. "Show me one item on this list you haven't heard anything about."

Surprised, Barton retreated. He stared back at Akita, then picked up the papers. He took out his glasses, and reconsidered them.

"This one, item 19, Data Interface—"

Jen Sharp, the CIO, spoke from a position further down the table from Akita. "That's the IT issue we discussed last week, if you'll remember, Jim. As you know, we need to be able to interface our systems with key partners. We need lots of their cooperation to do this. It's red because right now we're not getting the cooperation we need and so we don't see how to get all the interfaces in place in accordance with the timetable. It's red because we need your attention to it. We're going to need a high-level conversation with partner execs to get them to prioritize the issue. Right now we don't think they're taking our timetable seriously. It's something we need from you."

Barton remembered. He nodded.

"Okay. I can do that," he said. "I'll make some calls."

He flipped to the second page of the document, spotted another unfamiliar item. "How about this one?" he said. "Process for angled joining surfaces using composites? What the heck is that?"

Akita looked to Palepu. "Rajit? Want to take that one?"

The brilliant but cowed SMA engineer nodded. "Sure," he said. "We've been working with our partners' top experts on this one. It's something we don't know how to do yet. To be honest, we're pretty much going to need a scientific breakthrough here."

"And do you have that on the schedule yet?" asked Barton.

Palepu looked at Barton. Then over to Akita. Then back at Barton. Finally, Palepu spoke: "Do we have a scientific breakthrough on the schedule yet . . . ?"

Barton turned to Akita, the absurdity of his question dawning on him as he did so. Though he tried to avoid it, Barton began to smile and then laugh. "Yes," he said, "I guess I was wondering when we might expect this scientific breakthrough. Though I can see that such a thing might be hard to schedule exactly."

Laughter swept through room. Fueled by the tension built up from Barton's outburst, the hilarity ran a course longer than was probably warranted.

But the laughter changed the mood in the meeting. Barton nodded. "Okay," he said, getting a handle on his frustration. "Okay," he repeated.

"Maybe you'd like us to start lying to you," said a voice from somewhere in the row of people sitting behind those at the table. Barton couldn't tell exactly who said it. But that didn't matter. It was a good point.

"No," Barton said. "If there's this much red and yellow, I *do* want to know about it. I want you to tell me, even if it's bad news." He looked around the room, making eye contact with people. "I think I need to stay this involved," he said. "I think we need to keep having these meetings, and confronting these lists, and I need to help you solve these problems. Whether it's phone calls, or moving resources around, whatever. Do people here agree that I need to be involved in this conversation at this level of detail?"

He paused. People nodded.

"We appreciate the close attention," said Marochek.

"Yes," seconded Akita, "we do."

She exchanged glances with the members of her team sitting around the table and then continued: "There was a discussion, in fact, about how much bad news we should bring you. I insisted that we come clean on everything, and that we err on the side of calling out more yellows and reds. For example, we do think we can achieve the composites breakthrough Rajit mentioned in a reasonable amount of time, even if we're not sure of the exact timing. But if you've got a problem with this approach, with so many yellows and reds, it's my fault."

Barton shook his head. "No," he said. "That's the right approach. I see that now." It wasn't quite an apology. He didn't feel inclined to apologize. They all wanted the same thing, and if he'd succumbed to frustration for a moment . . . well, that conveyed an accurate sense of the importance of the schedule. It wasn't entirely misplaced, and everyone knew that. No apology, from anyone, was called for here.

"Let's go through these," said Barton. "I'd like to call off the presentations. Maybe we'll get back to them later. But right now I'd like to walk through these items one by one."

Barton felt agreement in the room and a sense of resolve.

"Okay," said Akita. "Change of plans. Rajit, how about you take these first three?"

Thursday, October 7, 2:23 p.m. . . .

"That all sounds brilliant, Susan," Barton said. "I'm not sure I see the problem."

Akita nodded. "I haven't come to the problem part yet," she said. "Ordinarily I'd just handle this myself, but I thought I should brief you on it and get your input, because now marketing and two customers are involved. It has the potential to become a bigger deal. I didn't want you to be blindsided by it."

"Well," said Barton, dismayed, "let's hear the rest of it."

Susan Akita and Jim Barton sat together in the conference room off Barton's office at SMA, engaged in what had become a weekly one-on-one update, in addition to the less frequent dashboard status meetings. Akita had been explaining how her product development engineers had implemented a very progressive approach to the design of the cockpit controls for the SMA plane.

The "human-machine interface" provided great opportunities for creating marketable selling points for the new plane, especially if the SMA cockpit could be arranged in a new way, still reliable and functional, in compliance with all safety standards and building on the great ideas of the past, but differentiated from that of other planes—an improvement on past designs. The details of which control resided where and how the system all fit together constituted just one of a large number of design challenges that remained after finalizing the conceptual design and securing the launch order and its dependent financing.

The launch order from a Chinese company had been bigger than anyone had ever dreamed, a huge win for SMA and Barton. But SMA executives believed the situation was even more favorable than the large original order would suggest. The Chinese government owned the airlines there, so winning the order had required convincing state officials. Those same officials would influence the decisions of other companies within China. Thus, this first order gave SMA a better chance at future orders. And there were a lot of companies in that country that needed to move cargo around.

As good as all this was, the launch order had come with strings attached. Ford had convinced Mr. Wu to put off his insistence on final assembly in China, even though all agreed that the possibility would be revisited later (in fact, at a time explicitly specified in the purchase agreement). In the six months since then, however, engineers from the Chinese company had become a fixture on the SMA project, ever present and involving themselves in a large number of design activities. Never before had customers been so involved in the details of design processes at SMA. Indeed, according to Akita, nothing quite like it had ever before been seen in the aerospace industry.

To be sure, customers had been involved in design decisions in the airline industry since early days. Tours of mock-ups of airplane interiors, discussions about major design decisions, that sort of thing, had long been commonplace. But Akita and her hotshot engineers had gone much, much further for the "SMA-7," as the new plane was now being called.

Influenced by the research of MIT scientist Eric von Hippel, Akita's engineers had developed "design toolkits" that allowed "lead users"—typically experienced pilots known for having expertise and strong opinions—to create their own prototype control arrangements to try out in simulation.* The toolkits, based on the SSEER environment technology developed by one of Jonathan Luce's new companies, allowed customers to fly simulated planes with cockpit control arrangements of their own design. Configurator software prevented impossible designs from being created and also made sure that designs adhered to certain principles of sound cockpit design, arrived at through careful learning within the industry over the years. But beyond these constraints, many new things remained possible.

Customers weren't sure what to make of the toolkits at first. Once they started to try them, though, they embraced the new approach. SMA had first shared the toolkits with domestic companies and later with the launch customer, which had raised enthusiasm about the approach to a new level. The result: rich conversations and collaboration between pilots and the engineers who developed the controls for the new SMA plane. Together, these teams of lead users and engineers had made breakthroughs, which, Akita assured Barton, should result in a cockpit interior vastly better and different from anything another airplane company could

*See, for example, Eric von Hippel, *Democratizing Innovation* (Cambridge, MA: MIT Press, 2005).

offer. Other ideas had come from a "crowdsourcing" project: the company offered monetary prizes to a web-based community of aviation enthusiasts, payable to the submitted ideas that the company chose to implement.

"We'll win design awards," Akita predicted. These processes and their results were what Barton had declared "brilliant" a mere few moments earlier.

"The problem," Akita said, "is that we now have too many design suggestions—suggestions in which different customers have become very invested."

"Can't we do different versions for each customer?" Barton asked.

"We could," said Akita, "but there's enthusiasm for very different designs. One might even say that the different designs represent very different human-machine interface paradigms. They're not that compatible. To accommodate all of them would involve a rather substantial degree of customization for each customer. Probably an economically infeasible degree. Also, common cockpit configurations solve a certification problem for pilots. Boeing's 757 and 767 airplanes have the same cockpit, which facilitates pilot certifications on both. A lot of variety in cockpits will lead to complexity in pilot certification."

Barton paused, thinking, trying to get his head around the problem. "So we asked customers what they wanted, they told us, and now we can't give everyone everything they've asked for," Barton summarized. "Do I have that right?"

Akita nodded. "Pretty much. Though there's one more wrinkle."

"Yes?"

"You probably remember Rick Arsenault. He's our best expert in cockpit controls. The really tall guy, with dark hair."

"Yes," said Barton, "I remember him. Pretty opinionated, as I recall."

"That's right," said Akita. "Well, he has his own ideas about how the cockpit should be laid out."

"And his ideas are different from what the customers want," Barton guessed.

"Not entirely, but yes, in important ways," said Akita. "Classic stuff, huh? I don't think we should discount this. The engineering tradition in this area takes as its basic assumption that there is no such thing as pilot error—the pilot is assumed to be an integral part of the human-machine interface. If a pilot gets information from the 'machine' and reacts to it in a way that causes a problem, the interface is presumed to need correcting. Based on this ethos, the design of the cockpit has evolved and been incrementally improved to a very high level of sophistication. Continuing in this tradition suggests that we begin with the current state of the art, probably the Boeing 787 cockpit design."

"Which is what Arsenault is arguing for," predicted Barton.

But Akita equivocated. "Not exactly. Arsenault is from this tradition, and he did start this way. But he's a pretty forward-looking guy. He would be happy to adopt some of the customer innovations, but he'd deliver a design quite different from what any customers have asked for. He says the designs the customers are advocating, while innovative and interesting in certain respects, are based on what pilots have already experienced."

"That would certainly be true," said Barton. "Wouldn't it? Isn't that the whole point? Customers know their own needs better than anyone else, so are best positioned to innovate—right?"

"Yes, of course," Akita answered. "The pilots who are our lead users are also aware of the traditional approach to cockpit design. But Arsenault says the lead-user suggestions are too incremental, insufficiently imaginative. Because customers can't imagine future possibilities fully, Rick says, they ask for incremental improvements in what they already know. He's inclined to favor more advanced configurations than the pilots suggest, which provides degrees of freedom that pilots don't think about."

"It's the pilots who have to fly the planes," said Barton.

Akita nodded: "Yes, but Rick's design, he says, represents a new approach that provides benefits customers—even lead users, the most progressive pilots—would never ask for because they don't yet know they actually want it. Once pilots see his design and get used to it, Arsenault thinks they'll see it for the breakthrough that it is."

"Will customers see any of their design in his?"

"Some. But just some."

"Can't we use some kind of objective, functional test to decide?" asked Barton. "Surely the different configurations perform differently. Can we just choose the best performer?"

"They're all pretty good," said Akita. "And it's hard to define performance in this case. Performance in human-machine interaction is the net effect of both the machine part and human part. It typically takes a whole lot of testing before we begin to see the subtle second-order effects, the unintended consequences, that sort of thing. We could test all of them, but that would be expensive since they're all so different. In my opinion, we really need to make a choice at this stage. Or narrow it down at least."

"You have a favored design?"

"I do," admitted Akita. "And I'll make that call if you want me too. But no matter what we choose, somebody's going to be unhappy. Customers who we've asked to be involved will be upset if we don't adopt their suggestions. They've put a lot of their own effort into this. Also, sales reps are taking up positions in favor of their specific customers' positions. It's getting to be a bit of a battle."

"Where did we go wrong?" Barton asked. "Involving our customers sounds like a good thing. Having guys like Arsenault involved sounds like a good thing."

"What we've got here is battling paradigms. On the one hand we've got user-driven innovation, as advocated by von Hippel. On the other, we've got designer-driven innovation, of the sort advocated by a guy named Roberto Verganti, a former engineer and expert on the design industry.[*] User-driven innovation fans say the large number of customers, relative to the number of designers, will come up with more ideas and better ideas because they know their own needs best, especially these lead users, who are the most expert and creative ones. Design-driven innovation fans say that user-suggested innovations will be constrained by what customers already know or can extrapolate from their individual, thus limited, experiences. Whereas designers, who are better able to anticipate future needs and trends, make innovative leaps that go beyond what customers can imagine, and propose to them a radically new—presumably 'better'—way of living, of interacting with things."

"So who's right?" Barton asked.

Akita shrugged. "There's evidence in both camps. I personally think both are very promising and useful approaches. I like what my people have done with the toolkits a lot. But I also deeply respect Rick Arsenault and really like his design. And I agree with him that no customer would ever have suggested it."

---

*See Roberto Verganti, *Design-Driven Innovation: Changing the Rules of Competition by Radically Innovating What Things Mean* (Boston: Harvard Business Press, 2009).

"So maybe we should have chosen one approach or the other, not both."

"Maybe," said Akita. "Or maybe there's a way we get the two approaches to sync up, to reinforce each other. Maybe not knowing enough about how to do that is where we ran into trouble."

Barton leaned back in his chair and put his hands behind his head, locking his fingers together in a weave. He bobbed back in forth in the chair. "Susan," he said, "I see the issue, and I appreciate your bringing it to my attention. But I don't feel at all qualified to help with the decision."

"I'll do that," she said. "But I want you to understand what has happened when you hear about this from someone else. Which I predict you will. When I make the decision, someone, probably someone in marketing, on behalf of one of our customers, will likely appeal the decision to you."

"I'll tell them what I just told you," Barton said. "That I'm not qualified to make this decision. And that I won't overrule you."

"That's fine," Akita said. "I appreciate your backing me up."

"Susan," said Barton, "I placed my bet on you a long time ago. It's a long-term bet, and I see no reason to go back on it now. Though I'm still waiting to see how it works out."

He winked at her and smiled. She smiled too, though less comfortably. "Thanks, Jim," she said. "I think."

Reflection

Should the engineering department be bringing so much "bad news" to Barton, as it does with the status dashboard? Do you agree with the consensus that Barton should be involved in the design and manufacture of the new plane at this level of detail? What alternatives, if any, would you recommend?

Which cockpit innovations should SMA favor in its final design decisions—those developed with lead-customer input or those developed by its lead designer? What are the benefits and challenges of choosing each option?

Would you advise SMA, in the future, to stick with one approach over the other, or do you agree with Akita that the two approaches might reinforce one another?

CHAPTER 18

Public Life, Private Life

Barton held the phone to his ear, listening to its ring, his anxiety rising as it always did when he made this call. Whether he worried that she wouldn't answer or that she would, he couldn't say. *Probably both*, he thought.

He leaned back in the chair and put his feet up on the desk, prepared to let the phone ring for a good long time.

Usually she didn't answer. He'd thought of calling her from a different phone, one with a number she wouldn't recognize. But that felt to Barton like a dumb, desperate trick. Though he felt sufficiently dumb, he'd wait until he felt really desperate to give that a try.

Which might not be a lot longer, he mused, listening to the ringing, ringing, and more ringing. Just when he had given up, as he began to withdraw the phone from his ear to return it to its cradle, the line clicked open.

"Hello," said a voice at the other end of the line.

"Veronica?" said Barton. He pulled his feet down to the floor and leaned forward, nestling the phone in both hands.

"Why do you keep calling?" she said. "What do you want, Jim?"

The questions threw him. So totally focused had he been on the challenge of reaching her that he'd lost any sense of what he wanted to say if she answered. And anyway, she always tipped him off balance. From the very beginning of their relationship, it had been the signature feature of their interactions. Her out in front, him struggling to keep up. Her witty, him awkward. She did it to other people, too, Barton knew, but knowing that didn't help.

"I want to talk," offered Barton.

"About what?" she pressed.

"About us?" Barton tried.

"There is no *us*," she responded, her tone businesslike.

"About how we were, then."

"Why talk about that?"

Barton shifted his strategy: "Because it could still cause complications for us."

"You mean Kohler's lawsuit."

"Yes," he said, hopeful that this would draw her into a deeper interaction. For some practical reasons, he did need to talk to her about it.

"What about it?"

He leaned back in the chair. "I was thinking that maybe we have a common interest in this matter," said Barton. "It could complicate your life, too."

"I'm not worried about it," said Perez. "She hasn't sued me."

"I realize that," Barton said, frustration slipping into his voice. "She hasn't sued anybody yet, but she's threatening."

"I'm not worried," Perez repeated.

He stopped himself and regrouped, trying another approach.

"There's a reputation issue, though, don't you think? There's what people might say if the visibility on this thing kicks way up."

"You want us to get our story straight?" she asked.

"Something like that," Barton said.

She laughed. Not a chuckle, not a momentary laugh, but a hearty, lengthening one, increasing in volume and pitch. It annoyed him and he tried to interrupt.

"What—?" he said. "What's so funny? Why does this amuse you?"

She stopped suddenly and spoke: "Because you're hopeless, Jim."

"Meaning . . . ?"

"You really think getting our stories straight will help? You don't understand the press, Jim. You don't understand the world. You've spent so much time living inside companies, among people who do your bidding, you really don't know how out of control things are going to get. You can't just tell the story your way and solve the problem here."

"I want to be proactive in getting our messaging out," said Barton.

"This is not a marketing campaign," said Perez. "They'll choose the message."

"Who will?" asked Barton.

"An amorphous entourage of reporters, their editors, and news execs who smell a controversy," Perez responded. "That gang of people who fall over each other to follow hot issues and people in trouble, and then fade away and lose interest when more mundane 'truths' come to light. A herd otherwise known as 'the press.'"

"Geez, Veronica," said Barton. "How can you stand to be a part of something you're so cynical about?"

But Perez was on a roll and didn't answer. She kept talking: "Their message will be simple and sensational. As sensational as they can make it. Also, it will be wrong. You'll try to correct it. To tell your story. Your story will be more factual, more complicated, presented indignantly. No one will hear it. Simple, wrong, and sensational beats complicated, correct, and boring every time. You have an unrealistic sense of control, Barton. These people don't work for you. They won't do your bidding."

"I don't think we're completely helpless," he said. "We have competent PR people. We can get out in front of some things, get some information out there, help frame people's interpretations."

"You can try," she said. "But there are a hundred ways they might play it when they decide to run with the story. And if you can think of fifty of them, you're a genius. And you, Jim, are no genius. You can't anticipate what they'll run with."

Barton sighed in genuine frustration and vented his sarcasm: "You must be very proud to be part of such a distinguished profession."

"You just keep saying things like that. It plays right into their hands. Self-righteous. Indignant. Like all guilty people. Because let's face it, Jim, you're the one who screwed up here. Nobody else. You."

"I screwed up by caring about you?"

"'Caring' about me? Is that what you call it? Or maybe you were flattered I'd pay attention to you? That I'd choose you? Maybe I was an ornament to hang on your arm? Befitting a CEO, right? Isn't that more like it, Jim?"

Barton didn't know how to respond, and Perez didn't give him much time. "Whatever it was that you felt, you screwed up by acting on the sentiment. No wrongdoing, nothing illegal, you want to say, but the way you acted doesn't *look* wise in retrospect. Probably wasn't wise. Wasn't good for SMA and the people who work there. Like so many others in positions of privilege and responsibility, you just couldn't keep control of yourself. And now look what's happened."

"I was spending time with *you*. A person I cared for."

Perez laughed again. "I'm a member of the press, Jim. It was always possible that I was *more* a member of the press than a friend of yours. Isn't that what you accused me of being the last time we spoke? Don't say you didn't wonder about me. You did."

"And should I have, Veronica?" he asked, suddenly desperate to know. "Should I have wondered about you in those private moments when we were together?"

She fell silent. Barton thought she might be feeling something, finally. But she put that hope to rest: "You couldn't afford to make assumptions about that. It was irresponsible of you."

"Irresponsible?" said Barton, aghast. "Why can't I act on my genuine and authentic feelings? I'm a person, too. It's my life."

"No," she said. "That's what you don't get, Jim. It's not your life. You have thousands of people working there whose jobs depend on you. It's not just your life. It's partly theirs. CEOs get confused about this all the time. Politicians, too. When you are that much responsible for other people, you can't keep your so-called 'personal life' off to the side. You can't do whatever you want in some segment of your life, because it leaks into your official life. Why do you think the news is so full of people who can't get this right, who lose their jobs as a result?"

"You think I should lose my job?" Barton asked, angry now. "Is that what you're hoping for?"

He said it because he thought it would wound her. Because he thought she would be offended that he would accuse her of wanting that, perhaps having wanted that all along. He expected her to object—tearfully, he dared hope. But again she surprised him.

"That's exactly what I want," she said. "I'd like to see you and all the others like you go down. That's why I'm in the business I'm in, in fact. To try to take people like you down. And in your case, I think it's likely to happen."

"Nonsense," said Barton. "I don't believe you. There's no fairness and no logic in what you're saying, only venom."

"You need to learn," said Perez. "You and too many others. Having a separate private life is a luxury you can't have. It's infinitely self-indulgent of you to think otherwise. Step up to that fact or turn down the top job."

"That's too harsh, Veronica," Barton said. "I don't buy it. It's not fair."

"It's real. Ask the people who might lose their jobs if you make the wrong decision. Who might lose their houses, or who can't afford to send their kids to school anymore. When you found that article I drafted, I thought, finally Jim Barton caught on. Had the guts to admit the mistake he was making. Hell, maybe I left that article for you to find on purpose, I was so sick of you thinking you could get away with it. But you haven't learned a thing, have you?"

For a few minutes, the line went completely silent. Then Barton heard the line click closed at the other end.

"Arrggghhhh!" he said, and slammed down the phone.

He sat, motionless for some time. Then he heard a sound, apparently from the adjoining conference room.

"Is someone there?" Barton said, anger still apparent in his voice.

Angel Crow emerged through the door. Barton remembered. She'd been working on the teleconference set up in the next room. How could he have forgotten?

"I'm really sorry, sir," she said. "I didn't mean to eavesdrop, but . . . well, you were pretty loud." The expression on her face, the posture of her body, radiated discomfort. Barton felt sheepish.

"It's okay, Angel," he said. Then, without thinking, he continued: "What do you think? Is it reasonable for the leader of an organization to have a personal life separate from his professional life?"

"A leader, sir?"

"Someone like me, for example," Barton said.

"Seems like you'd have a right to," she said. "But . . ."

She didn't continue.

"But what?" asked Barton.

"But I think a lot of people in leadership positions do cause trouble for a lot of the people they're leading when they make poor choices in their personal lives. I knew one who—" Crow faltered.

"Who what?" Barton prompted, with an edge of impatience, anger not yet fully dissipated.

Crow winced, as if regretting she'd started down this path. Then a new thought gave her courage, and she pressed on: "I'm sure it's not the same, but I knew one leader, a man, midforties, the head of a chain of low-cost, private schools, who messed up real bad. The schools served a mix of middle- and low-income students. He had this genius idea to transform education with a software system he'd been part of designing, open source, in his spare time. It did all sorts of cool stuff like aggregate all the latest learning materials, and it incorporated social networking tools for students to build knowledge collectively in this totally sweet way. It ran on these simple, inexpensive handheld devices, so kids wouldn't have to lug out-of-date textbooks around. He got this once-in-a-lifetime offer for funding. Two million to try it out in two schools with a promise for plenty more if the experiment worked. He had it up and running in eight months. Students were so fired up. Teachers were fighting for jobs at the school. Test scores shot up.

"Then they come to find out that the whole time, this jerk was hiding his pregnant, recently graduated from high school, little girlfriend in a trailer on school property. Fired him faster than you can say 'Jack Robinson.' Drove him out of town. Funders pulled out. The school was worse off than before. They'd tossed all their old books and materials; the teachers left. One of the schools was forced to close. You get the idea."

Barton looked at Crow a moment, trying to understand what link, precisely, she was making between this tale and him. "You're right, Angel, that's a good example of bad behavior, and he does sound like a jerk. But, we're talking about very different things here. What he did was possibly illegal, and definitely creepy. I'm not breaking any laws."

"Sorry, sir. Maybe it's not relevant." She turned toward the adjoining room, but teetered on one foot a moment and turned back. "But putting people at risk like that causes real damage."

Barton said nothing. Crow remained a moment longer, then winced again and started to leave.

"Tell me, Angel. You were one of the students who got cheated out of your high-tech program, weren't you?" He tried to smile. "Seems like you figured out computers just fine on your own."

"Nope. The jerk was my dad. We left town. I lost my full ride to Oberlin. Ended up in night classes, and taking care of my mom. At least I didn't have to see him again. But whatever, I'm fine. I survived. I just always feel bad about—" Barton heard her stifle a small sound rising in her throat before she finished. "—those kids."

Barton stood, but remained behind his desk. "Angel," Barton said, inhaling deeply. "I'm really sorry to hear that happened to you. I am. I just don't see it as the same thing."

"No, I guess you wouldn't, sir," she said. "But other people, Mr. Barton, maybe they will. Even if it is, maybe, unfair." Crow slipped out of the room.

"I'm afraid," said Barton to himself, "I still don't buy it."

Tuesday, October 12, 5:49 p.m. . . .

Barton looked up from his desk, responding to the sound of gentle knocking, seeing no one. Krishnan had gone somewhere, Barton couldn't remember where. To pick something up from another office, maybe.

"Yes?" said Barton.

Gardner stepped around the edge of the doorway.

"Oh, Clarke," Barton said. "I didn't realize you were still here. Come in."

"I just need a minute or two," said Gardner. "No need to get up. It's just something I need to make you aware of."

"Sure thing, Clarke," said Barton, getting up anyway and gesturing to a chair. He moved around the desk and sat on the couch. The SMA CFO remained standing. Something in his manner struck Barton as a little odd. Gardner was uncomfortable for some reason.

"What is it, Clarke?" asked Barton.

Gardner sat and started to speak: "I . . ." he began. He tried again, but again could not get anything out.

"Clarke? What's up? Is everything okay?"

Gardner exhaled. "Yes, fine. I don't want to make a big deal about this. It's awkward, that's all."

Barton waited.

"I had a meeting with my staff today," Gardner said. "The rumors about the Kohler lawsuit are flying around."

"There *is* no Kohler lawsuit yet," said Barton.

"Oh, I know," said Gardner. "I didn't mean to imply otherwise. But there are rumors that one might be coming."

"Is it really so big a deal?" said Barton. "I mean I get it that people like to gossip. But what does it really have to do with what we're trying to get done here?"

"That's just it," said Gardner. "Some of my guys think . . . Well, they think we might have a disclosure issue."

"A what?" asked Barton.

"They're suggesting," said Gardner, looking more uncomfortable than ever, "that the lawsuit, if it's filed, could have an impact on the SMA transformation. And that our knowledge of its likelihood might constitute an issue of potentially material impact on our financial outlook. Thus, that we might need to disclose it."

"How is it material?" asked Barton, incredulous. "Even if she files suit, even if it costs us something to settle it, the amount surely won't be enough to merit a disclosure now."

Gardner nodded. "Yes. But they're worried that she won't settle, that she'll take it to court, either to get a bigger settlement or to embarrass you and the company. It's not the amount of an award they're worried about. It's the cost of the negative publicity if the press goes crazy with it. Could reflect negatively on . . . the decision making of the SMA management."

"You mean my decision making," said Barton.

Gardner nodded.

"Did anyone suggest that maybe it's none of their business who I choose to date?" said Barton. "The claims Kohler is making are completely groundless. I don't think she'll win."

"But she could drag us through the mud."

"Are you telling me," Barton asked his friend and colleague, "that you agree with this? Do you think we need to disclose it?"

"I didn't say that," said Gardner. "I believe you have a right to privacy in your personal life. There are competing concerns. We have an obligation to shareholders to disclose our knowledge of future events that might impact the financial fortunes of SMA. But that obligation has to be balanced with the rights of an individual, even a CEO, to privacy. You haven't done anything wrong."

"No, I don't believe that I have."

"But it's a hazy area," said Gardner. "When Steve Jobs got sick, in the last couple of years before he died, Apple had an issue like this. Jobs didn't want anything about his health disclosed. Some board members thought it needed to be disclosed. But the press would have been all over it, all in his business."

"Have you taken this to *our* board?" Barton asked.

"No," said Gardner.

"Are you thinking you need to?"

"I don't know. That's partly why I'm here. I wonder if you, me, and Haas ought to have a conversation about it. Just a conversation. Obviously I would never have gone to the board about this without discussing it with you."

Barton nodded, thinking. "Jobs kept his illness private, right? Even though many investors would have considered his health very relevant to questions of the future success of the company."

"Yes," said Gardner. "But . . ."

"But what?" said Barton.

"As one of my guys pointed out this morning," he continued, "Jobs couldn't help getting sick. His claim on a right to privacy was partly based on the fact that getting sick was, for Jobs, pure misfortune. It was something that happened to him that he could not help. Whereas—"

"Whereas my issue," Barton interrupted, "was not something that happened to me, but something I did."

"That's it," said Gardner. "Something you had a choice about."

Barton sighed. "Smart guys you've got working for you."

"They are," Gardner agreed.

"Okay," said Barton. "A conversation with Haas. We'll see where to go with it from there."

"I just wanted you to be aware," said Gardner. "I especially didn't want you wondering whether I was talking to Haas about it behind your back."

"Hadn't occurred to me, Clarke. Not for an instant."

Gardner stood. "I'm glad. Have a good evening, Jim."

"You too, Clarke," Barton said, as the other man left the room.

Reflection

Do you agree with Perez's assertion that CEOs, politicians, and other people in official leadership positions don't get to do whatever they want with their "personal" lives? Should Barton lose his job over his decision to date a member of the press? Do you think Crow's story is relevant to Barton's situation?

Is there an issue of financial disclosure here? How might you decide? What would it depend on?

CHAPTER 19

Communicate, Communicate

Tuesday, April 12, 11:12 a.m. . . .

Clarke Gardner rapped his knuckles on the door frame to Barton's office. Barton looked up, peering over his glasses, holding aloft a piece of paper between his thumb and forefinger. When he saw it was Gardner, he let out an exclamation:

"Can you believe this?" Barton shook the paper, rattling it in the air.

"Which one is that?" Gardner asked.

"Which one do you think?" said Barton. He gestured toward a chair. "The one that arrived this morning, addressed to all executive team and board members."

"Oh," said Gardner, stepping into Barton's office and plopping down into a chair facing his boss's desk. "You mean the bad one."

"The bad one?" said Barton, puzzled.

"There's a good one this morning, too," said Gardner. He held aloft a piece of paper in his right hand, turned so Barton could see it.

"Oh, yeah," he said. "That one is pretty good. But this other one . . ."

"I've got that, too," said Gardner. He held up another piece of paper in his left hand. "Unbelievable irony."

"Irony?" Barton took off his glasses, set them on the table, and shifted back in his chair. "Clarke, what are you talking about? I'm not following you."

"Well," Gardner smiled, "if I'd asked you six months ago whether we'd have a bigger problem with this group—" he raised the page in his left hand—"or this one—" he raised the page in his right hand—" . . . which one would you have said?"

Barton chuckled. "The guys in the plants, of course," he said. "Yes, I see what you mean. But that's Ace who's doing that. I've always had more confidence in him than the rest of you have. He was never much for book learning, and he'll never be sympathetic with the management perspective. But he's one of the smartest guys I know. And he knows that we really are all in this together."

Gardner nodded. "You're right. I was skeptical. Now I'd have to agree. Anyway, this is the evidence." He waved the page in his right hand.

It was a letter, the formal legal notification of the completion of a restructuring transaction of formidable substance. Impressive amounts of SMA's component manufacturing organization had been sold to an investor group. SMA got an influx of cash, and the purchaser got more manufacturing capacity that it could match with its overabundance of orders, some from SMA competitors. And Jackson and his fellow workers got more long-term job security. This had all gone down without a peep of formal opposition from the unions. A year earlier, even six months earlier, no one would have considered that possible. The newspapers had been openly and loudly skeptical.

And wrong. But Barton doubted that they'd be apologetic after the fact.

This had happened partly because union officials had seen the writing on the wall for SMA and, by extension, its workers, if the company stuck with anything remotely like its old business model. Partly, too, it had been because SMA had lubricated the transaction with sweeteners for all involved parties. In the end, everybody won. The purchasers got an attractive price. Workers got some guarantees of orders from SMA and a promise of no layoffs in the first year. The whole thing had been expensive for SMA, more expensive than would have been acceptable to the former board, but Barton felt sure the deal was worth its cost. The business press had raked Barton over the coals because of the magnitude of those costs. But this morning, as word of the deal's completion spread in the public domain, the stock market seemed to be celebrating: SMA shares had jumped almost 15 percent. Barton had started the day feeling vindicated.

Then the other letter (or, rather, e-mail) had arrived.

"What do you make of it?" Gardner asked. "Are they bluffing?"

"Susan doesn't think so," said Barton. "She's meeting with them now, trying to talk them down. Bunch of prima donnas."

Gardner smiled, then suppressed it when the line of Barton's mouth stayed grim.

The page in Gardner's left hand contained an ultimatum issued by the SMA members of the professional engineers union (SPEEA), and supposedly agreed to by almost all of the product engineers at SMA: if SMA did not immediately abandon its plan to move key engineering groups to Washington State, they would initiate a work stoppage. Union members had repeatedly warned the executive team that they would not go along with this plan, the letter said.

Barton had sat down with groups of these engineers on several occasions, in sessions that he considered unproductive. They'd start out as meetings then turn into major whining sessions. Product engineers had a lot they wanted to complain about.

They didn't like outsourcing so much of the design to suppliers. It wouldn't work, they said. They knew from long experience with those suppliers that they weren't all that good at design, that they weren't very reliable.

They didn't like being forced into using so much composite technology. The technology was new and flaky, they said. Such technologies had unknown properties, and they weren't reliable.

But most of all, they did not want to move from California. They didn't need to be in close proximity to the engineering design community that had grown up around Boeing and the University of Washington, they said. The engineering design communities around Southern California companies and universities were just fine, they said. Better, in fact, than those to the north. Southern California had been a fine place to stimulate success for a very long time before Barton had arrived, they said. They didn't like the new guy coming in and saying what had served them so well for so long wasn't good enough. They didn't like it and wouldn't put up with it. Didn't he realize, they asked, how important the product engineering group was to SMA? They were, they said, the heart and soul of the company's past successes. The jewel in the company's crown. It was crazy, they said, to suggest that they could benefit from moving, since they had already eclipsed, in every important way, the community to the north. Those guys up there, they said, were a bunch of outdoor isolationist yahoos, truth be told.

Barton had listened, controlled his temper, and spoken kindly, even reverently to them. He'd told them how much they meant to the company. How delighted he'd been with their work and their openness to so much change. How much the company wanted to do what would be in the best interests of everyone, especially such an important group as product engineering.

But then he'd kept to his plan, assuming that they would never coordinate whispered threats to any degree, that SMA would lose a few, but not too many. Most people, Barton thought, would face reality and go along with the move. Now this letter made him realize that, even if they didn't all resign, they were capable of causing a lot of grief if their level of discontent was high enough and their intransigence coordinated. It was a serious problem.

"You going to call their bluff?" asked Gardner.

"I don't know what to do. What would you suggest?"

"Not much room to scale back your plans," said Gardner.

"We've already scaled back too much," said Barton. "I'd prefer we move more of engineering, but this group's the most important group to move, if you think about our strategy. Most of the people and many of the strategic partners they need to work with to transform us into a systems integration company are up there. And proximity matters. I'm already worried that we're not moving enough of the manufacturing engineering group. Why can't product engineering be as cooperative as the manufacturing guys? We heard some grumbling from them, but nothing like this craziness from product engineering."

"I wonder," said Gardner, "if there might be something else going on here. I mean, maybe it's moving to Seattle, but maybe it's something else. Something we're missing."

"Like what?" Barton asked. When Gardner didn't answer immediately, Barton's impatience got the better of him, and he added: "Come on, talk to me. Anything you've got might help in the conversation with them."

"Well," Gardner said, "I wonder if this might be general resistance to the fact that their jobs are changing in fundamental ways. You've heard Susan talk about how Boeing's propulsion engineers had a hard time giving up direct engine design and manufacture when Boeing started outsourcing. That all settled out over time. Today Boeing still has a bunch of propulsion engineers that have learned to work closely with the propulsion engineers at Pratt-Whitney, GE, and Rolls-Royce. But it didn't happen overnight. Maybe this is their way of working through this.

"If so, we might want to address this head on. Mention, when you talk to them, that we understand and appreciate the significant change in the way that they work that we're asking of them. But that the final result is likely to be a much more technologically advanced and sophisticated product than we could ever have built going it alone."

"Talk to them again," said Barton, his frustration unconcealed.

"Yes," said Gardner. "Again." He smiled and added, "You know, they really like the attention."

Barton cursed. "Why can't Susan keep her staff under control? They've been a nonstop pain in the butt almost since the day I arrived. Don't they know how high the stakes are? Don't they realize how much trouble this company is in?"

"It's a tough bunch," said Gardner. "Also, you are *not* their kind of guy. I know. I'm not their kind of guy either."

"Yeah, yeah," said Barton. "I know. I'm not an engineer. I get it. Maybe I ought to just fire the dude whose account this e-mail is sent from. Make an example of him. Mount his head on a stick. See if the rest of them have the courage of their convictions."

"Right," said Gardner, skeptically. "But you're not that kind of guy, either. And they know that. It's not a credible threat."

Barton agreed. "You're right. It wouldn't work. I didn't mean it. Just venting."

"So where does that leave you?"

"With higher blood pressure. This really makes me mad. We finalized a major restructuring agreement today. We should be celebrating."

"Might not hurt to point out to them how their stock is appreciating this morning," Gardner said. "They're prima donnas, but they like getting richer, just like everyone else. The market is showing some respect for your management this morning. Someone should point that out to them."

Barton sighed and reached for his glasses, folding them and depositing them in his shirt pocket. "I guess I better go talk to them again," he said.

He stood, moved to the door, lifted his coat from a hanger and started to pull it on. "Krish," he said, raising his voice to speak through the doorway into the next office. "Cancel my morning appointments. I've got to go over to the engineering building. I don't know how long it will take. Call them and tell them I'm on my way."

He stopped and turned back to Gardner. "Want to come?"

"Not on your life," the CFO said.

"Not feeling like a team player, eh?"

"Not this morning," Gardner said.

"Go crank on a spreadsheet, you lousy bean counter," Barton said.

Tuesday, April 12, 11:43 a.m. . . .

Much to his dismay, Barton had drawn a huge sedan from the company's large fleet of pool vehicles. The thing maneuvered like an ocean liner, but he supposed it would carry him to the meeting at the engineering building well enough.

While he drove, he thought through how he should handle the meeting. As in the past, he would need to listen a lot. Some of Bill Allen's points of advice came back to mind:

Must keep temper always—never get mad.

Be considerate of my associates' views.

Don't talk too much—let others talk.

Make a sincere effort to understand labor's viewpoint.

Be definite; don't vacillate.

Above all else be human—keep your sense of humor—learn to relax.

Be just, straightforward; invite criticism and learn to take it.

Be confident. Having once made the move, make the most of it.

Bring to the task great enthusiasm, unlimited energy.*

Barton remembered a story he'd heard about how Allen had handled a difficult meeting with members of the Seattle Chamber of Commerce.

Boeing's situation then had been analogous to SMA's now. Allen had to explain changes required to transform Boeing from a WWII manufacturer to a peacetime, commercially successful manufacturing firm. Giving a speech to the group, Allen had said, "I can assure you that the Boeing management will use diligent and aggressive effort to put our plants to use on a full-time basis."†

Right then, an angry man jumped up, shook a finger at Allen, and shouted: "I know these laid-off factory workers are not going back to work at Boeing, and you know it too." At which point, the meeting took a truly ominous turn: another person rose to propose that the government should take over the Boeing plant. Allen caught himself and remembered his principles, one in particular: *Never get mad.*

Then a "bluebird" flew into the room. Without prompting or comment from Allen, someone else in the room shouted a response: "That's a silly idea. It's the government canceling orders that's causing all the trouble in the first place."

The crowd laughed and settled down. The crisis moment resolved itself.

Three months later, several airlines placed big orders, and Boeing got some breathing room.

Barton remembered another story Maggie Landis had once told him, about how Scott McNealy, who was then CEO of Sun Microsystems, had handled a meeting with an angry crowd of software engineers. It was the early days of the web, and the enthusiasm of the company's employees for this new technology had increased network traffic so much that mainline business systems had begun to perform badly. Systems crashed. The company couldn't fill customer orders. To deter people from generating so much network traffic, McNealy had instituted a tax on departments

---

*The original source of these items is Harold Mansfield, *Vision: A Saga of the Sky* (New York: Duell, Sloan and Pearce, 1956), 150–151.

†Ibid., 265.

whose employees generated web-based traffic. A companywide revolt ensued. People were incensed. They believed that experimenting with new technology was part of their jobs, and to tax that experimentation was violation of a sacred norm.

In a scene that looked very bad for McNealy, a standing-room-only crowd gathered in the firm's largest auditorium for a meeting about the "web tax." Several other company sites used video teleconferencing to attend the meeting. McNealy sat with a small, lonely set of a few other execs up on stage, keenly aware of the anger in the looks sent their way by everyone in the crowd, waiting for the meeting to begin. It was like the villagers with pitchforks and torches come to roust the evildoers in their midst.

Unsure how to handle the meeting, McNeely opened the floor for comments. The first several were angry and predictable. But then a bluebird flew into his meeting, too. Someone from the network services group spoke next. He said something like, "Come on, people, think about it, and you'll realize there's a real issue here. We need networks to make and sell our products. Right now you're slamming the networks with this new web thing. We can add capacity to the network, but that will take time, and we can't suspend business operations that long."

After that, the anger subsided and a reasoned conversation about what to do ensued. In the end, McNeely rescinded the tax, but people in the room agreed to a short-term moratorium on web access.

Barton wondered whether he could count on a bluebird. He rather doubted it.

Reflection

What is your take on the SMA product engineering group's complaints regarding Barton's decision to outsource parts of design to suppliers, use more composite technology, and to move their group to a new location?

How do you think Barton should address the problem with the product engineering group? Which of Bill Allen's points do you anticipate will serve him best in this situation?

CHAPTER 20

Partnering Risks Realized

"What am I looking at?" Barton asked.

He stood with Paul Marochek on the metal-grated platform of a portable lift that a driver had steered onto the bare concrete floor of a production hangar. The driver had positioned the platform near the partially constructed fuselage of one of the new SMA planes, about thirty feet up from the floor. Then Marochek had pointed to a crack between the fuselage and the wing, right where the two connected. The crack widened as it extended from the front to the rear of the wing.

"That," said Marochek, "is what a hundreds-of-millions-of-dollars screwup looks like."

"That crack. Between the body of the plane and the wing," said Barton. "I gather it's not supposed to be there." Marochek nodded.

"These are the first wings flown in from our supplier in Japan that have come from their actual manufacturing process—their first wings made in a plant with all the tooling in place. To keep with our vision of SMA as a global systems integrator, those wings are supposed to snap flawlessly into place."

"With no cracks," said Barton.

"With no cracks," Marochek confirmed.

"The earlier prototypes did click together," Barton remembered. "I was there. I saw them."

"They did," said Marochek. "But those were not made in an actual plant. They were created in a prototype shop, using a process that won't scale up to production volumes."

"So, something has gone wrong with . . ." Barton began.

"With our partner's transfer of the product to manufacturing," Marochek finished.

"And that's expensive to fix," Barton said.

Marochek nodded. "Much of the investment they've made in tooling and some other equipment will probably be lost. They'll have to buy new tooling. Depending on what went wrong, their tooling supplier might be liable for some the costs. But, however that works out, it's going to be expensive. And it's definitely going to result in a substantial delay."

"Isn't it their problem?" asked Barton. "I mean, I see how the delay is our problem too, but the mistake was theirs, right? So *they'll* have to pay to fix it."

"Yes," said Marochek. "That would be our opening position. But we're talking a lot of money here. Enough to potentially make this an unprofitable arrangement for our partners. That's not good. We're making an airplane. If our partners start to see this program as an unprofitable millstone around their company's neck, they could divert resources to more profitable deals. They'll try to save as much money as possible in the fix, which might not be the mind-set we'd prefer they take to our program. And anyway, they'll probably argue we contributed to the problem in some way."

"Did we?" Barton asked.

"Maybe," said Marochek. "We were closely involved in development of the specs. Maybe they'll argue we designed something that couldn't be built. Maybe we did. Maybe it'll be something else. There might be IT issues. I still have to talk with Jen Sharp about it. But when you're talking about this much money, the gloves come off, and it's every firm for itself."

"The amount of money," Barton agreed, "makes it our problem, too. You're saying we might need to adjust the contract, to help them bear the cost of fixing this problem."

"The amount of money, the delay, and the global systems integrator concept—all suggest that," said Marochek. "In this model, we are relying on partners to carry out many of the tasks we would have kept internal traditionally, so we need to be more tightly integrated with our partners. And the viability of that partner integration rests firmly upon a presumption that 'we're all in this together'—a presumption we have been actively promoting. Which means it'll be hard for us to argue that it's their problem, theirs alone. Just tell me if I've got this wrong."

"No," said Barton, sagging against the rail of the lift platform, realizing the full implications of what Marochek was saying, "you're right." Then he asked the question he'd been putting off: "How much money do you think we're talking?"

Marochek shrugged. "Difficult to say."

"Hundreds of millions?"

"Maybe."

"Over a billion?"

"It's possible."

Barton sighed and cursed under his breath.

"How much delay?"

"Months at least."

Barton cursed again.

"With almost four hundred fifty advanced sales, the delay could be expensive, too," said Marochek.

"Late delivery penalties," said Barton.

"Right," said Marochek.

"Our Chinese customers have embraced the notion that cargo is not a second-class concern in comparison with commercial passenger travel," said Barton, "that cargo is really, for a developing country like China, what the twenty-first century is all about. Other airlines not in developing countries have gotten that news, too and placed orders for our new innovative plane to add air cargo capabilities into their portfolio of airline services. That's all good news. But all their big plans depend on our ability to deliver. Which we have now failed to prove."

"And there's potentially another problem," said Marochek.

Barton was already nodding. His thoughts had just started to go there. "The 'I told you so' problem," he said.

"That's one way of putting it," agreed Marochek. "This global systems integration model is new. It has had many detractors. People who said it wouldn't work."

"And this looks like evidence that they're right."

"Yes," said Marochek.

"Employees, especially in engineering. Especially those upset they had to move from California to Washington," Barton speculated. "They'll take it that way. The press. Maybe even investors."

"And the delay that will be noticeable to the outside world will be our delay in getting airplanes delivered. Even if we could get all the costs covered, no way is it *not* going to look like our problem. No way is it not going to *be* our problem. Lots of work for you, boss," said Marochek.

"This calls into question the main concept that has underlaid our transformation. And therefore the transformation itself."

"Some people will say that," agreed Marochek.

They'll also say, Barton thought, *that this is what happens when you hire a bean counter to run an airplane company.*

A silence descended over the two men. Marochek looked worried.

"Get us down from here," said Barton.

Marochek waved to the lift operator. The lift descended, the humming sound of the machinery serving to hold off any more conversation for a few minutes. When the platform had almost reached the ground, Marochek unhooked the safety gate, stepped aside to let Barton climb down, and then followed him. The two men stood awkwardly at the edge of the production floor, Barton seemingly lost in thought. Then he turned to Marochek:

"What do you think, Paul?" Barton asked. "Does this mean our concept is wrong? Or have we just not done it right yet?"

Surprised, Marochek did not answer immediately. Barton kept his eyes fixed on the manufacturing VP, probing. The situation demanded an honest answer. Marochek provided one:

"Personally, I think the concept is solid. It goes back to what my team proposed at the Edgewater meeting; I've been behind this all the way. But—like we acknowledged at that meeting but probably didn't fully realize—it's very, very different from how we have operated in the past. If you take into account how ambitious we're being—the change we're asking of our own people and our partners—I guess I'm not that surprised that we've had a big problem. But it doesn't invalidate the concept. Big change takes time. We're probably going to have more problems.

But it would be a mistake to pull back now. Things always look like a big mess before you get it all figured out."

"You're not just saying this because it's what I want to hear?" Barton asked. "It *is* what I want to hear."

"No," said Marochek, looking slightly hurt. "I'm not just saying this. Check with Akita and Sharp. I'll wager they'd say the same. But I do have a worry. A big one."

"What's that?" Barton asked.

"That the forces of skepticism—the naysayers, the press, weak-kneed investors—might prevail. That they might not be willing to wait long enough for us to get it right."

"It's a valid concern," Barton admitted. "I'll try to protect us from that. But I might not be able to. In a publicly traded company, you often don't get the opportunity to learn. This could cost me *my* job."

Marochek said nothing.

"That's mine to manage," said Barton. "You focus on the manufacturing problem. Get with Clarke. Get some of his people on this. We'll need to know as soon as possible how much it's going to cost to fix this, and how much SMA might reasonably end up needing to contribute. Also, how long a delay this means. We'll have to manage our customers. We don't want to lose sales over this. But again, that's not yours to manage. You focus on the core problem: get that fixed. I'll work with the board and the rest of the executive team on damage control."

"Will do, chief," said Marochek, trying—and not entirely succeeding— to add a portion of hope and optimism to the tone of his voice.

Barton smiled halfheartedly, thanked Marochek, and headed back toward the parking lot to return to his office.

Wednesday, October 19, 11:13 a.m. . . .

Driving a pool car on the way back to his office, navigating midmorning traffic on a beautiful fall day, Barton contemplated this most recent problem. By far, it was the most serious crisis he'd faced, with the possible exception of his initial failure to gain board approval for his transformation plan.

In fact, this could be round two of those tribulations. Once again, people would ask hard questions about whether Barton could really lead an airplane company. Some would argue that a CEO with an engineering background would have prevented the problems with the wing. Or, more likely, that such a CEO would have been wise enough to realize the folly in the expansive, overly ambitious, global systems integration concept.

Or, Barton thought, in protest, *such a CEO might've been so attached to the way things have always been done that he could not deliver on the promise of the global systems integration company.* Then he reprimanded himself for the uselessness of that thought. Trotting out that idea in public now, with a billion-dollar mistake in evidence, would appear more than naive. It would just reconfirm what detractors would say.

But damn it, I'm right about this, said Barton. *Even Marochek said so.*

So the real question would be how to weather the storm. He thought again of Bill Allen's advice. Several of his points now came to mind:

Try hard, but don't let obstacles get you down. Take things in stride.

Be just, straightforward; invite criticism and learn to take it.

Be confident. Having once made the move, make the most of it.

Bring to task great enthusiasm, unlimited energy.*

Barton had followed this advice as best he could. It had gotten him past many difficulties: the problems with the board early on, the rebellion in engineering against moving from California.

But this would be the toughest test yet.

How would he need to mobilize resources to handle this? The problem would ripple into every inlet and backwater of the company. No one would be untouched. And it would strain his and the rest of the executive team's ability to coordinate activity and control damage.

With that thought in mind, he thumbed the call button on the steering wheel to initiate a call to Krishnan. When he answered, Barton told him to call the executive team together for an emergency meeting that afternoon.

---

*The original source of these items is Harold Mansfield, *Vision: A Saga of the Sky* (New York: Duell, Sloan and Pearce, 1956), 150–151.

"What shall I tell them it's about?" asked Krishnan.

"Just tell them it's mandatory attendance," said Barton.

He disconnected the call. Soon he'd need to call Haas, but there was something he badly wanted to do first. Still running through the situation in his thoughts, he turned the car toward Venice.

Wednesday, October 19, 11:53 a.m. . . .

"Will the parachute ever open?" Barton asked Clara Jenkins. "Will I ever feel comfortable in this job? Or will I lose it before that happens?"

Jenkins tipped up a colorful ceramic pot, pouring fragrant and steaming dandelion tea into a cup resting in front of Barton. They sat in a small room at the front of her house, at an antique table, on chairs that creaked when Barton moved.

"There's sugar if you need it," she said. "But I don't think you need it. The flavor is quite nice without it."

Barton nodded, became cognizant of the full teacup, and lifted it to his lips. It smelled good, slightly earthy, but remained too hot to sip yet.

"You're already a lot more comfortable than you were," Jenkins said, in answer to Barton's question. "But will you ever get really comfortable? Maybe. If you last that long. But I don't really think comfort is what this is about. It might be an unreasonable expectation for someone in your position."

"Were you ever comfortable when you were a CEO?" Barton asked.

Jenkins thought about it. "Yes, for a while. But that proved to be a 'calm before the storm.' Not too long after that I was gone."

She sounded genuinely regretful, hurt even. Barton probed: "What happened?"

She shrugged. "Different worldviews. A board member who had always presented me with difficulties got a bright idea that I thought was a very bad one. The details don't matter much; I'm not sure I even remember them. It was all about some trendy notion in the business press at the time. Some of our competitors had jumped on board with it. He thought we should, too, and convinced enough of the other board members. I argued that the lemmings approach is not a business strategy. Probably could have been more diplomatic about that. But this was a really bad idea. Not too long after that I was out."

"How many years were you in?"

"Eight plus."

"And the company did well during that time?"

"Yes, on the whole. We had challenges. But overall performance had been good."

"And yet that had earned you no leeway? A trendy business notion overcame the years of good service you had provided? That's outrageous."

Jenkins laughed. "Jimmy, you're an idealist. In the final analysis, it was nothing personal, I think. But sometimes the bad ideas win. Maybe the good ideas win in the long run, but a CEO can certainly become a casualty before that happens. I personally think you can expect people to get it right in the long run, most of the time. But you and I and most people dealing with real problems must frequently operate in the short run."

"So," said Barton, now sipping his tea, "how do I go at this problem I'm facing? Any advice?"

She smiled. "Same way you've done everything else, Jimmy. You go straight at it. Earnestly. Openly. You do your best. You try to save the company, even if it might not save your job. You admit the mistake, explain it as best you can, and set the record straight when someone gets something wrong about what's happened. You won't win all those discussions. But it's a percentage game. You might win often enough."

"I *might*," said Barton.

"Yes," said Jenkins. "You *might*."

Barton nodded and stared into his teacup.

Reflection

How should SMA address the billion-dollar problem with its partner? What will serve it best in the short term and long term? How can it avoid these kinds of screwups in the future?

Harder Than I Thought

How should Barton address the problem with SMA stakeholders? How might he use his executive team to help? What is the biggest threat to SMA's future?

Is it possible to become comfortable in the CEO position? Is it desirable? How can a leader best cope with the continuous demands of such a position?

The Leadership Main Course

SSEER, a simulated senior executive experience role-play by Simavatar Studios

"May I take your order?" the waitress asks.

Neither Barton nor Jenkins responds to the young waitress. She waits. Luce looks across the table at his dinner companions.

Jenkins holds her glasses out of the way, studying the menu beneath them. Barton adjusts his own glasses to see through them better. Luce waves the waitress closer.

"These older folks," he whispers when she leans over, "need a bit more time." He winks, waggles his eyebrows, and places thumb and forefinger at the side of his head, as if position-ing his own imaginary glasses. "I fear," continues Luce, "that they may have also forgotten their hearing aids."

The waitress smiles, nods knowingly, and then departs.

"Kind of a jerk today, aren't you?" says Barton, not looking up from the menu.

"Apologies, Clara. I only tease the ones I love," says Luce. "No apology for you, Jim. You ought to know me by now. Anyway, today I jest in the spirit of celebration! I smell success. Don't you agree, Ms. Jenkins, that it looks like our Jimmy boy just might pull this off?

"Oh, I don't know," says Jenkins. "I wouldn't say he's in the clear yet. Not all the way in the clear."

"Jim's certainly not out of the deep end," says Luce. "But he's keeping his head above water and doing some real good for this company. I've just decided to invest in SMA."

"Well, my goodness!" says Jenkins. "Hear that, Jimmy?" Barton did not respond. "Jim! Did you hear that?"

"What?" says Barton, lowering the menu and taking off his glasses, seemingly annoyed.

"Jonathan just said he plans to invest in SMA," says Jenkins.

"Hmmph," says Barton. "About time."

"What's got you so absorbed over there?" Luce asks.

"Look at the menu, right after the appetizers," says Barton. He replaces his glasses on his nose and looks back down at his own menu.

"Oh. Wow. Interesting," says Luce.

"It's a good list," says Jenkins.

There, beneath the appetizers, emblazed on bold lettering, the menu reads "The Leadership Main Course." Following this title, a list includes numerous tasty items:

Get the Team Right
It'll take a while.

* * *

No Secrets
Get over it.

* * *

Partner Relationships
They need constant tending.

* * *

Managing Change
Your biggest challenge.

* * *

Enlist Key Constituencies
The unions, duh!

* * *

Address Governance Issues
Or nothing else works.

* * *

Rethink People Management
The old way won't work.

* * *

Set Direction and Keep Reminding
Keep after the details.

Trystorm and Learn
Cheap and rapid experiments.

* * *

In Crisis, Regroup
And change the game.

* * *

Lose the Parachute
Be all in.

* * *

Care for Customers
But never compromise on essentials.

* * *

Patience in Handling Revolt
Don't escalate.

* * *

Stay the Course
Reinforce weak knees—business is a contact sport.

"Check out dessert," says Luce.
The dessert menu included a few more items:

Go to the Future You Have
to live in the future

* * *

Everything Moves
Get things in sync.

"No prices," says Luce.

"If you have to ask, you can't afford these," Jenkins says, chuckling. She added, "I'm not sure I agree with all of these."

"Not sure I do either," says Barton.

"Nor I," says Luce. "But that's not the point. We're supposed to talk about them. Being a leader is not about analysis or technique. It's not fixed in time or place. It's about how you grow. About why people should do things you're asking them to do but you're not doing. The conversation has to stay alive. Right, Jim?"

"Uhh. I guess so," says Barton.

"May I take your order?" says the waitress, suddenly returned.

"We have not yet," says Jenkins, "made any decisions or commitments, young lady."

"Well, folks," says the waitress, who morphs suddenly into SMA's lead test pilot Shelly Kranz. "You've got to eat sometime," she says, pulling up a chair to sit and putting her feet up on a second chair. "And I'd recommend we all get on with it."

Luce breaks into a grin and nods with appreciation. Barton and Jenkins take off their glasses.

"Do you have any dandelion wine?" Jenkins asks.

CHAPTER 21

There Is a Time . . .

Wednesday, October 26, 11:35 a.m. . . .

Jim Barton could not remember another time when he had been this nervous.

For the past four hours, the new SMA plane had been airborne, on its maiden flight. Getting the plane off the ground for the first time was a milestone, a tremendous achievement, for the company and for Barton. But another even more crucial milestone remained: they had to land the new plane. If they failed to achieve that one, no one would remember anything else about this day.

Earlier that morning, before the takeoff, Barton had been almost this nervous. He'd rubbed his sweating palms on the sides of his pants and peered distrustingly at the hulking form of the new state-of-the-art air cargo carrier as it crept slowly from its spacious cocoon, an extra large, specially built hangar. The morning air at the new SMA flight test facility outside Seattle had been cool and pleasant. A gentle breeze from the west carried with it a few scattered clouds, but the sky stayed mostly bright and clear.

A perfect day for a first flight.

The beauty of the emerging plane's shape, so much more impressive in full size than in a model, awed Barton, as it had every time he'd seen it. Because of the properties of the composites used in its construction, and because this plane had been designed to move containerized cargo, it looked utterly unlike a commercial airliner. Wide, with swooping smooth curves around a roughly rectangular cross section that merged into a wider, yet shallow concave underside, it appeared vaguely saucerlike. Mostly due to its striking good looks, it had already won two industrial design awards given to concept "vehicles," usually cars, but sometimes motorcycles, boats, or aircraft.

Barton and a throng of board members, senior executives, engineers at work with equipment, and employees with family members who were there just to watch had positioned themselves a safe distance from the runway. Someone, probably the engineers, had painted a series of yellow hash marks at the edge of the tarmac; the biggest group of observers loitered near the widest of these marks. That wide paint mark showed where the plane would lift off, according to engineering calculations.

If it lifted off. Before the fact, they couldn't be sure, of course. This plane had never actually flown. And while all precautions had been taken, every analysis completed, every *t* crossed and every *i* dotted, there always remained a razor-thin but real possibility of a mishap. Something big *could* go wrong. Because of this, only three people flew in the plane: a test pilot, a copilot, and a flight engineer. Shelly Kranz was the pilot, and she had handpicked the other two.

The people on board had plans to bail out if the worst transpired. Every test pilot knew, however, that the parachutes, the bailout plans, all such preparations for emergencies, were mostly for show. If something went truly wrong, the circumstances that might actually allow bailout and recovery of those aboard comprised an exceedingly improbable subset of possibilities. If something went badly wrong, the crew would likely die, and that unmitigated disaster would negate all of the hard work of Barton and his team over the past two years.

But all had gone relatively well, so far. The takeoff had been dramatic. The crowd had gone silent as the plane accelerated down the runaway. The engines roared and grew deafening as the plane came closer, relentlessly closing in on the point of no return—that point at which the plane would either lift into the morning sky or the unthinkable would begin to happen. Barton and the others had watched, eyes riveted to the front wheels, straining to see some sign of a gap opening between rubber and tarmac.

Then it had happened, right on schedule. As the nose of the plane reached the heavily painted yellow line, weight lifted from the tires, uncompressing them, and then they rose, miraculously, into the air. The spectators inhaled audibly, in unison. The back wheels cleared the ground too, and the plane ascended majestically into the sky. Barton detected a change in the pitch of the engine noise and saw the angle of climb grow steeper: Kranz was gunning it, "seeing what this baby could do," and having a little fun, while staying well within the parameters of safety.

The crowd went wild. Applause echoed across the landscape, replacing the sound of the engines as the plane gained altitude.

Barton clapped, too, and then noticed that Gardner did not, nor did Akita. They were waiting, he realized, for the landing before they would allow themselves to celebrate. Ford, too. Barton kept on clapping, but restrained his enthusiasm.

As the plane turned for a ceremonial pass over the crowd, Barton found himself besieged by people wanting to shake his hand. He noticed a correlation between nontechnical specialization and willingness to celebrate before the flight had ended. Engineers remained on pins and needles, but marketers, HR people, some finance people, and many others had begun to rejoice in earnest. Montero came over and delivered a blow to Barton's back that nearly knocked him down.

"Geez, Jose," said Barton when he got his breath back, "take it easy, man. We've got to see that plane back on the ground before we can call this a success."

Montero laughed and then took in Barton's meaning and became more solemn. "It's going to happen, Jim," he said, his tone reassuring. "I can feel it." Barton wanted to agree but could not muster a commensurate level of confidence.

That had been four hours earlier. Now, not far away, members of the press stood with eyes again raised to the sky, cameras rolling. Having captured what had happened earlier, they stood ready to capture anything else that might. Among them, Barton spotted the devastatingly gorgeous Veronica Perez. Barton had passed near her earlier, but she had not even looked at him. It had been a long time since they'd spoken. She had written critical things about him and SMA in the paper in recent weeks. Annoying but not over-the-top or unfair things. Perhaps some modicum of respect for him lingered within her mind or heart.

He hoped so.

"This is it, Jim," said a voice at Barton's elbow, piercing his thoughts. He looked around and saw Gardner, but found no solace in his expression. The CFO didn't look at Barton, but moved his eyes across the sky, scanning for the plane returning from its flight out over the Pacific Ocean.

"Yes," Barton agreed. "This *is* it." He tried to enact a reassuring tone, but didn't pull it off. "They reported turbulence . . ."

"Yes," said Gardner, "I heard. About an hour into the flight. And then again a few minutes ago."

When a test pilot reported "turbulence" during a test flight, it was code for a problem with the plane. There had been some kind of problem, but it was too early for a full report. People were still busy testing and flying the plane.

"Any details?" Gardner asked.

"Some instability as they passed through 440 mph. That's all I've heard. The engineers saw something on their instruments about that time also."

"That doesn't sound too bad," Gardner observed.

"Impossible to say," Barton said. "As you know, Shelly is a master of understatement. The plane is still in the air, and that's good. But we'll need to get the full story from her after the landing before we know how serious it is."

Gardner swallowed hard and turned back toward the runway.

Barton saw Bill Ford standing nearby. He looked alternately hopeful and desperate. Susan Akita stood beside him. Her expression remained blank, unfazed, or, more likely, heavily guarded. Krishnan chattered nervously to anyone who stood too close to him. Montero was the lucky guy at the moment, but it made a good pairing, since you could tell that Montero didn't hear a thing Krishnan said.

As he awaited the plane's approach for its first landing, Barton's memory of Montero's confidence felt comforting, for reasons that had nothing to do with logic. Barton had never seen Montero wrong about anything. He'd hope for a continuation of that trend.

Looking around, Barton caught sight of Maggie Landis amid a group of engineers that included Paul Marochek. Though it startled him, it shouldn't have. He had invited her, and he knew she had accepted. But she had not coordinated her attendance at the event with him and was now making a point of not hovering near him. He saw her transmitting a concerned look in his direction. When their eyes met, she smiled gently and then went back to talking with Marochek.

Soon Barton would have to head back to the area where members of the board of directors and other dignitaries waited. He'd need to engage in the required chitchat. He knew of at least three congressmen who would expect his attention.

Still waiting for the plane to appear, he felt another presence near him and turned to see Ace Jackson standing by his side. Jackson didn't say anything, didn't try to shake hands. He stood stiff, reserved. Barton thought he might be angry, but then realized what he saw in the man's posture was anxiety.

"You look worried," Barton said.

"So do you," said Jackson.

"For the same reason," said Barton.

Jackson nodded. "The landing. These people celebrating, they're jinxing us. I'm worried that they're jinxing us."

Barton looked around again. Jackson was right. The buzz grew louder and too many people were shaking hands and congratulating each other. Reflexively, Barton raised his voice: "Let's wait for the landing, people," he said. A pall fell over the crowd, and Barton wondered if he'd done the right thing. Even people who couldn't have heard Barton became silent as the message traversed the crowd, person to person, in whispers.

Then someone gasped and pointed. Others raised their arms as well. The plane came into view. It expanded from a distant point to take on its familiar shape. Approaching quickly now, it straightened into its landing approach. Not a soul breathed a word during the last five minutes of the flight. But in the end, the newly designed SMA cargo plane touched gently down and slowed.

Barton realized that everyone was looking at him, awaiting a cue.

Quietly, he said: "We did it." Then louder, shouting: "We did it!"

He threw his arms into the air, and the celebrating commenced at a level not yet seen. The crowd quieted only when the plane's door opened and Kranz appeared at the top of a rolling stairway that had been pushed against the plane. She raised two thumbs up. "Flies like a dream!" she shouted.

And the celebration resumed.

Wednesday, October 26, 1:48 p.m. . . .

"That sounds eminently solvable," Barton said.

He sat with a group of engineers and executives huddled around Shelly Kranz at a makeshift table in the hangar, talking about the "turbulence" problem. Immediately behind them, the SMA-7 rested from its arduous morning flight, people swarming around it, under it, and up on it.

"It is solvable," said an aeronautical engineer, "it's definitely something we can work with—"

He stopped, realizing who had interjected the remark he'd just responded to. Faces turned toward Barton, each progressing from a routine problem-solving expression to surprise that Barton had jumped into the deeply technical engineering discussion, then to smiles that acknowledged that their bean-counter CEO had become one of them. He had followed the technical discussion in pretty much every detail.

"What?" said Barton. "I didn't mean to stop the conversation. Go on. Looks like we're onto something."

Within another five minutes, the group had arrived at the rough outlines of an approach to the problem. Eyes turned again to Barton. They'd need some additional resources to handle the problem quickly.

"Tell me what you need," said Barton, "and you'll have it."

The conversation continued, Barton weighing in from time to time, no longer drawing any sort of stare or smile. He was a member of the problem-solving team. This too was a milestone, a not-insignificant one. It had been a day of milestones. Barton felt a wave of deep satisfaction spread throughout his body, into his bones. Financial services had never been like this.

Then someone touched his elbow. Barton turned and saw Gardner.

"Jim, can you come with me?" he asked. Barton could tell from his voice that something was wrong.

"What is it, Clarke?" Barton asked. He saw distress in Gardner's eyes. Intense distress. Barton stood and put a hand on his CFO's shoulder.

"Ron Haas wants to see us," said Gardner.

Barton smiled. "He just wants a report on the problem, Clarke. Don't worry, it's solvable. We're going to have to spend a little more, but it's far from a showstopper."

Gardner shook his head. "No," he said, using confidential tones. "That's not what it's about. It's about the lawsuit, Jim."

Barton couldn't follow his meaning. Then it clicked. "The lawsuit?"

Gardner nodded.

"Now?" Barton said.

Gardner nodded again. He looked stricken.

"It must be bad," said Barton.

Yet again, Gardner nodded.

Jim Barton, CEO of Santa Monica Aerospace, took a deep breath.

"By all means, then," he said, "let's go see the chairman of the board."

Wednesday, October 26, 2:26 p.m. . . .

"You really think it's time?" said Barton. He sat in a small chair in an office at the edge of the hangar bay. He had no idea whose office it was, but at the moment it contained Ron Haas, Clarke Gardner, Hector Sacio, the PR consultant, and Jim Barton. Sacio sat across a table from Barton and took the lead in the conversation. Gardner sat close at Barton's side. Haas lurked at the far end of the table, quiet.

Sacio nodded. "Tough timing, I realize. Maiden flight of your airplane this morning and all." He tried to ooze compassion, but you could tell it wasn't his natural mode. "But, in a way," he continued, abandoning any attempt at sympathy, "that's the very reason it's time. This case is about to pop. They've filed this morning and scheduled a press conference for this afternoon. The legal proceedings will become very public. The press will feast on it. CEO sleeps with a gorgeous press opponent. PR director who warns against it gets fired, seemingly at the behest of the gorgeous reporter. Wrongfully dismissed. CEO swayed by sex with a beautiful woman to take actions detrimental to the company he leads."

"It wasn't like that," said Barton. He looked over at Haas and repeated it. "It wasn't like that."

Haas said nothing.

"Oh, I know," said Sacio. "We know. I expect we could win the lawsuit. The legal outcome is not the issue."

Barton grasped for a straw: "She won't settle?"

Sacio shook his head. "Not yet. We've tried. She and her attorneys know that their leverage builds with press attention. They know we'll want to eliminate the distraction. They've timed their action to coincide with the success of the new airplane. The spotlight is on us, now they're going to put something else in view. Something titillating and spectacular. Filing on the day of the successful maiden flight is a tactic. A good one."

Barton thought he detected a hint of admiration in Sacio's voice. That the PR consultant could indicate admiration for such a cynical and insignificant action on the day when Barton's whole company had beaten the odds and done the impossible irked Barton deep in his soul.

"We've achieved a great deal," said Barton.

"Yes, you have," agreed Sacio.

"And now," interjected Haas, "it's time to protect that achievement."

Barton looked down the table to Haas. The two men locked eyes for a moment before Haas looked away. Barton realized that the board had to be in agreement with this plan already or else the current conversation would not be taking place. Haas's remark sealed it. The deal was done, and Barton had played no part in it.

"I suppose that's the one thing they won't see coming," said Barton, for the first time managing a degree of clinical detachment. "That I might step down willingly."

"Exactly," said Sacio. "They're betting that you'll fight it. They're counting on your ego, your vanity, to win out," he explained. "That's the way it goes with most of these stories. 'I won't resign.' 'I have nothing to hide.' All that. Much damage incurred, and you end up stepping down in the end anyway."

"So if I step down, the story goes away?" asked Barton.

"Not completely," said Sacio, "but mostly. A wrongful dismissal suit is pretty boring without daily images of the scandalized CEO. Plus, once reporters bag their quarry, their editors quit giving them space to publish the story. Taking you out of the picture makes this a matter between SMA and a disgruntled former employee."

"And doing that moves attention back to the company, the plane, the future," said Barton.

"Right," said Sacio.

Barton turned to Haas and, at the same time, extended a hand backward to touch the arm of Gardner's suit coat.

"Clarke will take over, then," said Barton.

Haas nodded. "He'll be acting CEO. That's what the board has decided."

"Jim," said Gardner, his voice desperate, "you have to know—"

"It's okay, Clarke," Barton interrupted, not looking back at Gardner. "I do know."

Barton turned back to Sacio. "When do we need to do it?"

"The sooner, the better. Today would be my recommendation," said Sacio.

Barton leaned back in his chair and looked up at the ceiling.

The silence grew long. Sacio stood, bowed his head in Haas's direction, and then left the room. In a few more minutes, Haas stood, moved to a spot behind Barton, and rested one hand on his shoulder.

"I'm sorry, Jim," he said. "I wish it didn't have to go this way. We'll try to do something about that contract clause, get you some kind of parachute—"

Barton shook his head, not turning. "No. I agreed on that with Ace. If I lose my job, I'm just like one of the union guys. No gold, no parachute. They wanted me all in, and I have been. We've gotten it done as a result. I'm not going back on that now."

"You'll be snapped up quickly by another company," said Haas.

"Another company," said Barton. He ran his fingers along a line in the table, a minor imperfection in its surface.

"Yes," said Haas. "Another company. It's our loss."

"But it was my screwup," said Barton.

Haas said nothing. After another moment, he left the room.

Barton sat for a long time, lost in thought. Gardner stayed with him for a while, then, without saying anything, he too left.

Barton was alone.

Wednesday, October 26, 9:04 p.m. . . .

This is National Independent Radio. Now for today's business news headlines:

In a surprising development, Santa Monica Aerospace has announced the resignation of CEO, James Barton, on the same day that the company's new cargo plane made its first successful maiden flight. Chairman of the board Ronald Haas thanked Barton for his excellent work in delivering the company to this point, and said that Clarke Gardner, formerly the company's CFO, would take over the company's reins. Haas noted that the successful test flight represents a major milestone in the company's program to transform itself from a military defense contractor to a commercial cargo plane producer.

The official explanation for Barton's departure is that he wishes to pursue other opportunities, but sources we contacted speculate that the move is an effort to avoid distractions for the company that might arise from an emerging scandal related to Barton's relationship with a reporter who has written critically about the company, and a wrongful dismissal lawsuit filed by a former employee.

The company's stock rose 2.5 percent on the day.

In other news . . .

Reflection

What do you think of Barton's achievements as CEO of SMA? What features of the company's transformation seem most significant? To what do you attribute Barton's own transformation as a leader?

Do you think SMA's board is doing the right thing by asking Barton to step down at this point?

What do you think of the board's choice to appoint Gardner as the acting CEO? What does this indicate SMA might do next?

What should Barton do next?

FINALE

Still Figuring It Out

SSEER, a simulated senior executive experience role-play by Simavatar Studios

Barton stands in the courtroom where earlier he had presented his plan for the transformation of SMA—the plan accepted by the jury in the SSEER environment, but rejected later in real life by the SMA board. The furniture is still overly large and wildly colored, but it is no longer neatly arranged. Indeed, the setting looks as if a tornado might have swept through. The huge purplish mahogany judge's bench still towers over the room, but it sits at an odd angle. Several chairs are overturned, and one is broken into several pieces. Also, there's apparently no one in the room, in the jury box, or in the gallery.

Barton surveys the wreckage, looking for any signs of life or anything interesting. He rotates full circle, looking around, and when his eyes return to the judge's bench, he notices someone sitting in a chair next to it, half turned away from Barton, staring off into the distance.

It's Bob Goldman.

Barton walks closer to Goldman, stopping to grab and drag a chair along with him. Without saying a word, Barton sits down next to Goldman and also stares off in the same direction.

They remain there together for some time, neither man acknowledging the other. Finally, Barton speaks.

"You were right, Bob. I wasn't ready," says Barton. "I screwed up," he adds, his voice catching.

"No," Goldman says. "I was wrong. Jim, you did more with that company than I thought anyone could. You turned it around."

"I should still be there, though," says Barton.

"Yes," Goldman admits, "you should. The transition to a new leader should not be so abrupt. You should have planned for it intensely and then remained available to the new CEO while he or she got established in the role."

297

"It would have been Akita," says Barton. "Still will be. Gardner is acting CEO. When Susan finishes delivering that airplane, she'll be the one."

"I don't think she'll have any of the kind of trouble that undid you, Jim," says Goldman.

"No," Barton agrees. "She's as straitlaced as they come. And well qualified for the job."

"You would have lasted," says Goldman, "six to ten years. Probably closer to six, because you'd have thought through your exit strategy, and not overstayed your contribution window. Stay too long and you turn over a company that has plateaued at best or is in a tailspin at worst. Doing it the way you did, dropping out too early, unnecessarily complicates things that are already hard. Endangers the good you did. Sorry, Jim. I'm just telling it like it is here."

Barton nods.

Jenkins and Luce emerge from behind the judge's bench. Luce retrieves an overturned chair, and swings it under him, straddling its back, while Jenkins crosses to Barton and lays a hand on his shoulder. "Don't be too hard on yourself, Jimmy," she says.

"Yeah, Jimmy," adds Luce, "CEOs are human and flawed like the rest of us. They make mistakes. You made a doozy. But in this brave new world, leaders cannot allow themselves to be distracted from their great responsibilities. Your actions affected thousands of people. This kind of leadership role is a full-time job."

"I wonder what ever made me think I wanted this job," Barton says.

"You took up the mantle. You stepped up," says Goldman. "Nothing wrong with that. Don't kick yourself for the wrong things. It just compounds earlier errors."

"I still don't think I know how to do this job," says Barton. "I was still figuring it out."

"That's why you were good," says Luce. "You didn't think you had it all figured out. You were open to new ways of solving problems. And you helped others become open to new ways as well."

"Jonathan is right," Goldman admits. "The world has changed."

"And is still changing," says Luce. "Real changes. Information flows faster. Distance has contracted. People are more connected. There are opportunities and difficulty in all of this."

"But no formula," says Jenkins. "Nothing you can master and be done with. We have to keep talking about it. We have to keep discussing."

"We must 'think anew, and act anew,'" adds Luce.

"'Disenthrall ourselves', right, young man?" says Goldman.

"Yes, sir. Keep figuring it out," answers Luce.

"Be careful," Barton says. "The two of you wouldn't want to make agreeing too much of a habit."

Barton stands, turns to his three companions, and adds, "Let's pick up some of these chairs and straighten up a bit. This place is a mess."

Goldman smiles. "Thatta boy, Jimmy," says Jenkins. "Count me in," adds Luce.

WAYS OF USING THIS BOOK

Harder Than I Thought is written for new and potential CEO leaders, those working closely with CEOs, such as board members and senior leadership team executives, those interested in or studying general management who want to better understand the CEO's role, and those who are simply curious. Although our book is fiction, the story that we have told is being played out, with variation, in many modern corporations. We have used the cover of fiction to identify and elucidate the key challenges and decisions twenty-first-century CEOs face, with the intention to enable reflection.

While the book is useful and (we hope) interesting to an individual reader, we've also designed it to be the focus of discussion. We suggest reading and discussing the book with a peer, or convening a group of readers at a brown-bag lunch or other similar session to discuss the chapters one by one. We offer questions for reflection or discussion at the end of each chapter. There is no particular problem with reading ahead, although reading ahead will not reveal right answers. At SMA, as in life, there are no *right* answers, but rather a set of decisions made at a certain time by a group of actors with the information available, which results in specific consequences from which to profit or learn or recover.

CEO Jim Barton's story unfolds in twenty-one chapters. Experienced cumulatively, the story gains dramatic momentum, and later chapters provide opportunities to revisit key issues in more depth as readers gain deeper understanding and familiarity with the characters, the company, and SMA's transformation situation. The interludes are designed to explore and, at times, synthesize key issues and dilemmas Barton is addressing at given moments on his journey. Chapter notes occasionally recommend supplementary materials to enrich your reading and discussion as relevant.

The topics addressed in these twenty-one chapters, we propose, can constitute a course curriculum in general management or CEO leadership, which can be combined with supplementary materials and used at the undergraduate, graduate, or executive levels. If you are interested in using this book, or chapters selected from it, in a classroom setting, please contact Harvard Business School Publishing (www.hbsp.harvard.edu) for information about support materials.

To assist with whatever reading program you choose, we've provided a list of recurring main characters in order of appearance in the book (see "Cast of Main Characters") and a list of acronyms and terms (see "Glossary of Acronyms and Terms").

CAST OF MAIN CHARACTERS

In order of appearance...

James "Jim" Barton: The new CEO of SMA. Barton comes to his new position from a career in the financial services industry and service as governance committee chair on the SMA board of directors. Having grown up in Santa Monica, California, before pursuing a career on the East Coast, Barton is eager to prove a hero to his hometown and lead SMA's transition from a faltering defense contractor to a market-leading commercial cargo aircraft company.

Ben Krishnan, or "Krish": Barton's meticulous executive assistant.

Paul Marochek: SMA's exuberant, straight-talking vice president of manufacturing.

Acacio "Ace" Jackson: Barton's best friend in high school, now the formidable leader of the SMA mechanics union. Jackson's cooperation is key to Barton's plan for transformation at SMA.

Susan Akita: SMA's chief engineer, a tough and exceptionally competent leader in charge of the new SMA cargo plane design process.

Shelly Kranz: SMA's highest-profile test pilot.

Jennifer "Jen" Sharp: SMA's highly capable chief information officer.

Angel Crow: A young and unusually gifted employee in SMA's IT department with a reserved manner and an alternative appearance;

Barton recruits her to codevelop an advanced leadership simulation tool called SSEER, and continues to draw on her talents to assist with digital transformation at SMA.

Jonathan Luce: A serial entrepreneur and technology whiz kid, who, despite his youth, has become well known as a venture investor, philanthropist, board member, and nerd celebrity. Luce is a friend and unconventional mentor to Barton.

Robert "Bob" Goldman: Barton's former boss and longtime mentor, Goldman is CEO of Erlington Financial Group and a giant in the financial services industry. Barton recruits Goldman to the SMA board of directors.

SSEER: The "simulated senior executive experience role-play" is a virtual environment adapted, at Barton's request, from a video game under development by one of the companies in which Luce invests. In this experimental environment, Barton, as an avatar, interacts with his advisers as avatars to test out leadership and strategy ideas and learn quickly at low risk.

Clarke Gardner: SMA's chief financial officer. Barton sees Gardner as a critical member of the senior leadership team and potential confidant, but must first test Gardner's professional honesty and judgment in the wake of questionable accounting practices enacted under the former CEO.

Linda Kohler: SMA's director of public relations (PR) and communications. Early conflict between Kohler and Barton has unexpected repercussions for the latter.

Veronica Perez: A prominent, if controversial, local business journalist whose first priority is getting a great story. Despite her scathing editorial on Barton's appointment as CEO, Barton succumbs to Perez's renowned allure and begins a dangerous romance.

Martin Van Busin: Member of SMA's board of directors and dean of the school of engineering at MIT.

Edward "Ed" Frazier: A former SMA chairman and CEO, previously SMA's chief engineer. As Barton's predecessor, Frazier initiated the plan Barton inherits to design a state-of-the-art cargo plane and transition the organization from a defense contractor to a commercial business. Frazier was removed from the CEO position due to questionable accounting practices, but remains a member of the SMA board of directors.

William "Bill" Ford: A former SMA chairman and CEO, Ford was predecessor and mentor to Ed Frazier. As a current member of the SMA board of directors, Ford initially opposes the transformation strategy, but later makes an important contribution to its execution.

Ronald "Ron" Haas: Current chairman of the SMA board of directors.

Patricia Shanahan: Member of the SMA board of directors and a former pharmaceuticals company CIO.

Chris Harden: Member of the SMA board of directors. Harden is a retired US Air Force general, whose expertise is more suited to the military contracting company SMA has been than the commercial cargo aircraft company it is trying to become.

John Elliot: Member of the SMA board of directors. Elliot is a former ambassador to Japan and Wall Street securities lawyer, and advocates for the liquidation (rather than transformation) of SMA, based on responsibility to shareholders.

Bobbi Smithson: Member of the SMA board of directors. Smithson is a talented CFO and a strong advocate for SMA's transformation.

Russell Rigby: Member of the SMA board of directors and a former California lieutenant governor.

Charlotte Owens: Member of the SMA board of directors. Owens is a former Stanford Business School professor and currently active on a number of boards.

Philip "Phil" Shepard: Member of the SMA board of directors and an influential high-tech company CEO with a successful start-up and investment track record.

Jack Bruun: SMA's vice president of human resources (HR).

Rajit Paleplu: SMA's most talented R&D employee.

Clara Jenkins: Barton's eccentric neighbor in Venice Beach. A former pharmaceuticals CEO, Jenkins now specializes in raising dandelions and finds unusual ways to contribute to Barton's leadership development—and salvation.

Jose Montero: As part of SMA's transition to a commercial airplane company, Montero is hired as the new senior vice president of sales. Montero exudes confidence in his performance capabilities and expects everyone else in the organization to deliver as well.

Hector Sacio: A communications consultant brought in to aid Barton through crisis, in the absence of an SMA director of PR and communications.

Maggie Landis: A savvy management consultant, Landis grew up in Santa Monica knowing (and dating) both Barton and Jackson. She now lives on the East Coast, and was Barton's long-term girlfriend until his recent job transition.

GLOSSARY OF ACRONYMS AND TERMS

In alphabetical order...

AI	artificial intelligence
Biz dev	business development
CAD/CAM	computer-aided design and computer-aided manufacturing
CEO	chief executive officer
CFO	chief financial officer
CIO	chief information officer
COO	chief operating officer
CV	curriculum vitae, or résumé
DC	District of Columbia, capital of the United States of America
DOA	dead on arrival
EFG	Erlington Financial Group (*fictional*)
EVP	executive vice president
Exec	executive
GE	General Electric
HBS	Harvard Business School
HR	human resources

IBM	International Business Machines Corporation (IBM)
IP	intellectual property
IT	information technology
IVK	a fictional financial services firm; Barton was previously CIO at IVK
MBA	master's of business administration
MIT	Massachusetts Institute of Technology
NBA	National Basketball Association
NFL	National Football League
P&L	profit and loss statement
PR	public relations
QB	quarterback, a player's position in American football
Reps	representatives
R&D	research and development
ROE	return on equity
RFP	request for proposal
San Fran	San Francisco, California
SIM (or sim)	simulation; a virtually simulated game or activity
SMA	Santa Monica Aerospace (*fictional*)
Specs	specifications
SPEEA	Society of Professional Engineering Employees in Aerospace
SSEER	simulated senior executive experience role-play (*fictional*)
Tech	technology
US	United States (of America)
Vlog	a video blog
VP	vice president

ACKNOWLEDGMENTS

We owe thanks to a great many people who helped us conceive and execute this project.

We gratefully acknowledge the support of the dean and the Division of Research at Harvard Business School, the president of Copenhagen Business School, the president of the University of New Brunswick, the dean and senior associate dean of the Foster School of Business at the University of Washington, and the Boeing Company sponsors of the Philip M. Condit endowed chair at the University of Washington. All of these people and organizations enabled our research and collaborations, without which we could not have accomplished this project.

We are also indebted to the many people who generously gave their time to help us with this project. Deserving of special mention: our colleagues at Harvard Business School, Copenhagen Business School, the University of Washington, and the University of New Brunswick, many of whom provided encouragement and feedback throughout the writing of this book. Anna Ward and the other members of the dean's office staff at University of New Brunswick, Fredericton, who worked hard on the preparation of the manuscript and helped Rob Austin protect the time on his schedule to work on the final manuscript, also deserve warm thanks.

Rob wishes to thank the members of his family: Laurel, Lillian, Evelyn, and Daniel Austin, who supported me in many ways during the writing; and my parents, Bob and Sylvia Austin, who have made so many things possible over the years. My father, the original Robert Austin, departed from this world last year, and is greatly missed every day in many ways.

Dick wishes to thank his family: Pam, Sean, and Ben. Pam, my captive listener during more mornings than she would like to remember and avid Maine gardener, including being a docent at Boothbay's Botanical Gardeners, helped us to get Clara's gardening metaphors "right." Sean and Ben continue to teach me about their generations and the twenty-first-century world as it is.

Shannon wishes to thank her family: my husband, Thomas Hessel, for consistent patience and good humor, my mother Sandy O'Donnell for never-ending encouragement, and my father John O'Donnell for reading everything I write (twice) and offering the insightful comments of a talented educator. Warm gratitude to Jason Franklin for introducing me to the wonders of Joseph Campbell, and to my dramaturgical mentors: Geoff Proehl, Lee Devin, and Abigail Adams.

Also dear and departed, and due great thanks for his help with this work: José Royo, former CEO of Ascent Media Group, a former student and one of the greatest talents ever to emerge from Harvard Business School, who left this earth far too soon at the age of forty-four.

We greatly appreciate the important contributions of anonymous reviewers of the manuscript, and the many readers and advisers who have contributed to the development of our story.

We thank our patient, dauntless editor Jeff Kehoe, and, before him, Kathleen Carr, who believed in our "novel" approach and who helped us stay our course. We thank others at Harvard Business Review Press with whom we've had the good fortune to work: Erin Brown, Jenny Cromie, Mike DeRocco, Mary Dolan, Stephani Finks, Ralph Fowler, Jane Gebhart, Audra Longert, Allison Peter, Tim Sullivan, and Erica Truxler. Special thanks to the cover artist, Daniel Stolle, for adding his talent to the project.

The problem with making a list is that you always leave someone off it. Thanks too, then, to those whom we should have listed here but whom we've left off due to inexcusable oversight.

—Robert D. Austin
    Fredericton, New Brunswick, Canada
Richard L. Nolan
    Boston, Massachusetts, USA
Shannon O'Donnell
    Copenhagen, Denmark

ABOUT THE AUTHORS

Robert D. Austin is dean of the faculty of business at the University of New Brunswick, Fredericton, in Canada. This job and his former one as the CEO of the CBS-SIMI Executive Foundation (the largest executive education provider in Northern Europe) have provided many "harder than I thought" leadership experiences, for which he is sometimes grateful. He holds the chair in management of innovation and creativity at Copenhagen Business School, has been an associate professor of technology and operations management at Harvard Business School, and has been the author of publications in venues like *Harvard Business Review, MIT Sloan Management Review, Information Systems Research, Management Science, Organization Science,* and the *Wall Street Journal.* He's also authored or coauthored a number of books, most notably, *The Adventures of an IT Leader,* the prequel for this book. He lives in Fredericton, New Brunswick, with his wife, Laurel, and children, Lillian, Evelyn, and Daniel.

Richard L. Nolan grew up in Seattle and received three degrees from the University of Washington. His first full-time job was with the Boeing Company, first as a software engineer on the Minuteman missile program, and then as a financial systems manager on the 737 commercial airplane program. In 1969, he joined the faculty of Harvard Business School. After eight years on the faculty, he cofounded with Dave Norton the strategic IT consulting firm Nolan, Norton and Company, which they sold to KPMG in 1987. In 1991, he returned to Harvard Business School where he became the William Barclay Harding Endowed Professor of Business Administration. He became professor emeritus at HBS in 2003 and returned to the University of Washington as the first recipient of the Boeing Philip M. Condit Endowed Professor of Business Administration at the Foster School of Business. In 2012, he became University of Washington Professor Emeritus. Richard and Pamela Nolan have two sons: Sean Patrick and Benjamin Garrett.

Shannon O'Donnell is a PhD fellow at the Copenhagen Business School's Department of Management, Politics, and Philosophy. Her research focuses on collaborative creativity, innovation management, and the role of aesthetics and arts-based practices in processes of business value creation. She coauthored, with Austin and Nolan, the Harvard Business Press book *The Adventures of an IT Leader,* articles related to the special pedagogical approach developed for that book, as well as several HBS teaching cases. The Danish Ministry of Science, Technology, and Innovation awarded her an Elite Research Travel Stipend in 2010. She grew up in the Seattle area, graduated from the University of Puget Sound, and then spent eight years working as a director and dramaturg in professional theater, both in Seattle and at the People's Light & Theatre in Malvern, Pennsylvania. She currently lives in Copenhagen, Denmark, with her husband, Thomas.

Berkeley College

CAMPUSES: Brooklyn, NY * New York, NY * White Plains, NY
Newark, NJ * Paramus, NJ * Woodbridge, NJ * Woodland Park, NJ
* Berkeley College Online *

PLEASE KEEP DATE DUE CARD IN POCKET